How to Win Allah's Help and His Protection

Ibn Rajab al-Hanbali

Published by Muddassir Khan, 2024.

Table of Contents

How to Win
Allah's Help
And His Protection

Ibn Rajab al-Hanbali

Introduction

In the Name of Allaah, the Most Merciful, the Bestower of Mercy.

All praise belongs to Allaah, The Lord of the worlds.

Pure and blessed praise be to Him such as our Lord loves and accepts.

A praise which behoves the nobility of His Face and accords with His Magnificence.

May the peace and blessings of Allaah be upon Muhammad, the Unlettered Prophet, his family and his Companions.

Imam Ahmad relates the hadith of Hanash al-Sana'ani, on the authority of Ibn 'Abbas who said: One day when I was sitting [riding on the same mount] behind the Prophet (peace and blessings of Allaah be upon him), he said to me: "O young man! Shall I not teach you some words by which Allaah will enable you to benefit?"

I replied: "Of course!".

He (peace and blessings of Allaah be upon him) said:

"Safeuard (Be mindful of) Allaah and He will safeguard you.

Safeguard Allaah and you will find Him before you.

Know Allaah in ease and He will know you in difficulty.

When you ask, ask Allaah.

When you seek help, seek help from Allaah.

The pen is lifted and the pages are dried.

If all the creatures came together to try to benefit you through something that Allaah has not ordained, they would not be able to achieve it.

And if they joined together to harm you through something that Allaah has not decreed, they would not be able to achieve it.

Know that immense good lies in patiently enduring what you hate, that victory comes with patience, that relief comes with distress, and that ease accompanies difficulty."

This hadith contains advice of great importance and universal principles which deal with the greatest and noblest aspects of this religion.

So much so that Imam Abu al-Faraj (Allaah have mercy on him) said in his work Sayd al-Khatir: "I contemplated on this hadith and it struck me with wonder. I was so stunned that I almost became dizzy."

He then said: "The ignorance that reigns on the subject of this hadith and the resulting lack of understanding are truly distressing!"

Chapter 1: Being mindful of Allaah

The words of the Messenger of Allaah (peace and blessings of Allaah be upon him): "Safeguard (Be mindful of) Allaah and He will Safeguard you", means: to Safeguard (being mindful of) the limits of Allaah, His rights, His orders and His prohibitions.

All these elements are Safeguarded by respecting His orders with compliance, His prohibitions with abandonment, His limits by not crossing them and not transgressing them.

So, this phrase encompasses the fulfillment of all obligations and the abandonment of all prohibitions.

This is like what is mentioned in the hadith of Abu Tha'labah on the authority of which the Prophet (peace and blessings of Allaah be upon him) said:

"Allaah has prescribed obligations for you, do not neglect them.

He has forbidden you certain things, do not break His prohibitions.

He has set limits for you, do not transgress them."

All of the above is included in the term: "Safeguarding the limits of Allaah".

This is taken as it is in the Word of Allaah (approximate translation of the meanings):

"Those who Safeguard the limits of Allaah". (Surah 9: Tawbah, verse 112.)

"This is what has been promised to you [and]; it is for every person full of repentance and heedful [of divine orders] who fears the Most Merciful although he does not see Him, and who comes [to Him] with a heart inclined to obedience." (Surah 50: Qaf, verses 32-33.)

The term "heedful" in this verse has been explained by the following meaning: one who Safeguards the commandments of Allaah.

Another meaning was also given: one whose concern for his sins leads him to repent and renounce them.

The verse encompasses these two meanings.

Furthermore, all those who Safeguard and follow Allaah's legacy left to His servants come within the scope of this verse.

All these meanings revolve around the same fundamental meaning.

Thus, the advice he (peace be upon him) gives to Ibn 'Abbas regarding safeguarding Allaah encompasses everything previously mentioned.

To Safeguard the prayers

Among the most important things to Safeguard are the five daily prayers.

Allaah, the Most High, said: "Safeguard the prayers, especially the middle prayer." (Surah 2: al-Baqarah, verse 238)

"...those who Safeguard their prayer." (Surah 70: al-Ma'arij, verse 34)

The Prophet (peace and blessings of Allaah be upon him) said: "Whoever Safeguards them, Allaah promises him entry into Paradise."

In another hadith: "He who Safeguards them will receive light, proof and deliverance on the Day of Resurrection."

Safeguarding the purification

The same thing applies to purification, because it is the key to prayer.

The Prophet (peace and blessings of Allaah be upon him) said: "No one Safeguards ablution except a believer."

Indeed, the servant can very well cancel his state of purification without even realizing it.

Therefore, safeguarding the state of ablution for prayer is proof that faith has become firmly anchored in the heart.

Safeguarding of the oaths

Oaths are a part of what Allaah has ordered a person to Safeguard.

Mentioning the atonement for the breaking of oaths, He said:

"This is the atonement for your oaths, when you have sworn them. And keep your oaths." (Surah 5: al-Ma'isdah, verse 85)

People frequently make oaths.

The consequences of not keeping them (that is breaking them) vary. Sometimes it is the expiation for the breaking of oaths that is required. Other times, a more severe atonement is due. Still other times it requires divorce or similar things.

Faith has entered the heart of him who takes care of his oaths.

The Pious Predecessors (the Salaf) safeguarded their oaths carefully. Some among them would never take an oath by Allaah. Others were so cautious that they offered atonement for oaths they thought they might have broken.

Imam Ahmad (Allaah have mercy on him), on his deathbed, ordered that atonement for breaking an oath be given, saying: "I think I have broken an oath that I had made."

It is narrated that when [the Prophet] Job (Ayyub - peace be upon him) passed after two people swearing by Allaah, he went and made atonement (give expiation) on their behalf lest they commit a sin without realizing it. This is why, when he took an oath to whip his wife a hundred times, Allaah offered him a facility (flexibility), because he safeguarded his oaths as well as those of others. Scholars have differed as to whether this facility applies to other than Prophet Job (peace be upon him).

Yazid ibn Abi Habib said: It has come to me that, among the Throne Bearers, there is one whose eyes cry tears that flow like the rivers. When he raises his head, he says: "Glory to You, You are not feared as You deserve." Allaah then says: "Yet those who swear falsely in My Name do not know this!"

A severe warning has been reported regarding taking of false oaths. Frequent swearing in the Name of Allaah or false swearing in His Name comes from ignorance of Allaah and lack of reverence in the heart.

Safeguarding of the head and the stomach

Believers must Safeguard their head and their stomach.

Ibn Mas'ud reports that the Messenger of Allaah (peace and blessings of Allaah be upon him) said: "True modesty before Allaah consists in safeguarding the head and what it retains and the belly and what it contains."

Safeguarding the head and what it retains includes safeguarding the ears, eyes and tongue from falling into the forbidden.

Protecting the belly and what it contains includes safeguarding the heart against persisting in what is forbidden.

Allaah has mentioned all this in His Saying: "Hearing, sight and heart: concerning all these, verily, they will be questioned." (Surah 17: al-Isra verse 36)

Safeguarding the belly and all that it contains includes keeping it free from prohibited food and drink.

Safeguarding of the tongue and private parts

It is also obligatory to Safeguard the tongue and private parts from the transgression of prohibitions.

Abu Hurayrah (may Allaah be pleased with him) reported that the Prophet (peace and blessings of Allaah be upon him) said: "He who Safeguards what is between his jaws and what is between his legs will enter Paradise."

Ahmad reports the hadith of Abu Musa on the authority of which the Prophet (peace and blessings of Allaah be upon him) said: "He who Safeguards what is between his jaws and his private parts will enter Paradise."

Allaah, the Most High, has specifically ordered to Safeguard the private parts and praised those who do so: "Tell the believers to lower their gaze and Safeguard their private parts." (Surah 24: al-Nur, verse 30)

"... men and whome who guard their private parts..." (Surah 33: al-Ahzaab, verse 35)

"And who Safeguard their private parts – except from their wives or the slaves they own, because in which case there is no blame on them…" (Surah 23: The Believers, verses 5-6)

Chapter 2: He will Safeguard you

"He will Safeguard you" (in the Hadeeth) means that whoever Safeguards (is mindful of) the limits of Allaah and respects His rights, Allaah will Safeguard him.

This is because the recompense is of the same nature as the act.

Allaah, the Most High, said: "If you keep your commitments to Me, I will keep mine." (Surah 2: al-Baqarah, verse 40)

"Remember Me, I will remember you." (Surah 2: The Cow, verse 152)

"If you make (the cause of) Allaah triumph, He will make you triumph." (Surah 47: Muhammad, verse 7)

The Safeguarding of the servant by Allaah is of two categories.

The first is the safeguarding of what can benefit the servant in his life here below (in this world), such as his body, his children, his family and his property.

Ibn 'Umar reports that the Messenger of Allaah (peace and blessings of Allaah be upon him) never neglected the following invocation when he woke up and when he went to bed:

«اللَّهُمَّ إِنِّي أَسْأَلُكَ الْعَافِيَةَ فِي الدُّنْيَا وَالْآخِرَةِ، اللَّهُمَّ إِنِّي أَسْأَلُكَ الْعَفْوَ وَالْعَافِيَةَ فِي دِينِي وَدُنْيَايَ وَأَهْلِي وَمَالِي، اللَّهُمَّ اسْتُرْ عَوْرَتِي وَآمِنْ رَوْعَاتِي وَاحْفَظْنِي مِنْ بَيْنِ يَدَيَّ وَمِنْ خَلْفِي، وَعَنْ يَمِينِي وَعَنْ شِمَالِي وَمِنْ فَوْقِي، وَأَعُوذُ بِعَظَمَتِكَ أَنْ أُغْتَالَ مِنْ تَحْتِي».

"O Allaah! I ask you for well-being in this life and in the hereafter.

O Allaah! I ask You for forgiveness and well-being in my religion, my life, my family and my property.

O Allaah! Hide my faults and protect me from all my fears.

O Allaah! Protect me from the front, from behind, on my right, on my left and above me.

I place myself under the protection of Your greatness lest I be seized from beneath me."

This invocation is derived from His Saying:

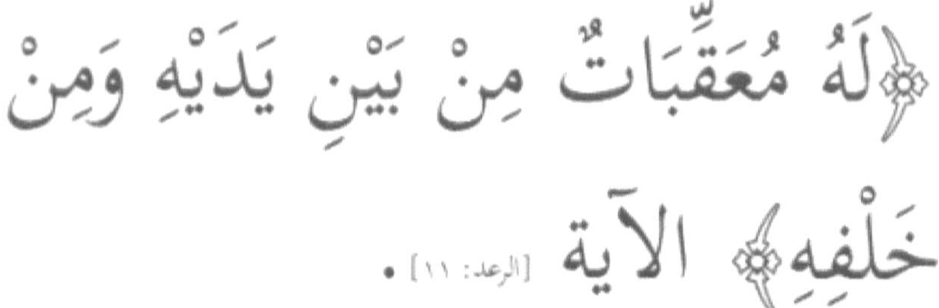

"He [man] has in front of him and behind him Angels who take turns guarding him by the order of Allaah." (Surah 13: al-Ra'd, verse 11.)

Ibn 'Abbas (may Allaah be pleased with him) said: "These are the angels who protect him by the order of Allaah. Then, when the decree comes, they withdraw from him."

'Ali (may Allaah be pleased with him) said: "Two angels accompany each person, protecting him against everything that has not been decreed. Then, when the decree comes, they withdraw, leaving him to it. See then how the appointed hour is a fortified shield."

Mujahid said: Every servant has an angel who protects him against Jinns, Men and dangerous animals during his waking and sleeping moments. Nothing comes to the servant without the angel saying, "Go away!", except for something to which Allaah has given permission and which will therefore affect him."

The safeguarding of health and property by Allaah

Another example of the Safeguarding of the servant by Allaah lies in the safeguarding of his health, his strength, his reason and his property.

One of the Pious Predecessors (Salaf) said: "The scholar does not become senile."

Another said: "He who memorizes the Quran will find blessing in his reason (intellect)."

Some explained His Saying:

"Then We reduced him to the lowest of the low..."

"...except for those who believe and do righteous deeds..." (Surah 95: at-Tiin, verses 5-6)

stating that "the lowest level" referred to the frailty of old age.

Abu al-Tayyib al-Tabari passed the age of one hundred, yet his reason remained intact as did his strength.

One day he jumped from a large boat he was on, landing directly on the ground.

When he was blamed for this, he said: "We Safeguarded these members from sin in our youth, so Allaah Safeguarded them for us in our old age."

On the other hand, Junayd saw an old man begging and remarked: "He neglected Allaah in his youth, so Allaah neglected him in his old age."

Allaah also Safeguards the servant, because of his piety, through his children and his grandchildren.

It is said, in explanation of His Saying:

"And as for the wall, it belonged to two orphan boys of the city, and there was under it a treasure of theirs;

and their father was a virtuous man." (Surah 18: al-Kahf, verse 82)

Your Lord therefore wanted that both of them reached maturity and that they extract [themselves] their treasure, by a mercy of your Lord.

That they were Safeguarded because of the virtue of their father.

Muhammad ibn al-Munkadir said: "Allaah Safeguards the children and grandchildren of an individual because of his virtue (righteousness). He will Safeguard the city in which he is located, as well as the surrounding villages. They will always be under the protection of Allaah."

Ibnal-Musayyiba said to his son: "My son, I increase my prayers because of you in the hope that I will be Safeguarded through you." Then he recited: "Their father was a virtuous man."

'Umar ibn 'Abd Al-'Aziz said: "No believer dies except that Allaah Safeguards him through his children and his grandchildren."

Yahya ibn Isma'il ibn Salamah ibn Kuhayl said: "I had an older sister who fell into madness and became uncontrollable. She stayed in a room located in the attic, the furthest part of our home. She stayed there for ten years. One day, there was a knock on the door in the middle of the night, while we were sleeping.

I said, "Who is it?"

She replied: "Kajjah."

I say: "My sister?"

She replied: "Yes, your sister."

I opened the door and she entered the house for the first time in ten years.

She said: "Someone appeared to me in a dream and said: "Allaah Safeguarded your father, Isma'il, by virtue of your grandfather, Salamah. He also Safeguarded you because of your father, so if you wish, invoke Allaah and what has afflicted you will leave you or be patient and Paradise will be yours. Abu Bakr and 'Umar have interceded in favor of you with Allaah, the Mighty, the Majestic, through the love that your father and your grandfather had for them."

I then said, "If I have to choose only one of these two outcomes, then I choose patience so that Paradise can be mine. On the other hand, Allaah is Generous with His creatures, nothing is too big for Him. If He wants to grant me both outcomes, He can."

I was then told: "Allaah has granted you both and is pleased with your father and grandfather because of their love for Abu Bakr and 'Umar. Get up and go downstairs."

This is how Allaah relieved her from her ordeal.

When the servant devotes himself to obedience to Allaah, the Mighty, the Majestic, Allaah Safeguards him in this state, as is reported in the Musnad of Imam Ahmad, on the authority of Humayd ibn Hilal on the authority of someone who said: I came to the Prophet (peace and blessings of Allaah be upon him) and he showed me a house.

He (peace and blessings of Allaah be upon him) said, "A woman lived here. She went out to take part in a battle by joining the ranks of the Muslims. She left behind twelve goats as well as the weavers hook with which she weaved. She lost a goat and her weaving hook. She then invoked (prayed to Allaah): "My Lord! You guarantee the safeguarding of a person who goes out on Your path. I lost one of my goats and my weaving hook. I implore you to return them to me!"

The Messenger of Allaah (peace and blessings of Allaah be upon him) described to us the intensity of her supplication to her Lord, the Exalted.

He then said: "Then she awoke in the morning and found her goat, her hook and the likes of them in addition. If you wish, go visit her and ask her."

I said, "I believe you."

Shayban al-Ra'i tended his flock in open ground. On Friday, he drew a line around his animals, then went off to pray. When he returned, he found them right where he had left them.

One of the Pious Predecessors had a scale with which he weighed dirhams. He heard the call to prayer. So he left them scattered on the ground and went to pray. When he returned, he counted the money again and nothing was missing.

Allaah's safeguarding against harm

Allaah also protects His servants here on earth against any jinn and human who would like to harm Him.

He, the Most High, said:

"And whoever fears (has Taqwa of) Allaah, He will give him a favorable outcome (a way out of every difficulty), and will grant him His gifts (provide for him) from where he does not expect." (Surah 65: al-Talaq, verses 2-3)

'Aishah (Allaah be pleased with her) said: "He will suffice him against the anxieties and worries of this world."

Rabi' ibn Khutaym said: "He will give him a way out of everything that overwhelms a man."

'Aishah (Allaah be pleased with her) wrote to Mu'awiyah: "If you fear Allaah, He will be enough for you in place of people. If you fear people, they will be of no use to you in anything before Allaah."

One of the Caliphs wrote a letter to Hakam ibn 'Amr al-Ghifari in which he ordered him to do something contrary to the Book of Allaah. Hakam wrote to him in response: "I looked in the Book of Allaah and saw that it came before the letter of the Commander of the Faithful. If the heavens and the earth were united into one entity and an individual fears Allaah, the Mighty, the Majestic, Allaah would give him a way out. Peace."

One of them composed the following verses:

By the fear of Allaah, Man is helped.

Victories are achieved and hopes obtained.

He who is endowed with piety, He will grant him a way out.

This is how He willed it.

One of the Pious Predecessors wrote to his brother: "He who fears Allaah has Safeguarded himself. He who neglects piety (Taqwa – the fear of Allaah) has neglected himself and Allaah has absolutely no need of him."

Allaah's safeguarding against animals

One of the most astonishing ways in which Allaah Safeguards those who Safeguard Him is in the fact that He makes usually dangerous animals to protect a person and help him.

This is what happened to Safinah, the freed slave of the Prophet (peace and blessings of Allaah be upon him), when his ship sank and he drifted to an island. He met a lion and said: "O Abu al-Harith, I am Safinah, the freed slave of the Messenger of Allaah."

It was then that the lion began to walk with him and guide him along the path.

He then purred as if saying goodbye, then left.

Abu Ibrahim al-Sa'ih fell ill while he was in a place near a monastery. He said: "If only I was in front of the monastery door, the monks would have found me and taken care of me." Suddenly, a lion approached. He carried him on his back and placed him in front of the monastery door. Four hundred monks saw him and embraced Islam.

Ibrahim ibn Adham slept one day in a garden. A snake in whose mouth were a circle of flowers was near him and kept guard for him until he woke up.

So whoever Safeguards Allaah, Allaah will protect him from dangerous animals. Better yet, these animals will protect him.

Whoever neglects Allaah, Allaah will neglect him to the point that he will suffer harm through things from which he expected to benefit.

He may even see the closest and most loved members of his family harming him!

[Al-Fudayl ibn 'Iyyad] said: "When I disobey Allaah, I see the effects in the behavior of my servant and my donkey." This means that his servant becomes disrespectful and disobedient and his donkey refuses to carry him.

All good is found in obedience to Allaah and turning to Him.

All evil lies in disobeying Allaah and turning away from Him.

A devotee said: "He who leaves his master's door will never be able to plant his feet firmly in the ground."

One of them composed the following verses:

> By Allaah, I never came to visit You
> Without the earth being compacted before me.
> I never resolved to leave Your door
> Without tripping over the clothes I am wearing
> Forgive, neglect and amend my sins in Your Name O Allaah!
> For my condition with You is as YOu see it.

The safeguarding of Allaah against doubts and desires

The second category of safeguarding is the most noble, the best.

This is the protection of the religion of the servant by Allaah.

During his life, Allaah Safeguards the religion of the servant, as well as his faith, by protecting him from base doubts, misleading innovations and prohibited desires.

Allaah also Safeguards his religion at the time of death, so that he dies on Islam.

Hakam ibn Aban reported that Abu Makki said: "When death comes to an individual, the angel is told: "Smell his head!"

The angel will respond: "I smell the fragrance of the Quran."

He will then be told: "Feel his heart!"

He will answer: "I smell the fragrance of fasting."

It will be said to him again: "Smell his feet!"

The angel will say: "I smell the fragrance of night prayer."

This person had Safeguarded himself so Allaah, the Mighty, the Majestic, Safeguarded him.

This was reported by Ibn Abi al-Dunya.

The two Sahihs report, on the authority of al-Bara'a ibn 'Azib, that the Prophet (peace and blessings of Allaah be upon him) taught him to say, when going to bed: "O Allaah, if You take my soul, have mercy on it. And if you grant it reprieve, Safeguard it by that with which You have Safeguarded Your righteous servants."

The hadith of 'Umar mentions that the Prophet (peace and blessings of Allaah be upon him) taught him to say: "O Allaah, Safeguard me with Islam when I am standing, Safeguard me with Islam when I am sitting, and Safeguard me with Islam when I am lying down. Do not respond to the request of a hidden and envious enemy about me." Reported by Ibn Hibban in his Sahih.

When the Prophet (peace and blessings of Allaah be upon him) bid farewell to a traveler, he said: "I entrust your religion, your trust and your last actions to the care of Allaah."

Another hadith states that he (peace and blessings of Allaah be upon him) said: "When Allaah entrusts something to His care, He Safeguards it."

'Umar ibn al-Khattab (may Allaah be pleased with him) said in his sermons: "O Allaah, protect us by Your safeguarding and hold us firmly to Your command."

A man said to one of the Pious Predecessors: "May Allaah Safeguard you."

He replied: "My brother, do not ask that he be Safeguarded, rather ask that his faith be Safeguarded!"

With this response he wanted to emphasize the importance of praying for the safeguarding of religion of others.

Indeed, worldly safeguarding can be granted to both the virtuous and the sinner.

However, Allaah only Safeguards the religion of the believer.

He puts himself between him (his religion) and anything that could corrupt it through various means, some of which the servant is unaware and others that he might hate.

This is how He Safeguarded Joseph (peace be upon him) as He said:

"Thus [We acted] so as to remove from him evil and immorality. He was certainly one of Our chosen servants." (Surah 12, verse 14)

The safeguarding of Allaah through His intervention

He who is sincere towards Allaah, He will Safeguard him against evil and indecency.

He will protect him against them in ways he is not even aware of.

He will come between him and the paths leading to destructive sins.

Ma'ruf al-Karkhi saw young people preparing to go into battle in a time of unrest (fitnah).

He said: "O Allaah, Safeguard them!"

They asked him: "Why do you pray for them?"

He replied: "If He were to Safeguard them, they would not go and accomplish what they intend to do."

'Umar heard someone say: "O Allaah, You come between a person and his heart, so come between me and my disobedience to You."

This pleased 'Umar who invoked in favor of this person.

In the exegesis of the Word of Allaah, the Most High:

"Know that Allaah intervenes between a man and his heart." (Surah 8, verse 24)

Ibn 'Abbas said: "He intervenes between the believer and (his committing of) the sins which would drag him to Hell."

A man from previous generations performed the Hajj.

While sleeping with a group of people in Makkah, he felt a sudden urge to commit a sin.

He heard a voice cry: "Woe to you! Are you not performing Hajj?"

Thus, Allaah Safeguarded him from committing this sin.

A man went out with a group of people, intending to commit a specific sin.

When he was about to accomplish it, a voice cried out:

"Every soul is a hostage to what it has earned." (Surah 74, verse 24)

He then abandoned the idea of committing it.

A man entered a dense grove, filled with trees.

He said: "I can commit my sin here without anyone seeing me.

He then heard a voice echoing through the grove (reciting the verse):

"Does He who created not know when He is the All-Pervading, the All-Aware? (Surah 67, verse 14)

Another was willing to commit a sin and went out to do it.

Along the way, he met a storyteller practicing his profession among the people.

He stopped to listen to him and heard him say: "O you who desire to commit a sin! Do you not know that the Creator of desires knows your intention perfectly?"

Hearing these words, he fainted.

When he regained consciousness, he repented immediately.

A righteous king once fell in love with one of his subjects endowed with great beauty.

He feared for his person.

So he remained in prayer during the night, seeking help from Allaah.

During that same night, the subject fell ill and died three days later.

The safeguarding of Allaah through exhortation

Some were Safeguarded through the exhortation given by a person whom they wanted to be their accomplice in sin.

An example of this is in the story of one of the three who entered the cave and were blocked by a rock.

[The hadith] mentions that one of them when he lay with a woman, ready to commit adultery, when she said to him: "Fear Allaah and do not break the seal except by due right."

It was then that he left her.

Another example is found in the story of Kifl, a man of the Children of Israel who frequently committed sins.

He was attracted by a woman and gave her sixty dinars.

He then lay down with her, ready to do the forbidden.

She began to tremble with fear.

He then asked her: "Am I forcing you?"

She replied: "No, but I have never done such a thing before and only need (such as hunger and poverty) that forces me to do it."

He said: "You fear Allaah, so must I not fear Him also?"

Then he left her, giving her the money as a gift.

He then said: "By Allaah, Kifl will never disobey Allaah again."

He died the same night.

The next morning, these words were written on his door: "Allaah has forgiven Kifl."

This was reported by Imam Ahmad and Tirmidhi on the authority of Ibn 'Umar (may Allaah be pleased with him), to the Messenger (peace and blessings of Allaah be upon him).

A man tried to seduce a woman and ordered her to lock the door, which she did.

She then said: "A door is still open."

He asked, "Which door is this?"

She replied: "That between Allaah, the Almighty, the Most High, and us."

He then turned away from her.

Another man tried to seduce a Bedouin woman.

He said: "Who can see us besides the stars?"

She replied: "What about the one who put them there?"

All these stories illustrate the providence of Allaah and His intervening between the servant and the fulfillment of his sin.

When speaking of sinners, al-Hasan said: "Their value diminished with Him, so they disobeyed Him."

If they had kept a valiant and honorable position with Him, He would have Safeguarded them."

Bishr said: "The noble and honorable never persist in disobeying Allaah. The wise man never gives preference to this lower world over the Hereafter."

Allaah ensures the best for his servant

Here is another example of the safeguarding of the servant's religion by Allaah.

The servant can pursue a worldly goal like power (leadership) or undertake a worldly activity like commerce and Allaah, knowing what is good for him, comes between him and his goal.

The servant, inattentive to this, then hates what happens.

Ibn Mas'uda says: The servant aims to undertake a trade or acquire power with the hope that this will be made easier for him. Allaah looks at him and say to the Angels: "Turn away from this, for if I made this matter easy for him, I would cause his entry into Hell!" Thus, Allaah prevents him from achieving what he aims for. The servant, all agitated, complains: "So-and-so beat me! So-and-so got me!" In reality, all this was nothing more than an expression of the grace of Allaah, the Almighty, the Most High!"

Even more astonishing is the fact that the servant tries so hard to perform an act of worship, when this specific work is not what is best for him.

It is then that Allaah intervenes between him and this act in order to Safeguard him.

All the while the servant remains inattentive to this.

Among the people of the first generations there was a man who frequently asked for martyrdom.

A voice then called him: "If you were embarked on a military expedition, you would be captured and converted to Christianity, so stop asking that."

So, in summary, he who Safeguards the limits of Allaah and carefully respects His rights, Allaah will take care of safeguarding him in his worldly and religious life, here on earth and in the Hereafter.

Allaah is the Protector of the Believers

In His Book, Allaah, the Most High, has informed us that He is the Protector of the Believers and that He protects the righteous.

This includes His safeguarding what is good for them in this life and the Hereafter and not abandoning them to another.

Allaah, the Most High, said:

"Allaah is the Protector of those who have faith: He brings them out of darkness into light." (Surah 2, verse 257.

"It is because Allaah is truly the Protector of those who believe; while the disbelievers have no protector." (Surah 47, verse 11)

"And whoever puts his trust in Allaah, He [Allaah] will be sufficient for him." (Surah 65, verse 3)

"Is Allaah not enough for His slave [as support]?" (Surah 39, verse 36)

Whoever establishes the rights of Allaah, Allaah will undertake to maintain everything that is beneficial to him in this life and in the next.

He who wishes that Allaah Safeguards him and takes care of all his affairs, let him first respect the rights that Allaah has over him.

He who does not wish to be afflicted with what he hates then let him not engage in what Allaah hates.

One among the Pious Predecessors went from assembly to assembly saying: "He who wishes that Allaah Safeguards his well-being, let him fear Allaah."

Al-'Umari, the devoted worshipper (of Allaah alone on the authority of the authentic Sunnah of the Prophet – peace and blessings of Allaah be upon him), said to anyone who asked him for advice: "Behave with Allaah, the Almighty, exactly as you would have Him behave with you."

Salih ibn 'Abd Al-Karim said: "Allaah, the Almighty says: "By My Might and My Majesty, I do not look at a heart which I know is filled with love towards respect for My obedience without Me taking charge of its protection and strengthening it."

One of the earlier scriptures mentions: Allaah, the Almighty, says: "Son of Adam, will you not tell me what makes you laugh? Son of Adam, fear Me and then sleep wherever you wish!"

This means that when you clothe yourself in the fear that is due to Allaah, then you no longer have to worry about what will be good for you, because Allaah knows them better than you and will lead them to you in the best of ways.

Narrated Jabir, the Prophet (peace and blessings of Allaah be upon him) said: "Whoever wishes to know his position with Allaah, let him examine himself and see the position that Allaah has with him. Allaah grants the individual the same position that He has with him."

This proves that the attention that Allaah pays to His servant and His safeguarding is proportional to the attention that the servant bears to the rights of Allaah, to their establishment, to respecting His limits and to their safeguarding.

He who aims to please Allaah, to draw near to Him, to know Him, to love Him and to serve Him, will find that Allaah will treat him in a similar way.

Allaah, the Most High, says: "Remember Me, I will remember you." (Surah 2, verse 152)

"Keep your commitments to Me, I will keep Mine." (Surah 2, verse 40)

Moreover, Allaah is the Most Benevolent of the benevolent.

He rewards a good deed by increasing it tenfold and more.

He who draws near to Him by a hand-span, He draws near to him by a cubit.

Whoever comes close to Him by a cubit, He approaches Him by a fathom, and whoever comes to Him walking, He hastens running towards Him.

Everything that is given to the individual comes from himself, and nothing afflicts him about what he hates without it being the result of his failures to respect the rights of his Lord.

'Ali (may Allaah be pleased with him) said: "The servant must place his hope in his Lord and his Lord only. There is nothing to fear except his sins."

It has been said: "He who clarifies and purifies will be purified, and he who mixes will be treated on the authority of it."

Masruq said: "He who scrupulously respects Allaah despite the instability and whims of his heart, Allaah will Safeguard for him the movements of his limbs."

There is much more to say about this, but what we have mentioned is enough and all praise belongs to Allaah.

Chapter 3: Allaah is with you

The Messenger of Allaah (peace and blessings of Allaah be upon him) said: "Safeguard Allaah and you will find Him in front of you."

Another narration says: "Safeguard Allaah and you will find him before you."

This means that he who Safeguards the limits of Allaah and carefully respects His rights will find Allaah with him in all his affairs.

He will surround him on all sides, help him, Safeguard him, support him, strengthen his steps and grant him His divine accord.

He is: "He who observes what each soul does," and He, the Most High, is: "With those who fear Him with piety and those who do good."

Qatadah said: "Allaah is with those who fear Him with piety. He who has Allaah with him is in the camp that will never be defeated, with the sentry who never sleeps and with the guide who never goes astray."

One of the Pious Predecessors wrote to his brother the following words: "If Allaah is with you, then who will you fear? If He is against you, then who will you place your hope on? Peace!"

This "company" is of a specific and special kind which is reserved only for the pious.

This is not the general "company" mentioned in His Saying: "He is with you wherever you are", "...But they do not hide from Allaah. He is with them when they spend the night saying words that He (Allaah) does not approve of."

And Allaah understands perfectly what they do.

This "specific companionship" implies help, support and safeguarding, such as Allaah said to Moses and Haroun (Allah have mercy on them): "Fear not. I am with you, All-Hearing and All-Seeing."

He, the Most High, said:

"He said to his companion: 'Do not grieve, Allaah is with us!'"

He (peace and blessings of Allaah be upon him) said to Abu Bakr, in that situation: "What do you think of two, of whom Allaah is the third?

The meaning of this "company" is not the same as that mentioned in His Saying:

"No secret conversation (can take place) between three without He being their fourth, nor between five without He being their sixth, neither less nor more than that without He being with them, there where they are located."

Here, the meaning is general and refers to any group of people.

The specific meaning corresponds to what the following hadith refers to: "My servant continues to draw closer to Me through supererogatory acts (optional actions) until I love him. Once I love him, I become his hearing with which he hears, his sight with which he sees, his hand with which he strikes and his foot with which he walks."

There are numerous texts from the Book and the Sun-nah which prove that the Lord, Glorified be He, is close to those who obey and fear Him, who Safeguard His limits and carefully respect His rights.

On the way to Tabuk, Bunan al-Hammal passed through vast lands and suddenly felt alone.

A voice shouted: "Why do you feel alone? Is not your Beloved with you?"

Thus, he who Safeguards Allaah carefully and fulfills His rights, will find Him in front of him and before him in every situation.

He will take comfort in Him and rely on Him instead of His creation.

Chapter 4: Knowing Allaah

The Messenger of Allaah (peace and blessings of Allaah be upon him) said: "Know Allaah in ease and He will know you in difficulty."

The meaning of these words is that the servant who fears Allaah, Safeguards His limits and carefully fulfills His rights in times of ease and comfort, ends up knowing Allaah.

This gives rise to spiritual knowledge between him and Allaah.

It follows then that his Lord will know him in times of difficulty.

He will know the works that his servant did in times of ease.

Because of this knowledge, He will provide him relief in times of adversity.

It is also a specific spiritual knowledge that leads to closeness to Allaah, the Almighty, to His love towards His servant and to His response to his supplications.

It is therefore not general spiritual knowledge which is designated here, that relating to His Creation of which nothing is hidden from Him.

Allaah, the Most High, said:

"He knows you best when He produced you from the earth, and also when you were embryos in the wombs of your mothers."

"We created Man and We know what his soul suggests to him"

Reference is made to this specific knowledge in the hadith qudsi: "My servant continues to draw closer to Me through supererogatory acts until I love him. Once I love him, I become his hearing with which he hears, his sight with which he sees, his hand with which he fights and his foot with which he walks. If he then asks Me for something, I give it to him and if he asks Me for My protection, I grant it to him."

Fudayl met Sha'wanah, the devotee, and asked her to pray for him.

She replied: "What separates you from Him? If you call upon Him, He will respond." After hearing these words he fainted and fell unconscious.

Abu Ja'far al-Sa'ih said that 'al-Hasan came to Habib, Abu Muhammad, on the run from Hajjaj.

He said: "Abu Muhammad! Hide me, because the police are on my steps!"

He replied: "Abu Sa'id, I am ashamed of you! Is there not a relationship of trust between you and your Lord, so that you can invoke Him and hide from them? Come into my house."

The police entered after him, but did not see him.

This was reported to Hajjaj who said: "He was rather in the house, but Allaah obscured their sight so that they would not see him."

When this specific knowledge arises, a special spiritual connection arises between the servant and his Lord that provides a feeling of comfort and intimacy with Him, coupled with a feeling of modesty towards Him.

This specific spiritual knowledge is different from that which is general and which applies to all believers.

It is this specific spiritual knowledge that the worshippers (of Allah on the authority of the authentic teachings of the Prophet – peace and blessings of Allah be upon him) aspire to and speak of.

Abu Sulayman heard a man say: "I spent all night talking about women."

He said: "Woe to you! Are you not ashamed of Him? He sees you spending the night mentioning other than Him! But anyway, how could you be modest towards the One you don't even know?"

Ahmad ibn 'Asim al-Antaki said: "My wish is to die after knowing my Master. Knowing Him does not mean affirming [His existence], but rather it is about the knowledge which leads to being modest towards Him."

This specific spiritual knowledge leads the servant to be satisfied with his Lord, to rely on Him, to trust on Him for deliverance from all difficulties and distress, just as it leads to the Lord answering his invocations.

When al-Hasan al-Basri hid from Hajjaj, it was suggested that he flee Basrah for fear that he would be discovered.

He wept and said, "Should I leave my city, my family and my brothers? My knowledge of my Lord, as well as of His blessings which He has bestowed upon me, leads me to believe that He will save me and deliver me from Him, if Allaah, the Most High, wills."

Hajjaj never harmed him.

Instead, after this incident, he honored him greatly and spoke well of him.

Ma'ruf was asked: "What gave rise to the desire in you to isolate yourself and devote yourself to worship?"

Some people mentioned death, barzakh, Paradise and Hell as possible causes.

Ma'ruf replied, "What is this? All this is in His Hand. When there is spiritual knowledge between you and Him, He is sufficient for you through all of this."

The hadith reported by Al-Tirmidhi, on the authority of Abu Hurayrah, clarifies this point.

The Prophet (peace and blessings of Allaah be upon him) said: "He who wishes Allaah to answer him in times of difficulty must frequently invoke Him in times of ease."

Ibn Abi al-Dunya, Ibn Abi Hatim, Ibn Jarir and others report the hadith of Yazid al-Raqashi, on the authority of Anas, that the Prophet (peace and blessings of Allaah be upon him) said: When Jonah (peace be upon him) invoked, while he was in the belly of the whale, the Angels said: "This is a familiar voice, but which comes from a strange place!"

Allaah says: "Do you know who this is?"

They asked, "Who is it?"

Allaah replied: "My servant, Jonah (Yunus)."

They said: "Jonah, Your servant, the one whose actions have always been accepted and whose supplications have always been answered?"

Allaah says: "Yes."

They said: "Lord! Are you not going to show him mercy in this difficult moment out of merit for what he did in times of ease?"

Allaah replied: "Of course!"

Then, He ordered the whale to throw him onto the deserted shore.

Dahhak ibn Qays said: "Remember Allaah in times of ease and He will remember you in times of difficulty."

Jonah (peace be upon him) remembered Allaah. Then, when he was swallowed by the whale, Allaah, the Most High, said:

"If he had not been among those who glorify Allaah, he would have remained in its belly until the Day of Resurrection."

Pharaoh was an oppressor, heedless of the remembrance of Allaah. When he was drowning, he said: "I believe!", and Allaah, the Most High, says:

"Will you believe now, when before you were disobedient and were among the corrupters?

Rishdin ibn Sa'da said: "A man asked Abual-Darda to advise him.

He replied: "Remember Allaah in ease, He will remember you in difficulty."

Salman al-Farisi said: "He who is given to prayer (to Allaah alone) in times of ease, and then faces difficulty and implores Allaah, the Angels say: "This is a familiar voice," and intercede on his behalf.

Whoever is not given to supplication in times of ease, and then faces difficulty and implores Allaah, the Almighty, the Angels say of him: "It is not a familiar voice," and do not intercede on his behalf.

The hadeeth about the three who got into a cave and then were blocked by a rock also supports this principle.

They were only saved because they invoked Allaah, citing the good works they had done before, that is what they accomplished while they were well off: respecting the rights of their parents, abandoning an act of sin and keeping a commitment that would not have been publicly known.

We therefore now understand that knowing Allaah in times of ease leads to Allaah knowing His servant in times of difficulty.

We also understand that there is no trial that the believer will face in this lower world worse than death. However, this test is actually lighter than what follows if the servant's destination is bad, or it is the worst if his destination is good.

Therefore, it becomes obligatory on the servant to prepare for death before it comes to him by performing good actions with haste.

No one knows what day or night they will be gripped by this ordeal.

Remembering good works at the time of death quickens the servant's good opinion of his Lord, helps relieve the pangs of death, and strengthens hope.

It was said: "It was considered advisable for the servant to have hidden good works which would serve to alleviate the onset of death."

It was also considered praiseworthy for a person to die after performing worship such as pilgrimage, jihad or fasting.

Al-Nakha'i said: "They considered it praiseworthy to remind the servant, on his deathbed, of his good works so that he would form a good opinion of his Lord."

While he was ill, Abu 'Abd Al-Rahman al-Sulami said: "How can I not have hope in my Lord who sees that I have fasted eighty months of Ramadan for Him?"

When death came to Abu Bakr ibn 'Ayyash and those around him were crying, he said: "Do not cry, for I have finished the Quran at this place of prayer thirteen thousand times!"

It is reported that he said to his son: "Do you think Allaah would waste forty years of your father's life, every night of which he completed the Quran?"

While on his deathbed, one of the Pious Predecessors saw his son crying.

He said to him: "Don't cry, because your father never committed an indecent act."

Adam ibn Abu Iyas completed the Quran while he was already wrapped, awaiting his death.

He exclaimed: "By my love for You! Be gentle with me during this terrible moment. My hopes and expectations have been placed on You all this time, in preparation for this day. No deity is worthy of worship except Allaah!"

He died with these words, may Allaah have mercy on him.

On his deathbed, 'Abd Al-Samad, the ascetic, said: "My Master, this is why I have kept You in my hidden store. It is for this moment that I have Safeguarded You. Give reality to my good opinion of You!"

At the time of his death, the women around Ibn 'Aqil were crying.

He said: "I have given legal verdicts for Him for fifty years, leave me alone to prepare my meeting with Him."

Whoever, during his life, obeys Allaah and Safeguards His limits, Allaah will take care of him on his deathbed and enable him to die on faith.

He will make him firm with firm words, in his grave, when he is questioned by the two angels.

He will put away from him the punishment of the grave.

He will give him comfort to his isolation in times of solitude and darkness.

One of the Pious Predecessors said: "If Allaah is with you when you enter the grave, you will suffer no harm and you will not be alone."

After his death, a scholar among the pious was seen in a dream.

He was questioned about his condition.

He replied: "My Lord, the Almighty, keeps me company."

He who, in this world, has Allaah as his Companion in moments of retirement and solitude can truly hope that Allaah will be his Companion in the darkness of the grave, when he leaves this world.

It is in this sense that it was said:

When I feel isolated, alone, My Lord! Be my Companion.

For I have completely believed in Your Revelation.

My journey to Allaah leaves me without any apprehension.

More than my family, He shows me gentleness and compassion!

The same applies to the terror of the Day of Resurrection, to its horrors and its trials.

When Allaah takes care of His obedient servant, He delivers him from all this.

Qatadaha said in his explanation of the Saying of the Most High:

"And whoever fears Allaah, He will give him a favorable outcome"

"(He will give him a favorable outcome) in relation to the test of death and the terrors of the Day of Resurrection."

'Ali ibn Abu Talha reports that Ibn 'Abbas (may Allaah be pleased with him) said in his commentary on this verse: "[This means] We will deliver him from all trials in this world and in the Hereafter."

Concerning the saying of Allaah, the Most High:

Those who say: "Our Lord is Allaah", and who stay in the right path, the Angels descend on them (saying): "Do not be afraid and do not grieve; but have the good news of Paradise which has been promised for you."

Zayd ibn Aslam said: "The good news will be announced to him at the time of death, in his grave and on the Day on which he is resurrected. He will find himself in Paradise before the joy of the good news has the chance to leave his heart!"

Thabit al-Bunani said in the commentary on this verse: It has been reported to us that two angels who accompanied the believer in this world will meet him when Allaah raises him from his grave.

They will say: "Do not be afraid, do not grieve."

Allaah will then relieve his fear and comfort his eye.

There is not a single terror that will strike down man on the Day of Resurrection without it being a source of comfort for the believer because of the fact that Allaah guided him and what he accomplished during his life.

All this was reported by Ibn Abi Hatim and others.

As for he who does not know Allaah in times of ease, he will have no one to know him in times of difficulty, neither in this life nor in the Hereafter. Noting the condition of this type of people in this world testifies to this reality and their condition in the afterlife will be even worse, because they will have neither protector nor support.

Chapter 5: Asking Allaah

The Messenger of Allaah (peace and blessings of Allaah be upon him) said: "When you ask, ask Allaah."

Allaah, the Exalted, has ordained that one should ask of Him, that He forbids that one should ask of another.

Allaah, the Most High, has ordered that one should ask Him: "Ask Allaah for His grace."

The hadith of Abu Hurayrah on the authority of which the Prophet (peace and blessings of Allaah be upon him) said: "Allaah is angry with the one who does not ask of Him."

He also reports the following hadith: "Allaah loves those who are the most sincere and the most persistent in invocation."

Another hadith mentions: "Each of you must ask your Lord for all your needs, even if the strap of your sandals if it should break."

Many ahadith have the same meaning.

There are also many authentic Ahadith which forbid asking creatures.

Ibn Mas'ud reports that the Messenger of Allaah (peace and blessings of Allaah be upon him) said: "A person, despite being rich, persists in asking (people) until his face wears out and then he has no face with Allaah."

The Prophet (peace and blessings of Allaah be upon him) took an oath of allegiance from a group of His Companions which mentioned the fact that they should not ask anything from people.

Among them were Abu Bakr Al-Siddiq, Abu Dharr and Thawban.

If their riding whip or the muzzle of their camels fell off, they didn't ask anyone to retrieve it for them.

Know that what is required is to ask Allaah, the Most High, rather than His creatures, whether from a rational or legal point of view.

Asking is a way of sacrificing one's honor and demeaning oneself in front of the one being asked, which (such a demeaning) is only viable towards Allaah.

Lowering oneself is only done for Allaah through worship and request.

This is a sincere sign of love.

Yusuf ibn al-Husayn was asked: "What drives lovers to take so much pleasure in humbling themselves in love?"

He replied: In love, the degradation of a person is nobility, and submission to the loved one is dignity.

This act of self-abasement and this love is valid only towards Allaah, and they make up true worship which is reserved only for the one True God.

Imam Ahmad, may Allaah have mercy on him, said in his invocations: "O Allaah! Just as you prevented my face from bowing down to anyone other than You, so prevent it from asking anyone other than You!"

Abu al-Khayr al-Aqta' said: While I was in Makkah for a year, I was afflicted by want and illness. Every time I went out to ask for help, a voice would cry out, "Do you want to offer a face that bows down for Me to someone else?"

In this sense, it was said:

He who offers Him his face will never agree to ask from anyone other than Him

Even if begging brings him wealth

When you compare the request

With any gift obtained

The request will prevail

And the gifts will be secondary

If you must offer Your face to begging

Offer it to Him Who is Gentle and Generous.

It is for this reason that he who engages in begging without being in need will come on the Day of Resurrection without any piece of flesh on his face as has been reported in the two Sahihs.

Indeed, in this world, he removed nobility, sacredness and honor from his face.

Thus, Allaah, on the Day of Resurrection, will strip away his physical beauty and grace, leaving in its place only a skeletal face devoid of flesh.

Furthermore, he will not hold any rank with Allaah.

The request to Allaah expresses deep servitude, because by performing this act, the servant displays his need for Him and recognizes His ability to respond.

To ask a creature is injustice, because he is incapable of attracting good for itself or repelling evil. What can we say then when he has to do it for someone other than himself?! Asking the creatures consists of choosing an incapable being in place of the One who is Capable.

This meaning is attested by the hadith in Sahih Muslim, on the authority of Abu Dharr, that the Prophet (peace and blessings of Allaah be upon him) said: "O My servants, if the first and the last of you, if the Men and the Jinns of you, stood on one plain, and if all of you asked Me for any favor and if I gave it to all those who ask for it, it would not diminish anything that I have, except what the needle dipped into the ocean decreases."

Al-Tirmidhi and others report the following addition: "... for I am the Generous, the Rich beyond need, the Glorious. I do what I wish. My gift is a word and My punishment is a word. When I want something to be, I just say 'Be!' and it is."

So, how can we ask the one who is in need and who is incapable and leave the Rich and the Capable?! This is certainly very surprising! One of the Pious Predecessors said: "I am ashamed to ask Allaah for anything in this world even though He owns it. How then can I ask someone who doesn't own it?!"

One of the Pious Predecessors was going through difficult times and decided to ask one of his brothers for help.

He saw a person in a dream saying:

Is it acceptable for one who is free

When he finds everything he desires with Allaah

To incline his heart towards the servants?

Then he woke up and noticed that among many people, he was the one with the most satisfied heart.

One of the Pious Predecessors said: I have read the following passage in one of the heavenly scriptures:

Allaah, the Almighty, said: "Can anyone hope for anything other than Me in difficult times? Adversity is in My Hand and I am the Ever-Living One, the Self-sufficient One.

Is there any hope other than Me to who you can knock on the door early in the morning? In My Hands are the keys to all treasures and My Door is open to anyone who calls on Me! Who can say that he placed his hopes in Me during the ordeal and that I abandoned him? Who can say that he placed his hopes in Me during adversity and that I cut short his hope? Who can say that he knocked on My door and I did not open it for him? I am the Source of hope, so how can hope be extinguished before Me? Am I a miser whom the servant finds miserly? What prevents those who hope to place their hopes in Me? If I united the inhabitants of the heavens and the earth, and gave to each of them the equivalent of what I give to all of them, and made the hope of each of them come true, my Kingdom would not diminish by the weight of a atom! How can a Kingdom diminish when I am its Manager? Miserable is he who despairs of My Mercy and transgresses My prohibitions with audacity!"

Allaah loves to be asked and is angry with anyone who does not ask Him.

He wants His servants to desire Him, ask Him, call upon Him, and display their need for Him.

He loves those who are fervent and persistent in their invocations.

Creatures (that is the creation of Allah), in general, hate being asked, because they are incapable and find themselves in need. So how can they fulfill someone else's need?

Ibnal-Sammaka said: "Do not ask him who will flee instead of listening to your request."

Instead, ask Him who commanded you to ask Him.

Abu al-'Atahiyyah said:

Allaah becomes angry if you neglect asking Him

The son of Adam becomes angry if you ask Him

Direct your request to Allah

Since we waver between the blessings of our Lord.

Yahya ibn Mu'adh said: "O You (that is Allah) who is angry with him who does not ask You, do not hold back from him who does ask You!"

Allaah, the Most High, requires His servants to ask Him.

Every night He calls: "Is there anyone who will call upon Me so that I may respond to his invocation? Is there anyone who will ask Me so that I may grant him his request?"

Allaah, the Most High, said:

"And when My servants ask you about Me, I am very close: I respond to the call of the one who prays to Me when he prays to Me."

No matter when the servant invokes Him, he will find Him listening, close and attentive.

There will be no guard at the door.

If he asked a creature, he would very quickly face erected barriers and closed doors.

He would realize that it is, most of the time, very difficult to reach the target person.

Tawus said to 'Ata: "Be careful and don't seek help from him who will shut his door in your face and who will erect a barrier. Instead, go to Him whose door is open until the Day of Judgment, who commanded you to ask Him and who promised you that He would answer you."

Wahb ibn Munabbih said to one of the scholars: "Have I not heard that you go to kings and princes (selling) your knowledge to them? Woe to you! You go to him who closes his door in your face and will make it understood (to you) that he is poor (and cannot help you), hiding his wealth, but you abandon Him who opened His door to you, noon and evening, presenting to you His wealth and saying to you: "Call on Me and I will answer you!"

Maymun ibn Mihran saw people gathering at the gate of one of the rulers and said: "He whose need is not met by the Sultan should know that the houses of the All-Merciful are always open. Let him go to the mosque and pray for two units, asking Him to fulfill his need."

Bakral-Muzani said: "Son of Adam, who is in a better situation than you? When you wish, you can purify yourself and speak privately with your Lord, without obstacles between you and without the need for a translator."

A man asked a righteous person to intercede on his behalf so that someone would answer his request.

He said: "I will not leave an open door to go to a closed door."

Regarding this, it has been said:

The courts of kings are closed

The gate of Allaah is open, not barricaded.

Another said:

Say to those who hide from the seekers

In houses where it is forbidden to approach

And whose sentries prevent entry

"At His gate, Allaah has no watchman."

Another said to a scholar:

Do not sit at the door of him Who refuses you entry.

Your reason: "My need will not be fulfilled If I do not visit his house."

Leave him and go instead to his Lord,

Your need will be fulfilled, unlike the previous one who balked!

Ibn Abi al-Dunya relates the hadith on the authority of which a man went to the Prophet (peace and blessings of Allaah be upon him) and said: "Messenger of Allaah, this tribe attacked me and captured my son and my camels."

The Prophet (peace and blessings of Allaah be upon him) said: "Muhammad's family lives in such a place that they don't even have a mudd or a sa' of food. So ask Allaah, the Almighty, the Most High."

He returned to his wife.

She asked: "What did he say to you?"

He then told her about their conversation.

She said: "What a great response!"

Shortly after, Allaah returned his son to him accompanied by a larger number of camels than before! They he went to the Prophet (peace and blessings of Allaah be upon him) and told him what had happened.

The Prophet (peace and blessings of Allaah be upon him) went up to the pulpit and praised Allaah, praising Him.

Then he ordered people to ask Allaah, the Almighty, the Most High, and to place their desires in Him.

He recited:

"And whoever fears Allaah, He will give him a favorable outcome"

A man asked Thabit al-Bunani to intercede in his favor with a judge so that his need is met.

Thabit rose to accompany him and each time he passed by a mosque on the way, he entered, prayed and invoked him.

When they arrived at their destination, the judge was no longer there.

The man was about to reprimand him, but he said: "All this time I have only been responding to your request."

Allaah fulfilled his need without it being necessary for him to go to the judge.

While Ishaq ibn 'Ubbad al-Basri was sleeping, he once saw a person in a dream saying to him: "Relieve the anguished!" ".

When he woke up, he asked, "Is there anyone in need nearby?"

He was told: "We don't know."

They then fell asleep and the same dream occurred a second time, then a third time during which the man said: "Are you falling asleep without relieving him?"

He woke up, took three hundred dirhams with him and went to Basra on his mule.

Once there, he stopped at the door of a mosque where some funeral prayers were being held.

He entered and saw a man praying.

When the latter realized his presence, he completed his prayer and approached him.

Ishaq said: "O servant of Allaah! (What are you doing) here at this time? What do you need ?"

He replied: "I am a man who only has one hundred dirhams in his possession that I have lost and I have a debt of two hundred dirhams."

Isahq took out his money and said: "Here are three hundred dirhams, take them."

The man accepted them and Ishaq asked: "Do you know me?"

He replied: "No."

He said: "I am Ishaq ibn 'Ubbad. If you encounter a difficulty, come see me, my house is in such and such a place."

The man replied: "May Allaah have mercy on you!" If adversity touches us, we will first rely on the One who brought you here!"

'Abd Al-Rahman ibn Zayd ibn Aslam said: "One morning, my mother said to my father: "By Allaah, there is no meat to eat in your house!"

They got up, performed ablutions, put on their usual clothes and prayed in the house.

My mother turned to me and said: "Your father is not going to do anything more than that, so go!"

I went out and a friend of our family who sold dates came to mind.

I then went to his market.

When he saw me, he called me, took me to his house and offered me something to eat.

Then, of his own free will, without me speaking to him about anything regarding our difficulties, he took out a purse containing thirty dinars and said: "Convey my greetings to your father and tell him that we have made him our partner in our business and that this is his share."

Ibrahim ibn Adham went on a military expedition with some of his colleagues.

They decided to share the expenses.

Everyone gave their part.

He began to think about which companion he was going to ask for a loan from.

Then he said to himself: "Woe is me! I run after the servants and abandon their Master?! He said to me: "Who deserves your request more, them or Me?"

He performed his ablutions, prayed two units, then once in prostration, he said: "My Lord! You knew what I did and I only did it by mistake and ignorance. If You punish me, I deserve it and if You forgive me, You can do so. You know my need well, so fulfil it with Your mercy!"

He looked up and found four hundred dinars near him.

He took a dinar from it and left.

Asbagh ibn Zayd said: "My family and I spent three days without eating anything. My two young daughters came to me crying: 'O father! We are hungry!' So I went to the pool, performed my ablutions, prayed two units and was inspired to utter a certain invocation, the last words of which were: "O Allaah, open the doors of provisions for me and do not leave me in debt to anyone nor make me responsible for this before You in the Hereafter, concerning this by Your mercy, O Most Merciful of the merciful."

I came back home and my eldest daughter was standing there.

She said: "Father, my uncle has just come with this purse containing dirhams, this box loaded with flour and this box loaded with everything he found at the market! He said: 'Give my greetings to my brother and tell him that every time he is in need, he should invoke with this invocation and his need will be fulfilled.'"

Asbagh then said: "By Allaah, I don't have a brother and I don't know who that person was. However, Allaah is Omnipotent!"

Hakam ibn Musa said: I got up one morning and my wife was complaining about not having flour or bread.

I walked out, knowing I wouldn't be able to get anything.

As I was walking down the street, I said, 'O Allaah! You know that I know that You know that I have neither flour, nor bread, nor money, so grant us all this!'

A man came up to me and asked: 'Would you like some bread or flour?'

I replied: "One or the other."

Then I started looking for ways to get what I needed throughout the day, but I couldn't.

When I returned home, my family had prepared a feast of bread and meat.

I then asked them: "Where did you find this?"

They replied: "From the person which you sent!"

I then kept silent.

Awza'i said: While I was performing tawaf, I saw a man clinging to the cloth of the Ka'aba saying: "My Lord! You see how poor I am.

You see my children undressed.

You see my emaciated camel.

So what sees You, O He who sees without being seen!"

A voice called from behind him saying: "Asim, Asim, go to your uncle, he has just died in Ta'if and left behind a thousand sheep, three hundred camels, four hundred dirhams, four slaves and three Yemeni swords. Go and take everything, for you are his only heir!"

I then said: "Asim, the One you invoked was close to you!"

He replied: Have you not heard His Word:

"And when My servants ask you about Me, then I am very close: I respond to the call of the one who prays to Me when he prays to Me."

The stories and events concerning these subjects are numerous.

Shaykh Abu al-Faraj reports in his great work on history, with his chain of transmission including Hasan ibn Sufyan al-Fasawi, that he resided in Egypt with a group of colleagues, writing the hadith.

They found themselves in need.

They therefore sold their goods.

They ended up having nothing left to sell.

They were therefore forced to starve for three days without finding anything to eat.

They woke up on the fourth day having made the decision to beg because of their vital need.

They decided to draw lots to choose the one who would go out to beg and this fell on Hasan ibn Sufyan.

He says: "I was confused and distraught.

I couldn't bring myself to beg.

Instead, I went to the mosque and prayed two units in which I begged Allaah, the Almighty, the Most High, to relieve us from our ordeal.

I had not yet finished my prayer when a man entered the mosque, accompanied by his servant who was wearing a cloth.

He asked: "Who is Ha-san ibn Sufyan?"

I raised my head from prostration and replied, "It's me."

He said: "'Amir ibn Tulun conveys his greetings to you and welcomes you.

He asks your forgiveness for not keeping up with you and not fulfilling your rights.

He has sent you everything you need to cover your expenses.

He will visit you himself tomorrow and asks that you excuse him."

He placed in the hands of each of us a purse containing one hundred dirhams.

We were astonished and then asked how this could have happened.

He replied: Today, while he was asleep, he saw in a dream a horseman in the sky saying: "Get up and go to Hasan ibn Sufyan and his companions at such and such a mosque.

They haven't eaten anything for three days!"

He asked: "Who are you?"

He replied: "I am Ridwan, the guardian of Paradise!"

Hasan said: "We thanked Allaah, the Almighty, the Most High.

Then we packed our things, put everything in order and left Egypt the same night, for fear that 'Amir would really visit us, and through this, we would gain fame and rank among people, which could lead to ostentation and self-importance.

Chapter 6: Seeking Help from Allaah

The Messenger of Allaah (peace and blessings of Allaah be upon him) said: "When you seek help, seek help from Allaah."

After ordering us to Safeguard Allaah and to know Him in times of ease, this being the very essence of worship, he directed us to asking Allaah Alone and invoking Him: "Invocation (Du'a) is worship", as mentioned in the hadith of Nu'man ibn Bashir.

After saying this, the Prophet (peace and blessings of Allaah be upon him) recited: And your Lord said:

"Call on Me, and I will answer you."

This hadith is reported by the authors of the Four Sunans.

After what he advised before, he (peace and blessings of Allah be upon him) directed us to seek help from Allaah Alone.

This is derived from His Saying:

"It is You alone that we worship and it is You alone from whom we ask for help."

This verse illustrates a comprehensive principle and it is said that the essential wisdom of all revealed scriptures revolves around this.

There are two benefits in seeking help from Allaah Alone:

– the servant does not possess the necessary strength to perform acts of obedience without the help of Allaah

– No one can help him improve his life in this world and the hereafter besides Allaah, the Almighty, the Most High.

He whom Allaah helps is certainly helped.

The one whom Allaah abandons has certainly been abandoned.

It is authentically stated that the Prophet (peace and blessings of Allaah be upon him) said: "Be desirous of all that will be profitable for you, seek help from Allaah and do not despair."

He (peace and blessings of Allah be upon him) said in his sermons and taught his Companions to say: "All praise belongs to Allaah, we ask for His help and seek His guidance."

He ordered Mu'adh never to abandon the following invocation: "O Allaah! Help me to remember You, to be grateful to You, and to make good my worship of You", at the end of each prayer.

One of his (peace and blessings of Allah be upon him) invocation was: "My Lord! Help me and don't help others against me!"

The invocation of the Qunut which was said by 'Umar and others mentions: "O Allaah! We ask for Your help!"

A known account mentions that after having struck the sea to split it, Moses (peace be upon him) said: "O Allaah! All praise belongs to You, to You we complain, to You whose help is sought, it is to You we turn for relief, it is in You we place our trust. There is no force or movement except by You."

The servant is in need of seeking help from Allaah in doing what is prescribed, in abandoning what is forbidden and in bearing with patience the ups and downs of the decree.

Jacob (peace be upon him) said:

"[It therefore remains] only a beautiful patience! It is Allaah alone who is my help against what you are saying!"

It is for this reason that 'Aishah (Allah be pleased with her) uttered the same words during the incident of Slander and Allaah cleared her of this false accusation.

Moses said to his people:

"Ask Allaah for help and be patient."

Allaah said to his Prophet (peace and blessings of Allaah be upon him):

Say: "Lord, judge with truth! Our Lord, the Most Merciful, it is Him whose help is implored in the face of what you describe".

When the Prophet (peace and blessings of Allaah be upon him) announced to 'Uthman the good news of his entry into Paradise after going through trials, he said: "And Allaah's help is sought!"

When they entered the house of 'Uthman and struck him, he said, with blood running down his body: "No deity is worthy of worship except You, Glory be to You, I have been one the wrong-doers. O Allaah! I seek refuge with You from them, I seek Your help in all my affairs and I ask You for patience to endure what You have tested me with!"

It is reported from Abu Talhah that the Prophet (peace and blessings of Allaah be upon him) said during one of his battles, at the time of encountering the enemy: "O the Master of the Day of Judgment, it is You alone whom we worship and it is from You alone whose help we seek!"

Abu Talhah said: "I saw the men falling down with seizures!"

The Prophet (peace and blessings of Allaah be upon him) said: The invocation of Dhun-Nun (Jonah) when he invoked his Lord from the belly of the whale: "None is worthy of worship except You! Glory be to You! I have been one of the wrong-doers": there is no servant who invokes this invocation without it being answered."

The servant needs to seek Allaah's help in acquiring good in his religious and worldly life, just as Zubayr said in his last advice to his son, 'Abdullah, asking him to pay off his debts: "If you are incapable of doing so, seek help from my Master."

He asked, "Father, who is your master?"

Zubayr replied: "Allaah."

His son said: When I had difficulty paying his debts, I said: "Master of Zubayr, pay off his debt!" and it was cleared."

During the first sermon that 'Umar ibn al-Khattab (may Allaah be pleased with him) delivered on the pulpit, he said: "The Arabs are like a long suffering camel whose muzzle I hold. I will lead him across the great plain and I seek Allaah's help in this."

The servant will also need Allaah's help to get through the terrors of the Day of Resurrection, from the moment of his death.

When Khalid ibn al-Walid was on his deathbed, one of the men around him said: "This is a very difficult thing."

Khalid replied: "Of course! But I seek help from Allaah, the Almighty, the Most High."

When 'Amir ibn 'Abdullah ibn al-Zubayr was on his deathbed, he wept and said: "I only cry because of (the losing of) the heat of the day and the coolness of standing," that is the fasting during the day and praying at night.

He said: "I seek help from Allaah in bearing this fatal injury that is affecting me."

One of the elders said: "My Lord! I am amazed at the one who knows You and how he can have hope in another. I am amazed at the one who knows You and how he can ask for help from another!"

Al-Hasan wrote to 'Umar ibn 'Abd Al-'Aziz, may Allaah have mercy on them: "Do not seek help from anyone besides Allaah or Allaah will leave you to Him."

It has been said: "Seek help from Allaah, seek His support, for He is the best of those whose help is sought."

Chapter 7: The Pens have Dried

He (peace be upon him) said: "The Pen has dried (after writing) everything that will happen." And in another version: "The Pens have been lifted and the pages have dried."

All these refer to the functioning of the decree and the fact that everything has been recorded in an erstwhile and comprehensive book.

It has been said about a book that was completed a long time ago: the quills have been lifted from it or the quills used to write it have dried up or the pages have dried up. This is a nice way to refer to the decree and a way to emphasize the seriousness of the meaning.

The Book and the authentic Sunnah also emphasize this meaning.

Allaah, the Almighty, the Most High, said:

"Nothing befalls in the earth or in yourseves that is not recorded in a Book before We make it happen; and this is certainly easy for Allaah." Surah 57, verse 22.

Dahhak reports that Ibn 'Abbas said: "Allaah created The Pen and ordered it to move by His permission.

The size of The Pen is equivalent to the space between the heavens and the earth.

The Pen said: "Lord, what should I write?"

He replied: "Everything that I am to create and everything that will happen to My creation: rain, vegetation, souls, actions, sustenance and lifespan."

The Pen then wrote down everything that would happen until the Day of Resurrection and Allaah placed it in a Book inscribed under the Throne, with Him.

Abu Zabyan reported that Ibn Abbas said: "The first thing that Allaah created was the Pen."

He ordered it: "Write!"

It asked, "What should I write?"

He replied: "The decree."

It then wrote down everything that will happen until the appearance of the Last Hour."

Then he recited:

"Nuun. By the pen and what they write!"

Muslim reports from 'Abdullah ibn 'Amr that the Prophet (peace and blessings of Allaah be upon him) said: "Allaah recorded the destinies of all creatures fifty thousand years before He created the heavens and the earth."

Imam Ahmad, Al-Tirmidhi and Al-Nasa'i report the hadith of 'Abdullah ibn 'Amr who said: "The Messenger of Allaah (peace and blessings of Allaah be upon him) returned to us.

He was carrying two books.

He asked, "Do you know what these books are?"

We replied: "No, Messenger of Allaah, unless you tell us."

He said about the book that was in his right hand: "This is a book from the Lord of the worlds. It contains the names of the inhabitants of Paradise, the names of their parents and their tribes. It contains to the last man and they will not increase or decrease in number."

He said of the book in his left hand: "This is a book from the Lord of the worlds.

It contains the names of the inhabitants of Fire, the names of their parents and their tribes.

It contains to the last man and they will neither increase nor decrease in number."

His Companions (Allah be pleased with them) asked: "Messenger of Allaah, if the matter is already decided, why do (good) actions?"

He replied: "Remain firm, perseverant and balanced.

The last act of an inhabitant of Paradise will be an act of the inhabitants of Paradise, whatever he may have accomplished previously, and the last act of an inhabitant of the Fire will be an act of the inhabitants of the Fire, whatever he may have accomplished previously."

Then the Messenger of Allaah (peace and blessings of Allaah be upon him) gestured with his hands, dropping the books: "Your Lord has decided everything about His servants: "One group in Paradise and one group in the fiery furnace."

Imam Ahmad relates the hadith of Abu al-Darda on the authority of which the Prophet (peace and blessings of Allaah be upon him) said: "Allaah has decided five things for every servant: His length of life, his sustenance, his deeds, his lying down, and whether he is unhappy or happy."

Imam Ahmad and Al-Tirmidhi relate the hadith of Ibn Mas'ud on the authority of which the Prophet (peace and blessings of Allaah be upon him) said: "Allaah created each soul and decreed its life, its sustenance and the trials it will face."

Muslim relates the hadith of Jabir on the authority of which a man asked the Messenger of Allaah (peace and blessings of Allaah be upon him): "Messenger of Allaah, what is the purpose of the (righteous) actions done today? Are they concerning the matters for which the pens have dried up and the destinies that have already been decided or do they concern something about our future?"

He replied: "They rather concern matters for which the pens have dried and the destinies have already been decided."

The man asked: "So why work deeds?"

He replied: "Work, because everyone will be eased (toward what he was created for)."

Many ahadith and words of Companions evoke this principle.

It was said:

Dedicate yourself completely to the matter.

The pen has dried up, writing down everything that will happen.

Man has a Creator, whose decree and order no one can prevent.

Chapter 8: Only the Decree of Allaah is in force

The Messenger of Allaah (peace and blessings of Allaah be upon him) said: "If all creatures came together to try to bring benefit to you through something which Allaah has not not decred, they will not be able to do so.

And if they joined together to harm you through something that Allaah has not decreed, they would not be able to do so."

This means that every harm or benefit that the servant encounters in this world has already been decreed for him.

It is impossible for him to face anything that has not been decreed for him, even if all creatures try their best to bring it about.

The Quran also proves this point in verses such as the following:

Say: "Nothing will overtake us except what Allaah has ordained for us."

"Nothing befalls either in the earth or in your selves that is not recorded in a Book before We make it happen; and this is certainly easy with Allaah..."

Say: "Had you been in your houses, those for whom death was decreed would have come out to the place where death awaited them."

Imam Ahmad relates the hadith of Abu al-Darda on the authority of which the Prophet (peace and blessings of Allaah be upon him) said: "Everything has a reality and the servant will not attain the reality of faith until he knows that what hit him could never have missed him and that what missed him could never have reached him."

Abu Dawud and Ibn Majah report a similar meaning hadith on the authority of Zayd ibn Thabit.

Know that this entire advice given to Ibn 'Abbas revolves around this central principle and the branches that derive from it.

When the servant understands that he will not encounter any good or evil, that is no benefit or harm, without Allaah having previously decreed it for him, when he realizes that if all creatures strive with all their might to try to produce something other than His decree, they would be powerless; he will then recognize that Allaah alone is the one who grants good and causes harm, and that He is the only one who gives and who withholds.

This recognition will lead the servant to perfect the Oneness (Tawheed) of his Lord, the Almighty, the Most High.

It is to Him alone that he will ask for help, it is to Him alone that he will beg, and it is to Him alone that he will submit and before whom he will humble himself.

It is Him alone that he will worship and it is Him alone that he will obey.

This is because something is worshiped in the hope that it attracts well-being or repels harm.

This is why Allaah blamed those who worship what can neither benefit nor harm them, that is whose worship is of no use.

Many who have not realized the reality of faith in their hearts actually place obedience to creatures before obedience to the Creator in the hope that they will bestow blessings on them and repel harm.

When the servant truly realizes that only Allaah can bring profit, cause or repel harm, give and deprive, he will necessarily unify only Him (perfect the Tawheed) in obedience and worship, favoring Him over obedience to all creatures.

This will also necessarily lead the servant to unify Him alone, Glorified be He, in asking for help and in supplication.

This magnificent comprehensive advice mentions all of these principles, each of which is of immense importance.

For a servant to Safeguard Allaah, the Almighty, the Most High, refers to safeguarding His boundaries and carefully fulfilling His rights.

This being the reality of His worship.

This is where this advice begins.

Then, this principle leads to the fact that Allaah Safeguards his servant.

This is the realization of the objective of each servant.

What is mentioned next is knowing Allaah in times of ease, leading to Allaah knowing His servant in times of difficulty.

This is part of Allaah's safeguarding of the servant and completes it.

Times of difficulty have been specifically mentioned here, because on such occasions servants find themselves in vital need of recourse to one who knows them and who can relieve them.

At such times, even polytheists invoke Him alone, pleading with Him, imploring Him, recognizing that Only He, Glorified be He, can make the evil and harm they face disappear.

However, once relieved, they return to polytheism, as Allaah mentioned in several places in His Book.

He blamed them for this.

The Prophet (peace and blessings of Allaah be upon him), in his advice, ordered us to oppose their practice by knowing Allaah in times of ease, through practicing religion for Him alone, obeying Him alone and seeking to get closer to Him alone.

This will necessarily lead to Him knowing us in times of difficulty and relieving us from it.

Next is mentioned asking Allaah Alone and seeking His help alone.

This principle incorporates both periods of ease and periods of difficulty.

Then is mentioned the principle on which everything that has preceded is based: Allaah, the Most High, is the Only One who produces benefits, who causes and repels harm, who gives and who withholds, only that which He decrees and predetermines will occur, all creation is physically incapable of causing any harm or benefit whatsoever which reaches a person without it not already been ordained in the Book.

Knowing and realizing this principle leads the servant to break all dependence on creatures.

This prevents him from asking them, soliciting their help and placing his hope in them in the search for good and in pushing back harm.

This also prevents him from fearing them, thinking that they can benefit or harm him.

This, then, implies that he unifies Allaah Alone in obedience and worship.

He will place obedience to Allaah in the first place, before obedience to creatures.

He will do everything possible to protect himself from His displeasure, even if he dissatisfies all creatures as a whole.

A hadith reported from Abu Sa'id mentions that the Messenger of Allaah (peace and blessings of Allaah be upon him) said: "It is part of the weakness of certainty that a person pleases people by displeasing Allaah, that he praises them for the sustenance that Allaah has given him and that he blames them for something of which Allaah has deprived him.

A person's greed will not bring him sustenance from Allaah and neither will the aversion of anyone repel it."

They are certainly beautiful, the words of the poet:

You would like to savor life even when it becomes bitter

You would like to be satisfied even when creatures are angry

Everything becomes easy, if your love is sincere

For everything that is on this earth is only dust.

Know that every creature that walks on the earth is dust. How then is it possible to obey such a creature before the Lord of lords? How can we please the dust by displeasing the King, the Giver? This is a very disturbing thing!

In many places, the Qur'an lays the foundation for the principle that Allaah, Glorified be He, is the One who gives and withholds:

"Whatever Allaah grants in mercy to people, no one can withhold.
And what He withholds, there is no one to release after Him.
And He is the Mighty, the Wise."
"And if Allaah causes you harm, no one can remove it except Him.
And if He wants good for you, no one can push away His favor."
Say: "So what do you think? If Allaah wished me harm, could [these deities] dispel His harm? Or if He wanted mercy on me, could they hold back His mercy?" - Say: "Allaah is sufficient for me: it is in Him that those who seek support place their trust."

He, the Most High, relates about His Prophet Noah (peace be upon him):

"O my people, our stay (among you), and my reminder of the signs of Allaah weighs too heavily on you, know that in Allaah that I place (entirely) my trust.
Consult with your gods, and do not hide your plans.
Then decide on me and be open about it."

He, the Most High, relates about His Prophet Hud (peace be upon him):

He said: "I call Allaah to witness—and you too are witnesses—that in truth, I disavow what you associate, apart from Him.
So scheme against me and give me no respite.
I have placed my trust in Allaah, my Lord and yours."

It has been said:
Whatever Allaah decrees for me must necessarily come to pass
Who can avoid the decree by carefulness?
Allaah deserves us more than we do
What are we other than His subjects, governed by His decree?

A man complained to Fudayl al-Faqah.

He replied: "Are you looking for someone other than Allaah to take charge of your affairs?"

It was said:
Govern! Your governance will be of no benefit

The decree will pass over everything you administer
The Lord regulates all affairs
The decree follows everything He ordains.

Chapter 9: The Merits of Patience

The Messenger of Allaah (peace and blessings of Allaah be upon him) said: "Know that there is great good in bearing with patience what you dislike."

The narration reported by 'Umar, the freed slave of Ghufrah, on the authority of Ibn 'Abbas, cites an additional sentence: "If you are able to work (do righteous actions) for Allaah, to be content and to find yourself in a state of certainty, do so. If you are unable to do so, know that great good lies in bearing with patience what you dislike."

Certainty here designates the actualisation of faith in the decree.

This is mentioned explicitly in the hadith of his son, 'Ali ibn 'Abdullah ibn 'Abbas, on the authority of his father which adds the following words:

I asked: "Messenger of Allaah, how can I act with certainty?"

He replied: "That you know that what you were afflicted with could never have missed you and that which you missed could never have afflicted you." However, the chain of transmission is weak.

When you have consolidated the certainty of the decree and pre-destination in your heart, it inevitably finds rest and peace in it.

This precise meaning is expressed by the Quran:

"Nothing will befall either in the earth or in your selves, without it being recorded in a Book before We make it happen…"

In the exegesis of this verse, Dahhak said: "He strengthened their resolve: "so that you do not worry about the things that passed you by", so do not grieve over what has escaped you in this life, for We have not decreed it for you.

"Or exult for what He gave you", do not exult for what We have given to you in this world, for it could never have been withheld from you. Narrated by Ibn Abi al-Dunya.

Sa'id ibn Jubayr explained this verse in the words: "so that you do not worry about what has escaped you" in matters of well-being and wealth, for you know that this was decreed for you even before He created you. Narrated by Ibn Abi Hatim.

It is in the light of this principle that one of the Pious Predecessors said: "Faith in the decree removes worry and suffering."

The Prophet (peace and blessings of Allaah be upon him) referred to this by saying:

"Be desirous of all that is profitable for you, seek help from Allaah, and do not despair. If something afflicts you, do not say: 'If only I had done this or that!' Rather say: 'This is the decree of Allaah, and He does what He wills.' Because [the particle] "if" opens the door to the devil's suggestions."

This hadith alludes to the fact that at the beginning of the affliction, the one who reminds himself of the decree will see the whisperings of Satan (that lead to worry, distress and sorrow) disappear.

Anas said: "I served the Prophet (peace and blessings of Allah be upon him) for ten years and he never reprimanded me for anything I did, saying: "Why did you do that?" or blamed me for something I didn't do by saying: "Why didn't you do that?!"

He also said, "When someone in his family remprimanded me, he would say, 'Leave him. If something has been decreed, it will happen.'"

The hadith with the additional wording was reported by Imam Ahmad.

Ibn Abi al-Dunya reports, with a problematic chain of transmission, that 'Aishah (Allah be pleased with her) said: "The most frequent words of the Prophet (peace and blessings of Allaah be upon him) when he came home were: "Whatever Allaah has decreed will happen."

He also reports, with a mursal transmission, that the Prophet (peace and blessings of Allaah be upon him) said to Ibn Mas'ud: "Do not worry excessively, what has been decreed will happen and the sustenance that is destined will come to you."

Putting this into practice necessarily leads to delegating all matters to Allaah and believing that nothing will happen unless Allaah wills it.

Faith in this principle makes worry and distress disappear.

The Prophet (peace and blessings of Allaah be upon him) advised a man saying: "Do not impugn Allaah for something He has decreed for you."

When the servant observes the effect of Allaah's Wisdom and Mercy through His decree and predestination, and knows that He should not be challenged for His decree, he attains the degree of satisfaction with destiny.

Allaah, the Almighty, said:

"No misfortune befalls [man] except by Allah's permission. And whoever believes in Allaah, [Allaah] guides his heart."

'Alqamah said in the exegesis of this verse: "It refers to a misfortune that befalls an individual, but the latter knows that it comes from Allaah, so he accepts it and is content."

In a authentic hadit, the Prophet (peace and blessings of Allaah be upon him) said: "How astonishing is the case of the believer! His case is always simple and this (characteristic) belongs only to the believer.

If ease touches him, he is grateful, which is good for him; and if a misfortune touches him, he is patient, which is good for him."

The Quran also proves this:

Say: "Nothing will harm us except what Allaah has ordained for us.

He is our Protector.

It is in Allaah that believers must place their trust."

Say: "What are you waiting for from us, except one of the two best things?"

Here He informs us that nothing can happen to them outside of what He has decreed.

This indicates that no matter what situation they encounter, difficult or easy, it is the same to them.

He then informs us that He is their Master and whoever finds himself in such a position will not be abandoned by Allaah.

Indeed, He is responsible for effectuating good for him:

"Know then that Allaah is your Master.

What an excellent Master and what an excellent Protector!"

"What are you waiting for from us, if not one of the two best things?"

That is to say, help and victory or martyrdom: both are the best things.

Tirmidhi reports from Anas that the Prophet (peace and blessings of Allaah be upon him) said: "When Allaah loves a people, He tests them.

He who is satisfied will obtain joy and he who is dissatisfied will obtain discontent."

Abu al-Darda said: "Allaah likes the servant to be satisfied with something that He has intended."

Umm al-Darda said: "Those who are truly satisfied with the destiny of Allaah are those who are satisfied with whatever has been destined.

On the Day of Resurrection, they will obtain such ranks in Paradise that they will make the martyrs jealous of them."

Ibn Mas'ud said: "By His Justice and Knowledge, Allaah has placed relief and joy in certainty and contentment, and worry and anguish in doubt and discontentment."

'Umar ibn 'Abd Al-'Aziz said: "These invocations left me with no further need, only submission to the decree of Allaah, the Almighty."

He often used the following words in his supplications: "O Allaah, make me satisfied with Your predestination and bless me in Your decree to the extent that I wish to hasten nothing of what You have delayed and not delay anything that You have hastened."

Ibn 'Awn said: "Be satisfied with the decree of Allaah in ease and in difficulty.

This will reduce your anxiety and will serve you better in your pursuit of the afterlife.

Know that the servant will never attain the reality of contentment until his contentment in times of poverty and hardship is the same as that in times of wealth and ease.

How can you go to Allaah so that He judges your affairs, and then be displeased when you see that what He has intended is not in accordance with your desires?! It is very possible that if these desires came to fruition, you would be destroyed! When His predestination is in accordance with your desires, you show yourself satisfied.

Both situations occur because of your meager knowledge of the invisible.

How can you entrust Him with Judgment when this is your condition?! You have not been fair to yourself and you will feel contentment."

These are fine words.

Their meaning is that when the servant turns to Allaah, the Almighty, for help in a decision (istikhara), he must be satisfied with what Allaah has chosen for him, whether it is in accordance with his desires or not.

Indeed, he does not know where he finds the good, and Allaah, Glorified be He, must not be disputed for His pre-destination.

It is for this reason that certain Pious Predecessors, like Ibn Mas'ud and others, ordered those who feared not being able to support a decision which opposes their desires, to add the words "in all good (well-being)" to his istikhara, since He could choose trial for him and he not be able to bear it.

Bakr al-Muzani reports that a man frequently did istikhara and was tested without being able to be patient, plunging instead into despair.

Then Allaah revealed to one of their Prophets: "Tell My servant that if he lacks determination, why does he not ask for one of My decisions [with the words] "in all good (well-being)"?

The hadith of Sa'd states that the Prophet (peace and blessings of Allaah be upon him) said: "It is part of the happiness of the servant that he seeks a decision from his Lord, the Almighty and is satisfied with that which He destines.

Part of an individual's unhappiness is his abandonment of seeking a decision and his dissatisfaction with what He intends."

This is reported by Tirmidhi and others.

There are many ways to achieve satisfaction (contentment) with the decree:

1. Feeling certainty in Allaah and firm confidence that whatever He decrees for the believer will be good for him.

Thus, the servant will be like a patient who has entrusted himself to the care of a competent doctor.

Such a patient will be satisfied with the care, whether painful or not, because he will have full confidence in the fact that the doctor only does what will benefit him.

This is what Ibn 'Awn was referring to in the comments mentioned above.

2. Expect the reward that Allaah has promised in exchange for contentment.

The servant might even be so absorbed in this thought that he would forget all the pain he is facing.

It is reported that a virtuous woman of the Pious Predecessors (Salaf) stumbled and broke one of her nails.

She laughed and said: "The delight of His reward made me forget the bitterness of His pain."

3- Immerse yourself in the love of the One who sends trials.

Be constantly aware of His infinite Majesty, Beauty, Greatness and Perfection.

The power of such awareness will lead the servant to submerge himself in it to the point that he no longer feels the pain, in the same way as the women who saw Joseph (peace be upon him): they forgot the pain of their cut hands.

This is a higher spiritual station than those previously mentioned.

Junayd reports that he asked Sirri if the lover felt the pain of the ordeal, to which he replied: "No."

In these words, he alludes to this spiritual station.

It is in light of this principle that a group of those who have faced trials said: "Let Him do what He wants of us.

Even if He cut us up, limb by limb, we would love Him even more."

It has been said:

If ardent love tears me limb from limb,

The pain will only increase my love.

I will remain a prisoner of love

Until I die in my pursuit of your satisfaction.

Ibrahim ibn Adham left his goods, his property, his children and his servants.

While he was doing the Tawaf, he saw his son, but he did not speak to him.

He said:

I have emigrated from everyone for love of You.

I have mourned those who are in my charge so that I can see You.

If You tear my limbs apart, for love

My heart will still yearn for You.

Lovers like Fuday and Fathal-Mawsili would cry with joy when they fell asleep without an evening meal and without a lit lamp.

During the winter nights, Fath would gather the members of his family and cover them with his cloak, saying:

"You starved me, so I starved my family.

You made me a stranger, so I made my family strangers.

You do this with your loved ones and your friends, am I one of them?

Should I exult with joy?"

People visited a pious predecessor who was ill.

They asked him: "Do you want anything?"

He replied: "What satisfies me most is whatever He finds satisfying."

It has been said on this subject:

For Your satisfaction, his punishment is sweet

For Your satisfaction, its distance is nearness

You are as dear as my soul,

Or rather, You are even dearer to me!

It is sufficient for me in my love,

That I only love what You love.

Abu al-Turab composed the following verses:

Do not be deceived, the lover is distinguished by signs

He holds paths to the gifts of his Beloved

Taking pleasure in the bitterness of His trial

His withholding is an accepted gift

Poverty is honor and generosity, fleeting.

A man whose son was martyred in jihad cried, saying: "I am not mourning his loss, I am only crying thinking of his state of satisfaction with Allaah when the swords struck!"

It was said:

If the people of Ghada want me dead, so be it.

By Allaah, I have never hesitated to respond to the wishes of the beloved!

I am in the likeness of a slave to them: I do not object.

What must be emphasized here is that the Prophet (peace and blessings of Allaah be upon him) enjoined Ibn 'Abbas to work (do righteous actions) while being in a state of contentment if he could.

If he was not able, he said: "If you are incapable, know that great good lies in bearing with patience what you dislike."

This therefore proves that being satisfied with decrees which are difficult to bear is not an obligation, but rather a recommendation, a state of excellence.

He who is unable to be satisfied must be patient.

Patience is required.

It must be present.

It contains immense good.

Allaah, the Most High, has commanded patience and promised a great reward for it:

"The patient will have their full reward without any reckoning."

"Most certainly, We will test you with a little fear, hunger and loss of possessions, people and fruits.

Give good tidings to the patient, who say, when misfortune strikes them: 'Certainly we belong to Allaah, and to Him we will return.'

These will receive blessings from their Lord, as well as mercy; and these are the rightly guided."

"And give good news to those who humble themselves, those whose hearts tremble when the name of Allaah is mentioned, those who endure what afflicts them and those who perform the prayer and spend from what We have provided for them."

Al-Hasan said: "The state of contentment is rare, but patience is the resort of the believer."

Sulayman al-Khawas said: "The station of patience is lower than that of contentment.

Contentment consists of the fact that a person, before the ordeal appears, is satisfied, whether the ordeal appears or not.

Patience consists of a person, after the appearance of the ordeal, enduring it with perseverance."

The difference between patience and contentment is the fact that patience consists of restraining the soul and preventing it from showing discontent, all this while we feel discomfort and pain.

Contentment requires the heart to readily accept what it faces.

Even if he comes to feel pain, the feeling of satisfaction will lessen it, or even make it disappear completely.

This, because the heart will have felt the soothing breath of certainty and knowledge.

This is why a large group of Pious Predecessors such as 'Umar ibn 'Abd Al-'Aziz, Abu Sulaiman and Ibn al-Mubarak said: "The satisfied (content) person does not desire any other state in which he finds himself unlike the one who is patient."

This way of being was reported from a group of Companions among whom were 'Umar and Ibn Mas'ud.

'Abd Al-'Aziz ibn Abu Ruwwada said: "Among the children of Israel there was a devotee.

He had a dream in which he was told that a certain woman would be his wife in Paradise.

So he went to her house as a guest for three nights to observe what she was doing.

She slept while he prayed at night and she ate while he fasted.

When he was about to leave her, he asked her what was the greatest work (righteous action) she thought she had accomplished.

She replied: "I do nothing more than what you have seen, but I have one quality: when I go through a trying period, I do not want to find myself in a period of comfort.

If I am sick, I do not want to be healthy.

If I'm hungry, I don't want to be full.

If I'm in the sun, I don't want to be in the shade."

He said: "By Allaah, this is a quality that is beyond the reach of servants!"

Patience must be displayed at the onset of trial, as is authentically reported from the Prophet (peace and blessings of Allaah be upon him).

Contentment is displayed after the appearance of the test, as the Prophet (peace and blessings of Allaah be upon him) said in his invocation: "I ask You for contentment after the decree."

This is because it could be that the servant resolves to be satisfied (content) with the decree before it occurs, and then his resolve dissipates when he faces it.

He who shows satisfaction after the decree falls is the one who displays true contentment.

So, to summarize, patience is mandatory and must necessarily be present.

Beyond patience lies dissatisfaction and discontent, and he who is dissatisfied with the decree of Allaah will only reap discontent.

Moreover, the pain he faces and the malice of his enemies will be much greater than his despair, just as it has been said:

Do not despair in the face of every problem that arises.

Do not let the malice of the enemy go free.

O People, through patience you will see your hopes.

When you encounter the enemy's army, be firm!

The Prophet (peace and blessings of Allaah be upon him) said:

"He who trains himself in patience, Allaah will grant him patience.

Allaah has not given a better and wider gift than patience."

'Umar said: "The best moments of our lives were those accompanied by patience."

'Ali said: "Patience in relation to faith is like the head in relation to the body: the person without patience has no faith."

Al-Hasan said: "Patience is one of the treasures of Paradise.

Allaah only bestows it on those whom He ennobles."

Maymun ibn Mihran said: "No Prophet or anyone else achieved goodness without it being through patience."

Ibrahim al-Taymi said: "Allaah does not give a servant patience in the face of harms, in the face of trials and in the face of calamities except that He has bestowed on him the best gift after faith in Allaah, the All-Mighty, the Most High."

He took this from the Word of Allaah, the Most High:

"But pious goodness is to believe in Allaah, the Last Day, the Angels, the Book and the prophets, to give one's wealth despite their love for it - to one's loved ones, to the orphans, the needy, the destitute travelers and those who ask for help and to set slaves free, to establish prayer and pay Zakah.

And those who fulfill their commitments (contracts) when they make them, those who are patient in poverty, illness and in battles, these are the truthful and these are the truly pious!"

'Umar ibn 'Abd Al-'Aziz said: "Allaah does not take away a blessing that He had given to an individual, leaving patience in its place, without He having replaced it with something better."

Then he recited:

"The patient will have their full reward without any reckoning."

Among the pious people was a man who kept a piece of paper in his pocket.

Every hour he looked at it and read it.

It was written: "And bear with patience the decision of your Lord.

For truly, you are before Our eyes."

Beautiful patience consists of the servant keeping the ordeal to himself and not telling anyone about it.

Allaah, the Most High, said:

"... Beauty lies in patience."

In the exegesis of this verse, a group of Pious Precessors explained that this referred to patience which was not accompanied by any form of complaint.

Ahnaf ibn Qays was blind for forty years without telling anyone.

'Abd Al-'Aziz ibn Abu Ruwwad was blinded in one eye for twenty years.

One day his son looked at him attentively and said, "Father, one of your eyes is blind!"

He replied: "Yes my son, for the last twenty years I have been pleased (content) with (the decree of) Allaah."

Imam Ahmad never complained to anyone about illnesses that affected him.

He had been informed that Mujahid hated to complain when he was sick.

So he decided to stop doing it and never did it again until his death.

He exhorted his soul, saying: "Be patient or you will regret it!"

A devous worshipper of Allah (according to the Quran and the authentic teachings of the Prophet – peace and blessings of Allah be upon him) once visited a sick person who said: "Ah! Ah!"

He asked him, "Who are you complaining about?"

It has been said:

The soul is eaten away by illness

But it hides it from visitors

The soul was not fair when it complained

Of its desires to someone other than its beloved

Yahya ibn Mu'adh said: "If you love your Lord and if He decrees hunger and destitution for you, it is obligatory on you to bear it and hide it from creatures.

The lover patiently bears the evil of his beloved, so why would you complain to them for something they didn't do?"

It was said:

In my eyes, the deeds done by other than You are detestable.

You do deeds and they are Magnificent from You.

The Messenger of Allaah (peace and blessings of Allaah be upon him) and his Companions attached stones to their bellies to combat the hunger they endured.

Uwais collected broken bones from the garbage in the middle of dogs who tried to do like him.

One day a dog barked at him.

He said: "Do not harm anyone who does not harm you, eat what is close to you and I will eat what is close to me.

If I enter Heaven, I will be better than you.

If I enter Hell, you will be better than me."

Ibrahim ibn Adham collected ears of grain along with the poor.

Seeing that the latter did not appreciate that he was competing with them in this harvest, he began to think: "I left my property in Balkh to compete with the poor in the collection of grain?"

After that, he only picked up the ears from among the animals that were grazing there.

Imam Ahmad also collected grains in the company of the poor.

Sufyan al-Thawri was employed to care for two camels while traveling to Makkah.

He cooked for a few people and it was so bad that they beat him for it.

Fath al-Mawsili lit fires for people in exchange for wages.

It was said:

For You, I have left the earth

To the malicious, to the envious.

Master, how long will I remain in Your good grace?

My life is passing by, my need is not fulfilled.

Another said:

How much have I submitted and labored

In pursuit of Your grace

How patient have I been for You

In the face of sickness and weakness

Do not abandon me

Without You, I am incapable of anything

If You desire wages

Take my soul

To satisfy You

An ardent love is born in me
My heart is infatuated with love
My tears suffocate me
My love for You
Make everything I bear easy
We do not savor the benefits
Without having known the ordeal.

In their eyes, the trials of this world were blessings.

One of them said: "The true scholar is the one who considers hardships as a blessing and comfort as a misfortune."

It was mentioned in a Judeo-Christian text: If you see a rich person approaching, say: "Here is a sin whose punishment has been hastened!"

If you see a poor person approaching, say: "This is the sign of virtue, welcome!"

One of the Pious Predecessors said: When I am tested by a misfortune, I praise Allaah four times.

I praise Allaah for sparing me from worse, for giving me the ability to bear it with patience, for enabling me to say: "To Allaah we belong and to Him we return." And for not having tested me in my religion.

Seeking relief in patience is an act of worship, because trial is never eternal.

It has been said:
Patiently bear each trial, with courage
Know that misfortune is never eternal.
Be patient, just like the nobles were.
It is only a fleeting moment, present today, gone tomorrow.

If the most tested of people were immersed even once in the delights of Paradise, ibnd were asked: "Have you ever experienced misfortune? Have you ever encountered the test?"

He would answer: "No, my Lord!"

It has been said:

O soul, be patient only for a few days, for a few fleeting dreams,

O soul, pass through this world with haste, turn away from it, true life is to come!

It was also said:

It is only an hour, then we will leave.

All this will go away, all this will disappear.

Chapter 10: Patience and Victory

The Messenger of Allaah (peace and blessings of Allaah be upon him) said (in his advice to Ibn 'Abbas): "Victory comes with patience."

This saying is in complete agreement with the Word of Allaah, the Most High:

"O you who believe! When you encounter an (enemy) troop, be firm, and invoke Allaah much in order to succeed."

"If they are found among you twenty believers who are patient, they will defeat two hundred; and if they are found among you a hundred, they will overcome a thousand unbelievers, for they are truly people who do not understand."

He said, regarding the story of Tâlut:

Then when he and those of the believers who accompanied him, they said: "Here we are without strength today against Goliath and his troops!" Those who were convinced that they would have to meet Allaah said: "How often has a small troop, by the grace of Allaah, defeated a very numerous troop! And Allaah is with the patient."

Allaah, the Most High, said:

"Yes! If you are patient and are pious (have Taqwa), and they [the enemies] attack you suddenly, your Lord will send you five thousand distinctly marked Angels to reinforce you."

Many other verses and ahadith about patience in the face of the enemy exist.

'Umar asked the elders of Banu 'Abasa: "With what tool do you fight your adversaries?"

They replied: "With patience.

We have never faced opponents without being patient and enduring just as they were patient and enduring."

One of the Pious Predecessors said: "Each of us hates death and the pain of injury.

However, we achieve varying degrees through patience."

Battal was asked about courage.

He replied: "It is to wait (be patient) for an hour."

All this refers to the fight against the external enemy, that is the fight against the unbelievers.

However, the same applies to the fight against the enemy within: the soul and base desires.

Moreover, this fight constitutes the greatest form of jihad.

The Prophet (peace and blessings of Allaah be upon him) said: "The Mujaahid is the one who fights against his soul for Allaah."

'Abdullahibn 'Amr replied to a person who asked him about jihad by saying:

"Start with your soul and fight against it.

Start with your soul and start a battle against it!"

When Abu Bakr al-Siddiq appointed 'Umar as Caliph, he advised in these terms: "The first thing you must guard against is your soul within you."

The poet 'Abbas ibn al-Ahnaf unites these meanings in a poem:

My heart calls me to that which will harm me

Will increase my sorrow and my pain

How can I protect myself from my enemy

When this enemy resides in me?

This jihad also requires patience. He who fights with endurance against his soul, his desires and his devil, will achieve victory.

On the other hand, he who despairs and abandons patience will be defeated, overcome, and imprisoned.

He will become submissive and vicious, imprisoned by his devil and his desires.

It has been said:

He who does not undo his desires

They will make the noble, ignoble.

Another said:

Perhaps a stranger is imprisoned by desires,

Yet in the face of patience they dissipate.

He who is subject to desires is a slave,

But if he dominates them, he is a king!

Ibn al-Mubarak said: "He who is patient will eventually find few things that require patience.

He who despairs will find few things that bring him pleasure."

Bukhari and Muslim report that the Prophet (peace and blessings of Allaah be upon him) said: "The strong man is not the one who wrestles, but it is the person who controls himself under the influence of anger."

Ahnafibn Qays was described in the following words:

"He had complete self-control when he became angry."

One person said, "So-and-so can walk on water."

He replied: "The one to whom Allaah grants the ability to oppose his desires is more impressive than the one who can walk on water."

Know that your soul is like an animal.

If it knows that you are firm and resolute, it will weaken.

On the other hand, if it knows that you are lazy and hesitant, it will take advantage of it, run after what it is looking for and pursue it desires.

Abu Sulayman al-Darani said: "While I was in Iraq, I was in charge of the palaces, dishes, clothes and food of the princes.

My soul wanted none of that.

Then, I was in charge of dates and my soul almost leaned towards them."

This story was mentioned to a devous worshipper who said: "He had no hope of attaining the things he mentioned first. So his desires did not pursue them. On the other hand, he wanted the second. So his desires ran after him."

It has been said: I patiently avoided delights until they disappeared.

I forced my soul to renounce them,

They remained absent.

The soul moves towards
The direction that the individual takes.
If it detects an opportunity,
It covets it,
Otherwise it doesn't move.
Several times a day,
My soul gains ascendancy.
Then, when it saw my resolution,
It submitted with humility.

Thus, his saying (peace and blessings of Allah be upon him): "Victory comes with patience", includes patience and endurance in the fight against both external and internal enemies.

The Pious Predecessors considered that fighting patiently against the soul and desires is better than patience in the face of trials.

Maymun ibn Mihran said: "Patience is of two categories: patience in the face of trial is good, and patience in avoiding sins is better."

Sa'id ibn Jubayr said: "Patience is of two types:

The best form of patience is to avoid what Allaah has forbidden and to do what He has made obligatory.

[The second type of] patience is that in the face of trials."

Chapter 11: Relief comes with distress

The Messenger of Allaah (peace and blessings of Allaah be upon him) said: "relief comes with distress"

This is proven by the Word of Allaah, the Most High:

"And it is He who sends down abundant rain after they have lost all hope, and unfolds His mercy.

And He is the Protector, the Praiseworthy."

"Allaah, it is He who sends the winds which raise up the clouds; then He spreads them in the sky as He wills; and He breaks them into dark clumps.

You then see the rain coming out of their depths.

Then, when He makes it fall on whoever He wants among His servants, there they are who rejoice, even though they were before it was brought down on them, in despair."

Allaah, Glorified be He, is surprised at the despondency of His servants, their fear, their apprehension and their despair in His Mercy, when He has decreed that their situation would soon change, without their awareness and that the rain is about to fall.

While the Prophet (peace and blessings of Allaah be upon him) was standing, delivering the Friday sermon, a man approached him to complain about the drought and the difficult situation in which everyone found themselves.

The Prophet (peace and blessings of Allaah be upon him) raised his hands and invoked for rain.

It was then that rain clouds gathered and it rained incessantly until the following Friday.

They then asked him (peace and blessings of Allah be upon him) to pray for the rain to stop.

This he did and the sky cleared up.

In His Book, Allaah has narrated many stories dealing with relief from distress and difficulty.

He told us how He rescued Noah (peace be upon him) from the "great anguish" and those with him on the ark, while the people remaining on dry land were all drowned.

He informed us of the way in which He saved Abraham (peace be upon him) from the fire lit by the polytheists and how He made it a "coolness and peace" for him.

He also told us about the moment when He ordered Abraham to sacrifice his son, then how He, at a later moment, replaced him with the ransom of a "mighty sacrifice".

He told us the story of Moses and his mother placing him in the river, and then how, as a result, he was found by Pharaoh's family.

He informed us of the story of Moses and Pharaoh, how He saved Moses and drowned his enemy.

He told us the stories of Job, Jonah, Jacob, Joseph, as well as that of the people of Jonah when they believed.

He told us about many events in the life of Muhammad (peace and blessings of Allah be upon him).

The times when He rescued him and saved him like when he was in the cave, during the Battle of Badr, during the Battle of Uhud or even during the Battle of Hunayn.

He told us the story of 'Aishah (Allah be pleased with her) when she was wrongly accused, as well as how He absolved her of that accusation.

He told us the story of the three:

"And [He welcomed the repentance] of the three who had remained behind so that, vast as it was, the earth seemed cramped to them; they felt cramped in their own person and they thought that there was no other refuge from Allaah except with Him.

Then He accepted their repentance so that they returned [to Him], because Allaah is the welcoming to repentance, the Merciful."

The Sunnah mentions numerous events, such as the story of the three who were trapped in the cave by a rock.

They called upon Allaah, mentioning their good deeds, and He freed them.

Likewise, we can cite the story of Abraham and Sarah, when the tyrant coveted her, but Allaah frustrated his evil plans.

Events of this type that have affected Muslims and those before Islam are too numerous to mention.

Several of them are collected in books such as Al-Farajba' dal-Shiddah and Mujabial-Du'ad'Ibn Abial-Dunya, Al-Mustaghithin billah wa Al-Mustasrikhina bihi as well as in books dealing with the miracles of the Awliyas, biographies of the virtuous and works of history.

A scholar, who I think came from Morocco, mentioned in one of his books that he heard Abu Dharral-Harawi, the Hafidh, recounting that while he was in Baghdad, reading to Abu Hafsibn Shahin, in a perfume shop, he saw a man approach the merchant.

The man gave ten dirhams in exchange for what he needed.

He placed his objects in a jar which he then placed on his head.

The man slipped, his jar fell and broke.

All the objects that were there were broken.

He then began to cry and said: "I lost, in a caravan, a camel which carried four hundred – or he said four thousand – dinars accompanied by precious stones which were worth even more.

However, I am not saddened by their loss.

However, my son has just been born and we need these things that a woman needs after giving birth.

Now, these ten dirhams are all I have.

So when what was decreed happened, I fell into distress.

I have nothing to give them tonight and I don't have a job that will allow me to bring something home tomorrow.

The only thing I can think of is to run away and let them die in peace."

Abu Dharr said: "An elder of the tribe of al-Jund, sitting at the threshold of his house, heard the story and asked permission from Abu Hafs to enter his house accompanied by his companions, while the afflicted man was still with him.

Entry permission was given.

The elder asked the man to repeat his story and asked him who was in the caravan he had spoken of and where he had lost a camel.

The man answered and was asked: "If you saw it, would you recognize it?"

The man replied: "Yes."

They brought him a camel and when he saw it he said: "It's this one!", then he described the precious stones it was carrying.

When the luggage attached to the camels was opened, the precious stones were discovered.

So the man became rich again.

When the man left, the Jundi man cried.

They asked him why.

He replied: "The only wish that remained for me in this world was that Allaah would bring me the owner of these goods so that he could recover them.

Now that Allaah has granted my wish by His grace, I no longer have any desire to fulfill, so I know that the time of my death is near."

Abu Dharr added: "He died less than a month later and we prayed over him, may Allaah have mercy on him."

The same author reports, on the authority of someone from Mawsul, that there was a merchant there who traveled to different countries for his trade.

He traveled one day to Koufah with all his merchandise and everything he owned.

During his trip, he met an individual who rendered him good services.

They quickly became friends and the merchant placed all his trust in him.

Later, when they stopped at a rest area, the individual took advantage of him and stole all his goods and provisions, leaving him with absolutely nothing.

The merchant searched tirelessly for him, but was unable to find him.

Being on foot and hungry, he returned home.

He entered his city by night and knocked on its door.

When his family members heard that it was him, they rejoiced and praised Allaah for his return, saying: "Your wife has just given birth to your son and we have no money to buy what a woman who has just given birth will need.

This evening we are very hungry.

So buy us flour and oil for the lamps."

When he heard this, the merchant's misfortune and distress intensified.

Not wanting to tell them what had happened, he went to a nearby shop, greeted the owner and took the oil and everything else he needed.

Then, while he was talking with him, he saw his bags on the floor in the store.

He asked the owner how they got here.

He replied: "A man bought me some food and asked me for shelter.

I put his bags in my store and I tied his beast to my neighbor's house.

The man sleeps in the mosque."

Taking his bag with him, the merchant went to the mosque where he found the individual sleeping.

He hit him and startled him awake.

"Thief ! Traitor! Where are my belongings located?" he shouted.

The individual replied: "It's in the bag that you hold around your neck."

When the merchant examined what was there, he noticed that nothing was missing at all.

He then retrieved his mount, and spent generously on his family and told them what had happened.

A similar story was related by Tinnawkani, in al-Faraj ba' d al-Shiddah.

It's a long story, but here's the summary.

In the time of al-Rashid there lived a money changer who bought a slave-girl for five hundred dinars.

He fell deeply in love with her.

As he wanted to spend all his time with her, such that his business suffered greatly.

He spent all his capital and had nothing left.

She became pregnant.

He then emptied his house and sold everything that was there, leaving nothing behind.

It was then that she felt labor beginning and asked him to buy what she needed to give birth, telling her that she might die if he did not hurry.

He immediately left his house in tears, determined to drown himself in the Tigris.

He was about to jump when the fear of Allaah struck him and stopped him.

He then decided to travel on foot from town to town until he reached Khorasan.

He stopped there and found a job.

He sent sixty-six letters home, asking for news of his slave-girl, but received no response.

He then deduced that she had indeed passed away.

Several years later, he decided to return to Baghdad with his possessions worth twenty-thousand dinars.

The caravan was attacked by highwaymen.

They stole everything he had, leaving him once again poor and in need.

He continued his journey until he reached Baghdad in the same state as when he left thirty years before.

He went to his house and found that his house was in excellent condition, with a beautiful entrance where there were guards, servants and mules.

He asked who lived in the house and was informed that it belonged to a money changer.

The name given to him was his own.

He was informed that the mother was the foster mother of the son of the Commander of the Faithful and that the owner of the house was in charge of the Public Treasury.

The person the man questioned added that his father had told him that the father of this money changer was also a rich money merchant in the past before he was hit by poverty, since he went in search of what his mother needed while she gave birth, got lost and died.

Her mother begged for help from the neighbors who rescued her.

Then, the Commander of the Faithful had a son, Ma'mun.

This one accepted milk from no nurse other than her.

Thus, while in his service, she obtained a respected and honored rank in this family.

Then, when Ma'mun became Caliph, he kept the woman and her son with him.

The son built the current house.

The son who was a trader then arrived with a group of people and entered his house.

The man also entered.

The son responded to their needs, then they departed, leaving the man alone.

The young man asked, "Old man, what do you need?"

He replied: "I am your father."

His face turned pale and he stood up suddenly, brought the man into his house and gave him a seat.

The man noticed that in the room there was a space hidden by a veil.

He said, "Maybe you should ask so-and-so I tell the truth?", mentioning his mother's name.

The mother, who was his slave, heard his voice, lifted the veil and ran to her master, embracing him and crying.

He informed them of his story.

They took him to al-Ma'mun who gave him his son's position and gave his son a promotion to the higher rank.

Ibn Abial-Dunya, in al-Farajba' dal-Shiddah, reports with his chain of transmission that Waddah ibn Khay-thamaa said: "'Umar ibn' Abd Al-'Aziz, may Allaah have mercy, ordered me to release all the prisoners of a prison.

So I released them with the exception of Yazid ibn Abi Muslim who swore revenge by shedding my blood.

I was in Africa when I was informed that Yazid ibn Abi Muslim, recently appointed Emir of the African provinces, had arrived.

I fled.

He sent people after me who captured me and brought me back to him.

He said: "By Allaah, I have urged Him to allow me to reach you! By Allaah, I have urged Him to protect me from your evil! By Allaah, He has not granted you safety and I will kill! If the Angel of Death himself were to race with me to take your soul, I would beat him! Bring a sword, as well as the executioner's rug!"

I was put on my knees, handcuffed.

The executioner stood above me, his sword ready.

Then the call to prayer sounded and he went to pray.

While he was prostrating, an army attacked and killed him.

A man freed me and told me to go away.

He also reports, with his chain of transmission on the authority of 'Umar al-Saraya, that he was once fighting in the Roman provinces alone.

One day, while he was sleeping, a Roman approached him and jostled him with his foot, which woke him up.

He said: "O Arab, you have a choice: I kill you with a spear, a sword or we fight!"

He replied: "Let us fight."

They fought and 'Umar was defeated.

While he was sitting on his chest, the Roman said: "How should I kill you?"

'Umar cried out: "I testify that everything that is worshiped under Your Throne is False except Your Noble Face.

You see the situation I'm in, so save me!"

'Umar said: "I then lost consciousness and when I awoke, I found the Roman dead, lying beside me."

Abu al-Hassan ibn al-Jahdam reports with his chain of transmission which goes back to Hatim al-Asamm who said: "We met the Turks with whom we had an joust combat.

A Turk threw me off my horse and I fell.

He got off his and sat on my chest.

He grabbed my beard, pulled a knife from his sock and prepared to slit my throat.

My heart, however, was not with him or his knife, but with my Master.

I began to think: "My Master, if You have decreed my death here, I submit completely to Your command.

I belong to You."

It was then that a Muslim shot an arrow which made him fall away from me.

I stood up, took his knife from his hand and stabbed him with it."

Let your heart remain with your Master and you will see wonders unfold from His providence, which your ancestors never witnessed! There are many other similar stories, but what we have mentioned is enough.

Chapter 12: Ease accompanies difficulty

The Messenger of Allaah (peace and blessings of Allaah be upon him) said: "Ease accompanies difficulty".

This saying comes from His statement, Glorified be He:

"Allaah will appoint ease after difficulty."

"For truly with difficulty comes ease, truly with difficulty comes ease."

Qatadah who said: "It was narrated to us that the Messenger of Allaah (peace and blessings of Allaah be upon him) announced to his Companions the good news of this verse saying: "One difficulty will never overcome two eases."

Ibn Abi al-Dunya reported the hadith of Mu'awiyah ibn Qurrah from someone who reported to him that Ibn Mas'ud said: "If difficulty entered a hole, ease would follow it."

Then he recited: "For truly with difficulty comes ease; truly with difficulty comes ease."

He also reports the hadith of 'Abd Al-Rahman ibn Zayd ibn Aslam, on the authority of his father, on the authority of his grandfather that when Abu 'Ubaydah was besieged, 'Umar wrote to him saying: "No matter what difficulty an individual faces, Allaah will send him relief thereafter, for one difficulty cannot overcome two eases and He says:

"O you who believe! Be patient.

Encourage yourself to have endurance.

Fight constantly (against the enemy) and fear Allaah, that you may succeed!"

This is also how Ibn 'Abbas and other exegetes explained the verse by saying: "One difficulty will never overcome two eases."

While an individual from the first generations found himself in the middle of the desert, in a state of extreme suffering, he was inspired by the following verses of poetry: When a man wakes up afflicted, I think that death is better for him.

When night fell, he heard a voice calling:

Be certain O you

Immersed in anguish

Poetry as he recited it

Remains higher in his mind

When the difficulty intensifies

Contemplate on: "Have We not expand for you" (Surah 94)

A difficulty lies between two eases

If you recognize this, rejoice!

The man said: "I loved memorizing these verses and Allaah relieved me of my distress."

Many poems of the same genre have been written.

Here is a selection:

Be patient, patience produces wonders

Do not despair in the face of misfortune

Ease follows difficulty closely

In difficult times, adversity is dissipated.

It has been said:

Many are those who despair in the face of events

Whose relief is imminent.

Another said: Maybe relief is coming soon. We treat our souls with "maybe." The individual is very close to relief when he gives in to despair.

It has also been said: When your situation becomes unbearable, expect relief. Relief is imminent when adversity intensifies.

Another composed the following verses:

Do not despair if you experience sorrow for a day

For you have lived in ease many times before

Do not think badly of your Lord

Beauty is what best suits Him

Do not give up hope, that is disbelief!

Allaah will make you satisfied with little

Know this: ease follows difficulty

Allaah is the most truthful of all those who speak.

It has been said:

Patience is the key to the door to relief

Ease follows every difficulty

Time does not stagnate

One event follows another.

We will conclude this treatise by evoking certain subtleties, certain benefits and certain wisdoms relating to trials.

1–Atonement for sins and the reward for bearing the trial with patience.

Scholars have differed: is the individual rewarded for the test itself or not?

2–The servant remembers his sins.

He can then repent and return to Allaah, the Most High.

3 – The heart softens after being hard and rough.

One of the Pious Predecessors said: "A person may fall ill and therefore be reminded of his sins.

Then, out of fear of Allaah, they (his sins) shattered and scattered like flies and Allaah pardoned them."

4–The servants humble themselves and submit before Allaah, the Almighty.

Indeed, such a state is more loved by Allaah than many acts of obedience.

5 – Trials lead the heart of the servant to return to Allaah, to stand before His door, to implore Him and to submit to Him.

This is one of the greatest benefits of the ordeal.

Allaah has blamed those who do not submit to Him in times of trial:

"We have certainly punished them, but they have not submitted to their Lord; just as they do not supplicate [Him]"

It is mentioned in the previous scriptures: "Allaah tests a servant, because He loves to hear his humble supplication."

Sa'id ibn 'Abd Al-'Aziz said: "David (peace be upon him) said: "Glory to Him who leads the servant to supplicate when he faces trial.

Glory to Him who gives gratitude to those in a state of ease."

Abu Ja'far Muhammad ibn 'Ali met Muhammad ibn al-Munkadir who was in a state of severe grief.

He asked regarding him and was informed that he was drowning in debt.

Abu Ja'far said: "Is the door of supplication open for him?"

He was told: "Yes."

He said: "The servant is truly blessed if, when he is in need, he frequently calls on his Lord, no matter what it is."

Some, while invoking in times of adversity, did not desire a quick response for fear that this state (of need for their Lord) in which they found themselves would cease.

Thabit said: When the believer calls on Allaah, Allaah entrusts Gabriel to fulfill his need, saying: "Do not hurry to fulfill his need, for I love to hear the voice of My servants who believe."

One of the Pious Predecessors saw the Lord Almighty in a dream and said: "My Lord, I invoked You so much without receiving a response!"

He replied: "I like to hear your voice."

6–Trials lead the heart to savor the delight of patience and contentment.

It is a spiritual station of great importance and immense rank.

We have already talked about its merits.

7 – The ordeal pushes the servant to abandon dependence on creatures and leads him to turn only to the Creator.

Allaah informed us that the polytheists sincerely turned to Him when supplicating in times of need.

So what should we say about the believer?!

8 – The test leads the servant to actualize and live monotheism (Tawheed) in his heart.

It is the most sublime of spiritual stations and the noblest of ranks.

A Judeo-Christian account states: "Trials have brought you and Me together.

(While) Well-being brings you and your self together."

Conclusion

Generally speaking, when the ordeal intensifies and the misfortune deepens, relief is near.

Allaah, the Most High, said: "When the Messengers almost lost hope (and their followers) thought that they were being denied, there came Our help to them.

And those We wanted were saved."

"Misery and sickness had touched them; and they were shaken until the Messenger, and with him, those who had believed, cried out: "When will the help of Allaah come?" – Be assured ! Allaah's help is very near."

He informs us that Jacob (peace be upon him) never gave up hope of seeing Joseph again and that he asked his (Yusuf's) brothers:

"O my sons! Go and ask about Joseph and his brother.

And do not despair of mercy from Allaah."

And he said: "It may be that Allaah will bring them both back to me."

Linking intense anguish and the onset of the relief contains wonderful wisdom.

Indeed, in such a situation, the individual abandons all hope that a creature will save them.

Instead, he turns to Allaah and depends only on Him.

When the individual cuts off all hope in creatures and places his dependence on Allaah, He responds and saves him.

Total trust in Allaah consists of stopping looking up at creatures and abandoning all hope in them.

This was indicated by Imam Ahmad.

He provided proof of this through the words of Abraham who (about to be thrown into the fire), when Gabriel asked him: "Do you need anything?", replied: "From you, nothing."

Full trust in Allaah is one of the greatest paths to meeting needs.

Indeed, Allaah is sufficient for him who puts his trust in Him:

"And whoever puts his trust in Allaah, He [Allaah] is sufficient for him."

Fudayl said: "By Allaah! If you abandon all hope in creatures to the point that you no longer desire anything from them, your Master will grant you everything you desire!"

Another wisdom lies in the fact that when the test intensifies, the servant must fight against Satan.

Indeed, it will inspire him to despair and abandon all hope.

The servant must repel these breaths and the reward of fighting the enemy, as well as repelling him, will be the dissipation of the ordeal.

An authentic hadith mentions: One of you never ceases to be heard until he becomes impatient and says: "I called on my Lord, but He did not hear me!" He then gets tired and abandons the invocation.

Another wisdom is that relief takes time to come.

The servant abandons hope of receiving it, especially after numerous invocations and humble supplications.

He will then examine his own person and blame his soul, saying: "I was only tested like this because of you.

If there was any good in you, I would have been answered."

This blame and this awareness are more loved by Allaah than many acts of obedience, because they lead the servant to break his soul for his Master.

The servant recognizes that his own person does not deserve a response.

Once in such a state, Allaah's hearing and relief are near.

Allaah is with those who have broken their souls for Him.

Its repair is then proportional to the shelter.

Wahb said: "A man worshiped Allaah for some time.

Then he was suddenly in need.

He then fasted seventy Saturdays, eating eleven dates each time.

He then invoked Allaah for his needs, but nothing was granted to him.

He examined himself and then said: "If there was any good in you, you would have been granted (an answer to your supplication)!"

At that moment an angel came down and said: "Son of Adam, this hour in which you find yourself is better for you than all your previous years of worship.

Allaah has now fulfilled your need!"

Whoever becomes aware of this, knows this and testifies of this in his heart, will understand that the blessings of Allaah in times of difficulty are greater than those in times of ease.

This principle is reflected in the authentic hadith in which the Prophet (peace and blessings of Allaah be upon him) said: "The believer has an amazing destiny! Everything that happens to him is beneficial, and that is reserved for him alone! Indeed, if he is the object of a happy event, he thanks Allaah and this is a good thing for him, and if he encounters misfortune, he endures it with patience and it is again a good thing for him.

And this is only for the believer."

It is because of this principle that devout worshippers do not prefer one state to another.

They are rather satisfied, regardless of what Allaah has decreed.

They then exercise the state of servitude which corresponds to each situation.

The Musnad and Al-Tirmidhi reports the hadith of Abu Umamah on the authority of which the Prophet, peace and blessings of Allah be upon him, said: My Lord proposed to me to transform the plains and stones of Makkah into gold, but I said: "No, my Lord! I prefer to eat what is enough for me one day and be hungry another day.

When I am sad, I turn to You, calling on You in humility and remembering You."

'Umar said: "I do not give importance to loving or hating the state in which I wake up, for I do not know in which of the two the good lies."

'Umar ibn 'Abd Al-'Aziz said: "I wake up in the morning keeping in mind that my delight and relief lie in the execution of the Order and the decree."

O human! Why, when We call you, do you flee from Us? We flood you with blessings, but you forget Us and remain careless! We afflict you with trials so that you return to Us, stand at Our door and invoke Us with humility! Trials bring you and Me together! Well-being reunites you with yourself!

Even if we blame each other

Or join distant lands

The love you know still exists

The benefits you know are still abundant

Many are the gifts wrapped in the ordeal

Many are the secrets hidden in the corners.

O human, your gratitude towards Our blessings is itself a blessing that We have given you.

So be thankful for that! If you are patient in times of difficulty, then patience is a grace We have bestowed on you.

So mention it! Every situation you go through is a blessing from Us.

So don't be ungrateful!

"And if you counted the blessings of Allaah, you would not be able to number them.

The man is truly very unfair, very ungrateful."

If my gratitude is a rewarded benefit

It is appropriate to show appreciation

How can gratitude not be a gift from Him?

The days pass, the years accumulate

He who meets ease knows joy

He who meets trial, the reward will soon follow

In both cases, He grants such grace

That not even faith, earth or sea can bear it .

Here ends this treatise, by the grace of Allaah, His providence and His divine accord.

All praise belongs to Allaah.

Mi sforzai di smettere di ossessionarmi su Liam e di concentrarmi sui numeri dell'ultimo mese.

Quando alzai di nuovo lo sguardo, il tempo era passato senza che mi rendessi conto di che ora fosse.

Una volta terminato il mio compito, mi alzai e mi distesi, il corpo dolorante per essere rimasta seduta quasi nella stessa posizione per così tanto tempo.

"Che diavolo ci fai qui così presto?" La voce maschile infastidita mi fece trasalire, mentre giravo la testa per guardare la fonte del baritono sexy.

Liam.

Abbassai le braccia lungo i fianchi, il cuore che mi batteva all'impazzata come faceva sempre, quando era nei paraggi.

Il mio corpo aveva una specie di sensore, che scattava come un fulmine nel momento in cui era a tiro di voce.

Cavolo, era stupendo. Anche con un vecchio paio di jeans e una maglietta dei Patriots, trasudava una calma sicurezza e un controllo che richiedevano alla maggior parte delle persone una vita per padroneggiarli.

Mi spostai. "Niente. Beh, non sto facendo niente *adesso*. Ho appena finito di caricare tutto per il tuo commercialista. I conti sono aggiornati."

Non sembrava ancora contento, ma quella era la sua solita espressione. "A che ora sei arrivata qui?"

Uscii da dietro la scrivania. "Presto" risposi.

"Quanto presto, Brooke?"

Non volevo dirgli che ero entrata prima dell'alba. Per qualche ragione, sembrava pensare che passassi troppe ore al ristorante, e forse era vero. Ma il lavoro era l'unica cosa che mi teneva sana di mente. "Cosa importa?" replicai sulla difensiva. "Il lavoro è finito."

Quando mi mossi per stare di fronte a lui, dovetti piegare un po' indietro la testa per guardarlo in faccia.

Ero di altezza media, ma lui era così alto che mi faceva sentire minuta.

La stanza era improvvisamente troppo calda e piccola.

Provai a superarlo per uscire dall'ufficio, ma fermò facilmente i miei progressi con una mano potente sul mio braccio. "È importante per me, Brooke. Non sei la proprietaria del posto, e non mi aspetto che tu trascorra qui le mie stesse ore."

Sinceramente, ero stufa di avere quella discussione. Mi ero seppellita nel lavoro per un motivo, e per aiutarlo il più possibile. Mi aveva fatto un favore assumendomi. Avevo voluto ricambiare.

Mi sentivo torturata e tormentata, quindi sputai fuori la prima cosa che mi venne in mente. "Mi dimetto. Sto dando il mio preavviso di due settimane."

Scrollando le spalle dalla sua presa, mi spinsi fuori dalla stanza. Il mio unico rifugio era il bagno, e chiusi velocemente la porta, a chiave, appoggiandomi alla superficie di legno, mentre cercavo di far rallentare il battito cardiaco.

Ora tutto quello che dovevo fare era vivere due settimane di inferno, prima di capire come avrei mai potuto togliermi dalla testa l'unico ragazzo che poteva farmi perdere completamente l'autocontrollo.

Liam

Cosa diavolo era appena successo?

Aveva davvero appena detto che si stava... *dimettendo?*

Oh, accidenti, no. Non poteva semplicemente andarsene. Avevo bisogno di lei.

Forse averla qui mi tormentava a morte, ma sapevo benissimo che Brooke era la ragione per cui mi alzavo dal letto così in fretta la mattina. Forse ero un masochista, e mettevo in dubbio il mio giudizio sul desiderare una donna che era già stata presa. Ma non vederla affatto era peggio che dovermi comportare come se non mi facesse indurire l'uccello ogni volta che la vedevo.

Sì, sapevo che aveva già un ragazzo nella sua vita, e non avrei oltrepassato quella linea, anche se volevo. Ma ero abituato a vedere la sua faccia quasi ogni giorno. La volevo lì al Sullivan.

Andai in bagno a grandi passi e bussai alla porta. "Non accetto il tuo preavviso" urlai.

Impiegò un momento per rispondere. "Non hai scelta. Non puoi tenermi qui, se non voglio restare. Ho pensato di essere onesta dandoti il preavviso."

In realtà, era stata *onesta*. Ero io ad essere completamente irrazionale. Due settimane erano una buona quantità di tempo, ed erano più che sufficienti. Avevo avuto dipendenti inaffidabili che non si erano più presentati, dopo aver trovato un altro lavoro. Pochissime persone prendevano sul serio un lavoro di cameriera come lei. "Possiamo parlarne?" chiesi in un tono più ragionevole.

Sentii un po' di rumore nel bagno, ma Brooke finalmente aprì la porta. "Liam, non ho altro da dire. Sapevi che questo lavoro era temporaneo per me. Apprezzo tutto quello che hai fatto. Mi hai dato un'occupazione, quando ne avevo bisogno, e te ne sono grata."

La guardai accigliato. Non volevo la sua gratitudine. Volevo che il suo culo rimanesse qui ad Amesport.

Forse ancora non sapevo esattamente *perché* fosse lì, ma non mi importava più. Avevo tentato senza successo di ottenere più informazioni da Evan, ma tutto quello che quel bastardo mi avrebbe detto era che Brooke aveva bisogno di stare un po' di tempo lontano dalla Costa Occidentale. Avevo persino minacciato di licenziarla, se lui non avesse sputato il rospo. Ma aveva chiamato il mio bluff, sapendo che non avrei mai lasciato andare una brava dipendente.

"Cos'è cambiato?» le domandai. "Perché proprio ora?"

Scrollò le spalle: "Perché è ora. Le mie ragioni per essere qui sono superate. Posso andare a casa."

"Non sei qui nemmeno da un anno" borbottai, sapendo che non potevo contestare la sua decisione. Era solo una dipendente, e aveva tutto il diritto di rinunciare, se voleva, ma non l'avrei lasciata andare senza discutere.

Rise. "Un anno è molto tempo. Non ho mai programmato di restare così a lungo."

Probabilmente le mancava il suo ragazzo, anche se avevo i miei dubbi su quanto fosse serio nei suoi confronti. Era venuto a trovarla solo un paio di volte, e non era rimasto a lungo. "Oltre al tuo ragazzo, cos'hai sulla Costa Occidentale? Almeno hai un lavoro qui."

"Tutta la mia famiglia è lì, Liam. Ho tre fratelli maggiori, una sorella gemella, e un fratello minore che studia medicina."

Ero sorpreso. Non parlava molto della sua vita personale. Non avevo idea che avesse molti parenti. "Hai una gemella? Ti somiglia?"

Scosse la testa. "Non siamo identiche, ma puoi dire che siamo sorelle. Mi manca. Parliamo al telefono, ma non sono mai stata lontana da lei per così tanto tempo."

"Perché non mi hai detto che avevi dei parenti lì?"

Fece spallucce. "Non potevo rivelare molto sulla mia vita personale."

Fanculo! Odiavo il fatto che Brooke e io non ci fossimo mai veramente conosciuti. Avremmo dovuto. Era stata qui abbastanza a lungo. Ma ovviamente non voleva essere trovata, ed io ero troppo occupato a farle credere che la mia attrazione per lei fosse storia. Avevamo passato molto tempo nello stesso spazio, ma non avevamo mai parlato veramente.

Onestamente, mi ero incolpato per questo. Se non fossi stato così coinvolto nel cercare di dire a me stesso che non volevo scoparla, avremmo potuto essere amici.

Difficile essere amici, quando tutto quello a cui riesco a pensare è farla venire.

"Hai una famiglia numerosa" osservai, non sapendo cos'altro dire.

Sbuffò. "Non hai idea di quanto l'ho odiato a volte. Avere tre fratelli maggiori che cercavano di dominarmi non è mai stato facile. Ma li amo tutti. I miei genitori sono morti, quindi tutto quello che avevamo davvero eravamo l'un l'altro."

"Mi dispiace" risposi automaticamente, empatizzando con la sua perdita, dato che anch'io avevo perso mia madre e mio padre.

"Sono morti molto tempo fa" replicò in tono malinconico, prima di aggiungere: "Vado a preparare un caffè."

Mi spostai da lei e poi la seguii in cucina. "Quindi, dev'essere stata dura stare dall'altra parte del Paese lontano da tutta quella famiglia."

Armeggiò per preparare una nuova caraffa, mentre rispondeva: "È stato un bene per me. Avevo bisogno di tempo per me stessa."

Le sue risposte erano vaghe, e sapevo che non voleva parlare delle ragioni per aver lasciato la California in primo luogo. "Sono sicuro che non vedi l'ora di riabbracciare il tuo ragazzo" commentai, avendo problemi a immaginarla di nuovo con un ragazzo a tempo pieno.

Ero abituato a vederla da sola, e mi piaceva così.

In realtà, mi dava fastidio pensare a lei come impegnata, anche se sapevo che lo era.

Ma non avevo intenzione di dirglielo. Se lo avessi fatto, avrei dovuto ammettere che non avevo mai superato la mia attrazione per lei, e questo era qualcosa di cui probabilmente non avevamo bisogno di discutere.

Premette il pulsante *Caffè* sulla macchinetta, prima di dire: "Non vedo l'ora di riabbracciare tutti a casa."

Come potevo competere con un'intera dannata famiglia e un ragazzo? Non avevo mai veramente stretto amicizia con lei. Non potevo. Non quando il mio uccello diventava duro ogni volta che la vedevo. "Ci mancherai qui" dissi scontento.

Si voltò a guardarmi. "A chi mancherò? Non ho mai davvero fatto amicizia con qualcuno qui, e tu hai detto che non avresti mai potuto essere mio amico."

L'avevo detto. Subito dopo essermi lasciato sfuggire che ero attratto da lei. Ma nei mesi successivi alla mia confessione, avrei voluto non averlo detto. Brooke era il tipo di donna che vedeva del buono in tutti. Era ottimista per la maggior parte del tempo, e il genere di persona che mi faceva desiderare di essere sua amico, anche se volevo disperatamente scoparla. "Ci mancherai comunque" mormorai.

"Ti mancherò?" chiese con voce curiosa.

"Certo. Ti sei fatta il culo per me. Mi hai coperto, quando avevo bisogno di stare con mia sorella per i suoi impianti cocleari e il trattamento a New York. Hai fatto molto per me, Brooke." Mia sorella non era più sorda. Gli impianti acustici avevano avuto successo, e Tessa aveva sposato Micah Sinclair, un altro miliardario della famiglia Sinclair, che si era trasferito qui ad Amesport.

Si voltò, cercando di nascondere un'espressione di delusione che avevo scorto poco prima che nascondesse il viso.

"Sono sicura che troverai un buon sostituto" replicò, avvicinandosi al bancone vicino al bagno e saltando su per sedersi.

Era l'unica volta in cui quel particolare spazio avesse mai avuto un uso. Da quando avevo ristrutturato il ristorante, c'erano diverse aree antiche di cui non avevamo più bisogno.

"Starai bene?" chiesi, non del tutto sicuro del motivo per cui avevo mormorato quella domanda.

Forse non sapevo perché avesse dovuto lasciare la sua famiglia, ma ora che ero a conoscenza dei suoi fratelli e della vita che si era lasciata alle spalle, sapevo che doveva essere qualcosa di serio.

Mi guardò con un paio di bellissimi occhi azzurri espressivi. "Sto meglio" spiegò. "Avevo bisogno di un po' di tempo da sola, e l'ho trovato qui nel Maine. Tutti sono stati perlopiù gentili. È una città fantastica."

"A parte il fatto che è invasa da miliardari" borbottai.

Uno per uno, tutti i fratelli Sinclair avevano fatto di Amesport la loro casa. Non che non andassero bene per la città. Tutti avevano fatto investimenti significativi nella piccola area costiera per migliorare l'economia e la qualità della vita dei suoi residenti. Ma era ancora strano vedere i loro jet decollare e atterrare all'aeroporto fuori Amesport.

"Lo dici come se fosse una brutta cosa" prese in giro. "Non sei esattamente povero."

Si era occupata delle mie tasse, quindi conosceva la mia situazione finanziaria. Ero ben lungi dall'essere al verde, e anche se non ero un miliardario, avevo milioni nei miei investimenti e liquidità sui conti proveniente dal mercato di attrezzature di sicurezza e altri macchinari che avevo brevettato, mentre stavo ancora lavorando agli effetti speciali a Hollywood. "Ma non sono un Sinclair" replicai.

"Chi se ne frega" ribatté. "Sei comunque pieno di soldi."

Lo ero, ma i soldi non erano mai stati così importanti per me. Avevo cercato di risparmiare, quando i miei genitori erano morti, e mia sorella, Tessa, si era ammalata e aveva perso l'udito. Avevo voluto assicurarmi che potesse permettersi i migliori dottori e le migliori cure mediche disponibili. Ma dopo aver riacquistato l'udito e sposato Micah, tutto quel denaro aveva continuato ad accumularsi. Avevo la vita che desideravo, quindi non ne avevo mai speso la gran parte.

Alzai le spalle. "Non mi importa più molto dei soldi."

"Adori il ristorante" disse.

"Credo di sì. Non sapevo che gestire il Sullivan fosse davvero il mio sogno, finché non sono tornato a casa. Immagino che gli involtini di aragosta siano nel mio sangue."

"I migliori involtini di aragosta della Costa Orientale" mi ricordò. "E anche le tue bistecche sono dannatamente buone."

"È meglio che lo siano" replicai. "Altrimenti, passerei un sacco di tempo a mangiare carne di merda."

Ero orgoglioso di avere le migliori bistecche che potessi ottenere. Avevo passato molto tempo a cercare il meglio sul mercato.

"Avresti potuto semplicemente sedere su una spiaggia da qualche parte e raccogliere milioni" sottolineò. "Ma non l'hai fatto."

"Non credo che potrei mai smettere di lavorare" ammisi.

"Perché vuoi che la tua vita abbia uno scopo?" indagò.

"Non c'ho mai riflettuto davvero. Il Sullivan è un luogo iconico. È nella nostra famiglia da generazioni."

"Ammiro questo di te" disse con sincerità. "Continui sempre a sforzarti di migliorare il ristorante, quando avresti potuto facilmente assumere un manager e non lavorare affatto qui."

"Siamo simili in questo senso" osservai riluttante. "Avresti potuto essere una dipendente nella norma, invece di fare la tua missione dell'essere la miglior dipendente che potresti essere. La maggior parte dei ragazzi che lavora qui si presenta e fa solo quello che deve fare."

La vidi sussultare visibilmente al mio commento. "Non sono una bambina, Liam. Ho ventisei anni e non sono mai stata una bambina. La nostra famiglia era povera. Ognuno di noi ha dovuto fare un passo in avanti per rimanere uniti. Siamo diventati tutti adulti abbastanza presto."

Dovevo ammettere che non avevo mai *sentito* tanto la differenza di età tra noi, anche se avevo cercato di usare quel divario di nove anni per allontanarmi da lei. Accidenti, avevo provato praticamente di tutto per tenerla a distanza. "Sei sicura di voler andare?" chiesi burbero. "Posso farti dirigere, darti un titolo e uno stipendio più alto."

"Mi paghi già abbastanza bene" sostenne. "Guadagno abbastanza bene per essere una cameriera."

"Sei molto di più, e penso che tu lo sappia. Ne sai quasi quanto me sulla gestione di questo posto."

Saltò giù dal bancone. "È un'offerta davvero allettante, ma posso trovare qualcosa in California. Non ho motivo di restare."

Ci pensai per un minuto. Non aveva amici qui, perché non si era mai veramente avvicinata a nessuno. Mi piaceva la mia privacy, ma Brooke era isolata in un modo che doveva essere quasi insopportabile. Poteva stare in una stanza piena di persone e finire sola, perché non era mai stata libera di parlare di se stessa. "Mi dispiace, Brooke. Avrei dovuto essere un amico migliore."

Mi sorrise debolmente. "Va tutto bene. Capisco perché non potevamo essere amici."

Si diresse verso la porta.

"Dove stai andando?" gridai.

"Sto tornando al mio appartamento. Voglio pulire e vestirmi per il mio turno."

Ora che se ne stava andando, odiavo davvero vederla allontanarsi da me.

Lasciò il ristorante chiudendo la porta dietro di sé.

Volevo seguirla, ma cosa diavolo potevo dire?

Non potevo dirle quanto sarebbe stata incredibilmente solitaria Amesport senza di lei.

L'aria si fece tranquilla, come se fosse un segno di ciò che stava per accadere.

Sarebbe stata troppo tranquilla, troppo silenziosa una volta che se ne fosse andata.

Mentre iniziavo a prepararmi per l'apertura pomeridiana, mi dissi che avrei dovuto abituarmi.

Brooke stava tornando in California, e io avrei dovuto abituarmi alla mia solitudine.

Capitolo 3

Brooke

"**V**olevo ringraziarti per tutto quello che hai fatto per me" dissi a Evan Sinclair, mentre sorseggiavamo un caffè al bar locale, Brew Magic, più tardi quella sera.

L'avevo chiamato e gli avevo chiesto se potessimo parlare. Volevo ringraziarlo di persona per avermi dato la possibilità di scappare dalla California per un po'.

Sollevò un sopracciglio con fare arrogante. "Sei sicura di essere pronta per partire?"

Mi ero abituata alle sue stronzate e al suo comportamento schietto. Poteva sembrare piuttosto distaccato, ma ero convinta che avesse un buon cuore. Quale altro magnate super ricco avrebbe trovato il tempo di aiutare una donna normale come me?

Annuii, mentre bevevo un sorso di caffè. Mi sarebbe mancato davvero Brew Magic. La California aveva un buon caffè, ma quel particolare bar produceva *davvero* un po' di magia, quando si trattava di fornire ai clienti una gustosa dose di caffeina. "Sono pronta. Devo tornare alla mia vita reale. Devo trovarmi un altro lavoro e cercare di riprendermi."

Vivevo i postumi di un incidente devastante da quasi un anno. Sapevo che era ora di lasciarmi tutto alle spalle e andare avanti.

"Posso aiutarti a trovare un lavoro" offrì.

"Non avrò problemi. Ho esperienza. Non credo che sarà così difficile trovarlo."

"Ho molti contatti, se ne hai bisogno."

Quasi soffocai sul caffè. Evan Sinclair aveva più contatti di quasi ogni altra persona sul pianeta. "Lo apprezzo molto."

"Felice di dare una mano."

Lo guardai e capii che era sincero. Se avessi davvero avuto bisogno della sua assistenza, non avevo dubbi che mi avrebbe trovato un lavoro l'indomani stesso. "Resterò per due settimane. Ho promesso a Liam quel periodo di tempo per sostituirmi."

Annuì. "Bene. Forse possiamo passare un po' di tempo insieme, prima che tu vada. So che Miranda voleva invitarti a cena."

Lo osservai attentamente. "È molto gentile da parte tua. Ma sono sicura che sei un ragazzo impegnato."

Non volevo occupare altro del suo tempo. Era un amico di *Noah*, e aveva già fatto abbastanza per me.

"Non è un problema" mi assicurò.

"Va bene, allora. Mi piacerebbe." Ora che non dovevo nascondere il mio passato, volevo essere solo me stessa. E di solito facevo amicizia facilmente.

Evan rimise il caffè sul tavolo, prima di chiedere: "Come si sente Liam all'idea della tua partenza?"

Lo guardai con sorpresa. "Sta bene. Ha sempre saputo che sarebbe stata una cosa temporanea, giusto?"

Annuì bruscamente. "Sì. Ma Xander ha accennato al fatto che sembra molto... affezionato a te."

"Xander ha detto questo?" Sapevo che Liam e il fratello più piccolo di Evan erano amici, ma non avevo idea di come il mio nome fosse venuto fuori in una conversazione tra loro.

"L'ha fatto. Ha anche predetto che Liam non ti avrebbe mai permesso di lasciare Amesport."

"Non può esattamente fermarmi. Sono decisamente maggiorenne, e lui non è mio padre." Sarebbe stato più che inquietante, se lo fosse stato. Dopotutto, lo desideravo da quando ero arrivata ad Amesport. E sicuramente non avevo strane perversioni.

"Penso che gli mancherai, ma ha molti soldi. Potrebbe riportarti qui o prendere un aereo privato per volare avanti e indietro per la California."

Sbuffai. "Non farebbe mai tutto questo per tenersi in contatto. Credo di metterlo a disagio a volte."

Evan sorrise. "Quel disagio non significa sempre che un ragazzo non si preoccupi per te. Mi sono sentito completamente a disagio, quando ho incontrato Miranda per la prima volta."

"Perché?"

"Ad alcuni uomini piace avere sempre il controllo. Quando incontriamo qualcuno che ci travolge, non è facile non prendere il sopravvento."

"Quindi, stai dicendo che tua moglie ti rende davvero irrazionale?"

"Purtroppo, sì. Ma non scambierei lo sbarazzarmi di quella sensazione col non averla nella mia vita. Penso di aver bisogno di essere scosso ogni tanto. Probabilmente è così anche per Liam."

Era divertente pensare che l'adorabile moglie di Evan fosse in grado di avere la meglio con un uomo potente come lui. "Beh, Liam non è interessato."

"Come fai a saperlo?"

Rimasi in silenzio per un momento, prima di confessare: "Gliel'ho chiesto. Diversi mesi fa. Ha ammesso di essere attratto da me, ma ha mantenuto le distanze."

"Interessante" rifletté.

"Non è stato *interessante*" replicai. "In realtà, è stato piuttosto umiliante. Pensa di essere troppo vecchio per me, e mi tratta come una bambina. È anche incline a credere che io abbia un ragazzo."

Le sopracciglia di Evan si inarcarono. "Ce l'hai?"

"Ovviamente no. Mi piacerebbe pensare che se avessi avuto un interesse amoroso, quell'uomo mi avrebbe voluta far tornare in California prima."

"Allora, perché non gli dici semplicemente la verità?"

Lascio uscire un sospiro di resa. "È complicato."

"Sono bravo con le complicazioni" insistette.

"La prima volta che hai portato Noah qui a farci visita su uno dei tuoi aerei, Liam mi ha vista con lui. Non potevo dirgli la verità, quindi ha fatto le sue ipotesi. Pensa che io abbia un ragazzo schifosamente ricco."

"Non c'è niente di male in questo. Il denaro rende la vita più facile."

"Ma molto più complicata" ribattei.

Si strinse nelle spalle. "Può essere. Ma è tutto quello che abbia mai conosciuto. Liam non può pensare che ci sia qualcosa di sbagliato nell'essere ricchi. Lui stesso sta abbastanza bene."

Annuii. "Lo so. Mi sono occupata io delle sue tasse."

"Allora, perché non puoi dirglielo adesso?"

Mi ero posta la stessa domanda più volte. Certo, Liam si sarebbe probabilmente sentito meglio sapendo che non ero innamorata di un altro ragazzo, perché sapeva che una volta ero stata attratta da lui. "Capirebbe che ho mentito" risposi tristemente.

"È una bugia solo perché non hai mai detto nulla in contrario."

"No, Evan. Ho mentito. Quando ha fatto domande, ho mentito."

Bevve un altro sorso di caffè, prima di dire: "È venuto anche da me a fare domande. Suppongo sia stato più o meno il periodo in cui pensava che avessi un uomo nella tua vita. Ha minacciato di licenziarti, se non gli avessi detto perché eri qui."

Lo guardai acutamente. "Davvero? Perché non hai detto niente?"

"Perché non ti avrebbe licenziata, anche se gli avessi negato qualsiasi informazione, cosa che ho fatto."

"E se lo avesse fatto?"

"Allora, ti avrei trovato un altro lavoro. Ma sapevo che non sarebbe arrivato a tanto. Ha un innato senso di decenza. Non aveva intenzione di scaricarti, dopo che avevi fatto un ottimo lavoro per lui" spiegò compiaciuto.

"Cosa voleva sapere?" Non riuscivo ancora a credere che Liam fosse andato da Evan in cerca della verità.

"Tutto" replicò. "Ma non spettava a me rispondere a quelle domande. Ho pensato che gli avresti detto tu quello che volevi dirgli."

"Ci sono state così tante volte in cui avrei voluto dirglielo" ammisi. "Ma ho promesso a te e Noah che non avrei detto niente."

"Non c'è niente che ti impedisca di farlo ora. Stai tornando a casa. I tuoi giorni passati a nasconderti sono finiti."

"Penso che sarebbe troppo tardi per quello" condivisi. "Da allora non ha più menzionato la sua attrazione, ed è tornato a trattarmi come un'adolescente."

"E come ti senti?"

"Male" dissi tristemente. "Non posso davvero vincere in nessun caso. O mi disprezzerà per essere stata attratta da lui, mentre stavo con qualcun altro, o mi odierà per avergli mentito. È una situazione in cui perderò comunque. Ma non importa. Sto andando a casa, e non lo rivedrò mai più."

Il petto mi faceva male per aver detto le parole che non volevo davvero pronunciare.

Non l'avrei mai più visto.

Evan si appoggiò allo schienale della sedia. "Negli affari, non si perde mai del tutto" rifletté. "È solo una mancanza della capacità di vedere gli aspetti positivi."

Tranguggiai il resto del caffè, prima di ribattere: "Questi non sono affari, e non ci sono aspetti positivi, Evan. Il tempo di dire la verità è passato, e non mi aiuterebbe ora. Liam ed io abbiamo una relazione strettamente professionale. Ha superato la sua attrazione, ne sono sicura."

"E tu?" sondò senza pietà.

Dio, potevo capire perché Evan avesse così tanto successo negli affari. Mi stavo quasi contorcendo, perché si comportava come se mi avesse messa al microscopio dopo avermi sezionata. E avrebbe dovuto essere dalla mia parte. Di sicuro non l'avrei voluto come nemico.

"Sì" mentii. Ma poi, ricordai che odiavo mentire e ritrattai: "No."

Sorrise. "Difficilmente può essere entrambe le cose."

Esasperata, gli dissi: "Va bene, sì. Sono attratta da lui. Non mi è mai passato. Ma so che è bene non desiderare cose inutili. Mi sentirò meglio una volta tornata a casa a una vita normale. Liam non era altro che una fantasia. Forse ero annoiata. Forse mi mancavano la mia famiglia e i miei amici. Qualunque sia la causa di queste folli emozioni, scomparirà una volta tornata sulla Costa Occidentale."

"E se alla fine non scomparirà?"

Gli lanciai un'occhiata irritata. "Allora, sarò completamente fregata" risposi alla fine, esausta per il suo serrato interrogatorio. Cominciavo a sentirmi come una testimone di spicco interrogata dalla squadra di difesa durante un processo per omicidio.

I suoi modi erano disinvolti, ma la sua espressione era intensa.

"Non deve essere così, Brooke. Potresti dirgli tutto. Non c'è vergogna in quello che hai fatto. Se hai mentito, l'hai fatto perché dovevi. Penso che capirebbe."

"Non credo che lo farebbe." Evan non aveva idea di come fosse stata tesa la mia relazione con lui. "Per favore. Voglio solo andare a casa."

"La decisione spetta a te" affermò. "Ma posso dirti per esperienza che ci sono sempre aspetti positivi anche nella vita reale. Non solo negli affari. Sfortunatamente, a volte si deve cercare davvero duramente per trovarli."

Eravamo caduti in un'altra conversazione, e fui sollevata dal fatto che non dovevamo più parlare di Liam. Era troppo doloroso chiedersi come sarebbe andata, se fossi stata solo una dipendente e non una pretendente.

Ma sapevo che le bugie mi impedivano di sapere cosa sarebbe successo tra me e Liam, se tutto fosse stato diverso.

Non pensarci. Devi solo superare le prossime due settimane.

Le cose non sarebbero mai state diverse, e non aveva senso pensare a cosa avrebbe potuto essere.

Dovevo affrontare la realtà.

Il mondo reale a volte faceva schifo.

Capitolo 4

Brooke

Dopo aver lasciato Brew Magic, mi infilai nel piccolo negozio di dolciumi di Main Street, felice di vedere che era ancora aperto. C'era solo un'altra persona all'interno, e la riconobbi immediatamente.

"Ciao, Tessa" salutai cordialmente l'altra avventrice. Non conoscevo bene la sorella di Liam, ma era stata molto gentile con me ogni volta che ci incontravamo o quando mi sostituiva al ristorante.

La bella bionda girò la testa dalla cassa per salutarmi. "Brooke" disse con un sorriso. "È bello vederti. Vieni anche tu per uno spuntino a tarda notte?"

Le sorrisi di rimando. "Più per nutrire la mia ossessione. Adoro il croccante alle mandorle. Ti prego, dimmi che l'hai appena comprato tutto, così non dovrò portarne a casa una busta."

Rise, i suoi occhi scintillanti di malizia. "Mi dispiace. Ne ho preso un po', ma ce n'è rimasto ancora metà vassoio."

E io che speravo di non poter avere la mia dose. Il dolce sarebbe andato dritto sui miei fianchi, ma non riuscivo a resistere alla possibilità di prenderne un po', dato che il negozio era ancora aperto. "Allora, non c'è speranza per me. Dovrò fare più esercizio."

Il piccolo negozio era avvolto nel profumo stuzzicante delle mandorle, e avevo già l'acquolina in bocca.

"Penso che tu possa permetterti qualche caloria in più" rispose Tessa. "Io proprio no, ma io e Micah possiamo tornare fuori per correre ora, quindi non sarà poi così male."

"Dov'è Micah?" domandai. Il bel marito della ragazza era quasi sempre con lei.

"Evento notturno in North Carolina. La sua azienda tiene lì l'evento annuale di sport estremi."

Tessa finì di pagare, e io diedi l'ordinazione alla dipendente. Mi aspettavo che se ne andasse dopo aver concluso, ma aspettò finché non ebbi finito di parlare con la cassiera, e poi disse: "Ho visto Liam prima al ristorante. Ha detto che vuoi andartene."

Sospirai. Le notizie viaggiavano veloci ad Amesport. "Non è che *voglio* davvero andare, ma ho una vita in California. È sempre stato un lavoro temporaneo per me."

Annuì. "Lo so. Liam mi ha detto tutto stasera. Vorrei che tu restassi. Mio fratello è molto più felice con te in giro."

Sorrisi. "Vuoi dire che quello che ho visto è il suo umore ottimista?"

"So che suona strano, ma mio fratello è sempre stato tranquillo. Non è mai stato un gran chiacchierone."

"*Questo* lo credo."

"So che non si è mai aperto molto con me" confidò. "Forse si è sempre sentito come se avesse bisogno di prendersi cura di me, perché prima ero la sua sorellina e poi la sua sorellina sorda."

"So cosa vuol dire avere un fratello maggiore" le dissi. "Ne ho tre."

Scosse la testa e mi lanciò un'occhiata comprensiva. "Non riesco a immaginare di avere tre fratelli maggiori. Solo Liam è più che sufficiente."

Noah, Seth e Aiden non erano intensi come Liam, ma Jade e io venivamo comandate da ogni direzione. "Non è sempre brutto" spiegai. "Almeno ho un ragazzo in giro per riparare la mia macchina, quando ne ho bisogno. Sono tutti abbastanza meccanici."

"È già qualcosa" replicò scettica, come se non avesse assolutamente bisogno di tanti uomini prepotenti nella sua vita. "Quando parti?"

"Ho appena dato a Liam il mio preavviso. Gli ho dato due settimane per trovare qualcun altro."

"Posso aiutarlo a sostituirti per un po', ma so che gli mancherai. Non credo che si renda conto di quanto parli di te."

"Lo fa?" risposi sorpresa. "Parla a malapena con *me*."

Mi studiò attentamente, il che era un po' imbarazzante, prima di dire: "Speravo un po' che voi due vi metteste insieme."

Alzai le spalle. "Non era qualcosa che Liam fosse interessato a perseguire."

Non vedevo più alcun motivo per mentirle. Non sarei rimasta ancora per molto.

"Era decisamente interessato" ribatté. "Non sono sicura del motivo per cui non si sia proposto."

Sapevo perché, ma non volevo spiegarle tutto. Ovviamente Liam non le aveva detto del mio cosiddetto ragazzo. "Semplicemente non ha mai funzionato" dissi vagamente. "Immagino sia meglio così, dato che tutta la mia vita è su un'altra costa."

Tessa cambiò argomento, mentre pagavo il mio malvagio spuntino. "Ti ho vista al bar con Evan."

"Siamo amici" mi affrettai a informarla. "Conosce mio fratello maggiore, Noah."

L'ultima cosa che chiunque avrebbe pensato era che Evan sarebbe mai uscito con un altro interesse amoroso, quando aveva una donna che adorava come faceva con sua moglie, Miranda. Ma volevo chiarire.

Roteò gli occhi. "Lo so. Evan morirebbe per Randi. Non devi difenderti per aver preso un caffè con lui. Ma sembravate così a vostro agio. Evan non è un gran chiacchierone, proprio come Liam."

"Parla quando vuole" dissi, pensando a come aveva appena finito di interrogarmi su Liam.

"La maggior parte degli uomini lo fa" replicò con un sorriso. "Brooke, so che non sarai in giro a lungo, ma se hai bisogno di qualcuno con cui parlare, sono una buona ascoltatrice. Vorrei che avessimo avuto più tempo per conoscerci, ma al ristorante eravamo sempre così impegnate."

"Grazie" risposi, afferrando la busta dalla dipendente. "Penso che starò bene. Avevo solo bisogno di un po' di tempo per me stessa. Essere qui mi ha dato questo."

Una parte di me voleva spifferarle tutto. Era solo una di quelle persone gentili che mi facevano desiderare di essere sua amica. Ma sapendo che l'avrebbe detto a Liam, tenni le labbra serrate.

"L'offerta è sempre lì" confermò.

Presi un pezzo di croccante alle mandorle dal sacchetto e me lo misi in bocca. Deglutii, prima di rispondere: "Grazie. Apprezzo che nessuno abbia insistito molto. Non ero pronta a parlare di quello che è successo in California."

Lasciammo il negozio insieme, entrambe che ci nutrivamo dei nostri sacchetti.

"Posso darti un passaggio?" offrì.

"No. Non è il caso. Abito a pochi isolati da qui." Vivevo in un minuscolo monolocale vicino al centro. Era arredato, con vista sul retro dei negozi di Main Street, ma ero grata che Evan fosse riuscito a trovarmelo. Non avevo mai avuto bisogno di una macchina, dato che ero vicina a tutto in città.

"Ci vediamo presto, spero" disse Tessa.

La salutai, mentre si affrettava verso il suo veicolo, desiderando di averla conosciuta meglio. Aveva affrontato tante sfide nella vita. Probabilmente sarebbe stata una persona fantastica da avere come amica.

Iniziai a camminare verso il mio appartamento. Era primavera, ma faceva ancora freddo nel Maine. Indossavo una giacca leggera con jeans, maglioncino e camicia a maniche lunghe, ma gli indumenti non erano abbastanza caldi per la primavera in questo Stato. Mi ero abituata al clima gelido durante l'inverno, ma ero più che pronta al riscaldamento delle cose.

Il mio appartamento era già in vista, quando un braccio uscì dall'oscurità. Fui sorpresa, quando fui costretta a fermarmi per la forte stretta di una mano sul mio braccio.

"Che diavolo ci fai qui fuori così tardi?"

Riconobbi la voce, prima di vedere il suo corpo entrare nella fioca illuminazione dei lampioni.

"Liam?"

"Sono quasi le undici" borbottò.

Volevo dirgli che gli adolescenti hanno il coprifuoco più tardi, ma diedi un'occhiata al suo viso e chiusi la bocca.

La sua espressione era cupa, ma potevo vedere che era preoccupato.

Mentre pensavo a quanto fosse irrazionale, il mio cuore si sciolse un po'.

"Non è esattamente il cuore della notte" dissi con calma.

"È buio" borbottò. "Troppo tardi per girovagare al freddo."

"Sto tornando a casa" spiegai. "Ho solo preso un caffè con Evan al Brew Magic."

"Perché?"

Ero perplessa. Si comportava in modo così strano che non sapevo come rispondere. Impiegai un momento per farlo: "Volevo ringraziarlo per avermi aiutata."

"Perché stai partendo" disse scontento.

"Sì. Perché sto partendo."

Un lungo silenzio si protese per quella che sembrava un'eternità, prima che replicasse: "Hai freddo. Ti accompagno al tuo appartamento."

Ero quasi arrivata. Potevo già vedere l'ingresso del mio edificio. "Nessun problema. Me la caverò. Posso vedere il mio appartamento."

Fece cenno all'ingresso. "Verrò con te."

Iniziai a camminare, e Liam si mise al mio fianco. Non aveva senso discutere con lui. Stavamo al freddo, quando potevamo essere entrambi al caldo in pochi minuti. "Hai appena lasciato il ristorante?"

Chiudeva alle nove in quel periodo dell'anno, quindi pensai che avesse appena chiuso e mi avesse vista camminare al buio.

"Solo pochi minuti fa" confermò.

Anche se le sue parole spiegavano perché si trovava in zona, non capivo ancora perché mi avesse seguita, quando ero a pochi passi da casa.

Non era insolito per Liam assicurarsi che arrivassi a casa mia sana e salva. Nei mesi più caldi, mi aveva accompagnata a casa. D'inverno, mi aveva guidata per la breve distanza dal ristorante al mio edificio. Mi aveva sempre tenuta d'occhio in quel modo. Ma non c'era motivo per lui di accompagnarmi ad una porta che potevo effettivamente vedere dalla mia posizione sul marciapiede.

"Grazie" mormorai, quando arrivai all'ingresso del mio edificio.

"Chiamami la prossima volta" pretese. "Amesport è relativamente sicura, ma ho visto alcune persone strane qui in estate."

"Non è estate" ribattei.

Rispetto alla California, la piccola città costiera del Maine sembrava il posto più sicuro del mondo.

"Chiamami e basta" ripeté. "Ti porterò ovunque tu voglia andare."

Annuii. "Vuoi venire su?" Invitarlo ad entrare sembrava la cosa giusta da fare. Glielo avevo chiesto in passato, e lui aveva sempre rifiutato. Ma lo chiesi comunque.

"Sì. Penso di sì" disse goffamente, come se fosse abituato a dare una risposta diversa—cosa che era vera.

"Posso preparare un caffè" offrii, armeggiando per trovare la chiave della porta d'ingresso.

"Penso di aver bisogno di un drink" rispose.

Trovai la chiave giusta e la inserii nella serratura, prima di voltarmi a guardarlo. Liam non beveva. Mi aveva detto che si era sballato così tanto in California che raramente toccava ancora l'alcol. Nei mesi in cui l'avevo conosciuto, non l'avevo mai visto bere una sola bevanda alcolica.

"Prenderò birra e vino." La birra era stata lasciata a casa mia da mio fratello. E il vino era mio. Dio sapeva che ogni tanto avevo bisogno di bere, soprattutto dopo aver passato l'intera serata con Liam al ristorante.

"D'accordo."

Aprii la porta ed entrai nell'atrio del mio edificio. Era tranquillo. Non era monitorato dalla sicurezza in tempo reale. Non che fosse necessario.

Questo sarà imbarazzante.

Passavamo del tempo insieme da soli al lavoro, ma lasciarlo entrare nella mia vita privata era tutta un'altra cosa.

Salimmo in silenzio con l'ascensore fino al secondo piano. Quando finalmente le porte si spalancarono, chiesi: "Perché finalmente hai deciso di salire?"

Gliel'avevo offerto almeno un centinaio di volte, e lui non aveva mai accettato di venire con me.

"Penso che dobbiamo parlare." Uscì dall'ascensore senza ulteriori spiegazioni.

Lo seguii, prendendo l'iniziativa per mostrargli quale appartamento fosse il mio.

Non volevo parlare di nuovo della partenza, ma sembrava che avessi poca scelta.

Brooke

Il mio appartamento sembrava piccolissimo con Liam dentro. Non per la sua taglia, anche se era un ragazzo grosso. Era la sua presenza. Mi sentivo come se succhiasse ogni piccola quantità di ossigeno, e questo mi lasciava senza fiato.

Gli dissi di mettersi a suo agio nel soggiorno, mentre io preparavo le bevande. Quando entrai in cucina, premetti automaticamente il pulsante per ascoltare i miei messaggi. Ce n'era solo uno.

So che tornerai a casa presto, ma immagino che volessi solo sentire la tua voce. Sarò felice, quando tornerai in California. Ci sentiamo più tardi. Ti adoro, Brooke.

Sorrisi, mentre ascoltavo il messaggio di Noah. La mia famiglia mi mancava davvero. Volevo anche rivedere tutti i miei fratelli rompiscatole in quel momento.

Avevo i drink in mano, quando mi voltai per tornare nel soggiorno, ma non andai lontano. Liam era in piedi all'ingresso della cucina, e non sembrava molto felice.

"Non ti ama, e tu non ami lui" disse in tono rude.

Lo spinsi via, e lui mi seguì nel soggiorno. Gli passai una birra, prima di dire: "Lo amo. Moltissimo."

Ovviamente aveva sentito il messaggio di Noah e pensava che fosse il mio ragazzo inesistente.

"Come diavolo può avere una donna come te e non aver bisogno di vederla ogni fottuto giorno?"

Liam si era seduto all'estremità del divano, quindi mi sedetti dall'altra parte. "Non sono *sua*."

La sua testa si voltò bruscamente per guardarmi. "Stai rompendo con lui?"

Gli sorrisi. "Sfortunatamente, non credo che sia possibile."

C'erano state molte volte in cui i miei fratelli mi avevano fatta impazzire, ma siccome eravamo legati dal sangue, o dovevo sopportarli o non li avevo nella mia vita. Dato che avevano alcune buone qualità, avevo deciso di ignorare le loro sciocchezze.

"Perché? Se non lo ami e lui non ti ama, sarebbe meglio lasciarlo."

"Non posso scaricare mio fratello" lo informai, e poi bevvi un bel sorso del mio Merlot dal bicchiere.

"Quello era tuo fratello?"

Annuii. "Noah. Il maggiore."

Sembrava sollevato, mentre rispondeva. "Scusa. Immagino di non essere abituato al fatto che tu abbia dei fratelli."

"Non sono nemmeno sicura di esserci abituata io" scherzai. "E sono miei fratelli da ventisei anni. Noah è protettivo, visto che ha cresciuto tutti noi, ma non riusciamo mai a convincerlo che siamo tutti adulti."

Trangugiò metà della bottiglia di birra che aveva in mano, prima di rispondere: "Vorrà sempre proteggerti. Tessa è sposata, e io voglio ancora dirle cosa fare. Non credo che l'istinto se ne andrà mai."

"Gli voglio bene. Ha dedicato tutta la sua vita alla famiglia, quando era a malapena un adulto."

"Ha fatto quello che doveva fare per tenervi tutti insieme. Lo rispetto."

"Ma pensavi che fosse il mio ragazzo?"

Annuì. "Sì. Puoi ancora rompere con lui, Brooke."

"Non posso." Come potevo scaricare un ragazzo che non esisteva?

"Fondamentalmente ti ha lasciata da sola nell'ultimo anno. È stato qui per farti visita un giorno o due un paio di volte, ma se ti avesse davvero amata, sarebbe stato qui con te."

Il mio cuore si sciolse ancora un po'. Liam stava ovviamente cercando di aiutarmi, e non potevo ignorare il fatto che sembrava importargli se fossi felice. "Se fossi stato nella stessa situazione, avresti abbandonato tutta la tua vita per una donna?"

"Se fosse stata la donna giusta, sì."

Stranamente, gli credevo. Era leale e risoluto con le persone a cui teneva. "Non ci sono molti ragazzi che lo farebbero" spiegai.

"Cazzate! Non conosco molti ragazzi che non lo farebbero." Bevve un altro salutare sorso della sua birra.

Conoscevo un sacco di uomini che non avrebbero abbandonato la loro vita per seguire una donna, anche se avessero avuto una relazione. Ma Liam evidentemente frequentava ragazzi che avevano altre priorità.

Cambiai argomento, prima di dover dire una vera bugia. "Di cosa volevi parlare?"

"Volevo vedere se potessi convincerti a restare, ma dopo aver ascoltato il messaggio di tuo fratello, so che non succederà. E sicuramente non posso convincerti a sbarazzarti del fidanzato inutile." Si fermò un attimo, prima di aggiungere: "Ma non mi sembra giusto lasciarti andare."

Bevvi un altro lungo sorso del mio vino. "Perché vuoi così tanto che rimanga? Hai detto che non avremmo mai potuto essere amici. E non hai mai detto un'altra parola sul fatto che fossimo attratti l'uno dall'altra. Faccio fatica a credere che tutto questo riguardi il ristorante."

"Non è così" confermò. "Non ha nulla a che fare con il Sullivan."

Il mio cuore sussultò. "Allora, di cosa si tratta, Liam?"

"Non voglio che tu vada."

"Perché?" Adesso volevo davvero la sua risposta a quella domanda.

"L'attrazione non è mai svanita, Brooke. Ma mi rifiuto di intromettermi nel territorio di un altro ragazzo. Ogni volta che ti vedo, il mio uccello è duro, ma non posso farci niente."

Lo vidi alzarsi e prendere il mio bicchiere. Si diresse in cucina, e io lo seguii. Mi appoggiai alla piccola isola, mentre lui tirava fuori un'altra birra, poi riempì il mio bicchiere di vino quasi fino all'orlo.

Lo mise di fronte a me, mentre beveva un'altra bottiglia e gettava via quella vuota.

Sollevai il bicchiere di vino e bevvi, chiedendomi cosa dire. Nemmeno io avevo mai superato la mia lussuria per lui. In effetti, più a lungo rimanevo, più peggiorava. Se dovevo essere onesta con me stessa, quella era la ragione per cui dovevo andarmene. Non potevo sopportare molte altre notti passate a masturbarmi e a fantasticare su di lui. Stava diventando quasi doloroso, e sapevo benissimo che era patetico.

"Non sono sicura che la chimica andrà mai via." Dovevo essere sincera con lui. Glielo dovevo.

Adesso stavo bevendo il mio vino, cercando di calmare i nervi.

Liam finì la sua bottiglia di birra e la buttò nella spazzatura, prima di avvicinarsi a me. "Senza dubbio non lo farà" concordò. "Allora, cosa faremo?"

Il mio bicchiere da vino era vuoto, così lo misi da parte e lo guardai. Era vicino, così vicino che potevo sentire il suo respiro caldo sul mio viso. "Non faremo nulla" dissi in fretta. "Cos'altro possiamo fare? Spero che passerà una volta tornata in California. Te ne dimenticherai, dopo un po' di tempo che me ne sarò andata."

"Riprova, Brooke" sfidò. "Il mio uccello è duro da quasi un anno ormai. Tutto quello che devo fare è pensare a te."

Ero abbastanza sicura che la mia bocca fosse aperta, ma non mi importava. Mi chiedevo se si masturbasse come me, sdraiato sul letto ogni singola notte con un orgasmo insoddisfacente, perché tutto quello che voleva era stare con me. Sapevo che era quello che facevo io. "Mi masturbo davvero con pensieri molto sporchi su di te."

Gli avevo detto che lo facevo al pensiero di lui, quando avevamo ammesso la nostra attrazione reciproca. Era stata l'unica volta in cui mi ero aperta con lui, e mi si era ritorto contro. Non gli avevo mai più confessato niente.

"Lo so. Anch'io lo faccio" disse con voce roca. "Non so te, ma io sono dannatamente stufo. Non so quale impegno hai preso con questo ragazzo in California, ma so che non lo ami. Non se sei attratta da me. Ti conosco abbastanza bene da sapere che non è così."

Ero un po' stordita dal vino che avevo bevuto, ed ero pronta a sputare il rospo. Forse non avremmo mai fatto sesso, ma questo non mi impediva di dirgli quello che pensavo.

Annuii. "Sta iniziando a far male. Questo è uno dei motivi per cui voglio andare."

Il suo sguardo era fisso sul mio, i suoi occhi verdi intensi. "Posso fare in modo che smetta di far male, Brooke. Non credi che dovremmo concederci una pausa?"

Voleva scoparmi. Lo vedevo nei suoi occhi. Gli avvolsi le braccia intorno al collo. Al diavolo le mie inibizioni. Volevo provare come sarebbe stato fare sesso con un uomo che mi voleva davvero.

Adesso era la mia occasione.

Tra due settimane, non l'avrei mai più visto, ed era l'unico che mi facesse ardere così tanto.

Chiusi gli occhi, lasciando che le mie mani gli accarezzassero la schiena. Si era tolto la giacca, e tutto quello che dovevo fare era trovare la sua pelle nuda.

Gli tolsi la maglietta e gemetti ad alta voce, quando i miei palmi stabilirono una calda connessione con la sua schiena nuda. "Questo è molto meglio della fantasia" dissi senza fiato.

Con mio dispiacere, fece un passo indietro, ma solo per strapparmi il maglione e lasciarlo cadere sul pavimento. "Toccami, Brooke. Fanculo! Ti volevo da troppo tempo."

I miei occhi si spalancarono così da poterlo guardare. Aveva il corpo più bello che avessi mai visto, ed essendo in grado di studiarne effettivamente la parte superiore nuda, mi sentivo quasi stordita.

I suoi capelli biondi erano arruffati per avergli tolto la maglietta, ma era lo spettacolo più bello che avessi mai visto. Il suo corpo era tonico da morire. Mi protesi in avanti e gli passai le mani sul petto e sull'addome scolpito. Tracciando la sexy scia di peli che scompariva all'interno della cintura dei suoi jeans, rabbrividii. La sua pelle era morbida, ma potevo sentire ogni muscolo duro sotto di essa.

Anche se era inverno, la sua carnagione era leggermente abbronzata, un colore che gli veniva naturale. "Sei così dannatamente perfetto" dissi in fretta.

"Sono tutt'altro che perfetto" grugnì a denti stretti, segno che stava cercando di trattenersi.

"Questi non sono mai stati nelle mie fantasie" replicai, toccando i tatuaggi sul suo torace. Un lato aveva un cuore spezzato con ali d'angelo. L'altro aveva un'immagine più grande: un feroce drago che sembrava pronto a saltare fuori dalla sua pelle per attaccare.

Mi prese la mano e la portò sul suo cuore. "Questo era per i miei genitori dopo la loro morte." Si mosse in modo che il mio palmo toccasse il drago. "L'ho fatto quando Tessa si è ammalata. Volevo qualcosa che significasse forza, perché sapevo che ne avremmo avuto bisogno entrambi."

Ero ipnotizzata dai tatuaggi, probabilmente perché non lo vedevo come il tipo di ragazzo che li avrebbe avuti. Ma li aveva fatti entrambi per amore della sua famiglia, e lo trovavo straordinario.

"Ti hanno fatto male?"

"Non così tanto quanto il vero motivo per cui li ho fatti. Immagino di aver avuto bisogno di una sorta di distacco da mia madre e mio padre. E quando Tessa si è ammalata, ho dovuto trovare un modo per superarlo."

"Sono bellissimi" dissi, tracciando la forma del drago.

Lasciai che le mie mani gli accarezzassero la schiena nuda, sentendomi come se fossi in una sorta di trance surreale. In quel momento, tutto il mio mondo era l'uomo che mi teneva e, se stavo sognando, di sicuro non volevo svegliarmi. Sapevo che le sensazioni non erano causate dall'aver bevuto più vino del solito. Era tutto... Liam.

Lo guardai, mentre afferrava l'orlo della mia camicia, e alzai le braccia come se fosse la cosa più naturale al mondo.

Aveva bisogno di essere nudo.

Io avevo bisogno di essere nuda.

Morivo dal desiderio di sentire la nostra pelle fondersi insieme.

Non esitai, quando rimosse il mio reggiseno.

Lo volevo.

Volevo *lui*.

Sentii il calore scorrere tra le mie cosce, mentre osservavo lo sguardo affamato sul suo viso con gli occhi che divoravano i miei seni nudi. "Fanculo, Brooke!" Li prese entrambi. "Non posso credere che sia vero."

Sapevo esattamente cosa intendeva, ma lo presi in giro comunque. "È vero al cento per cento. Non mi piace la chirurgia plastica."

Avevo sempre pensato che si dovesse accettare qualunque DNA ci fosse stato dato alla nascita. Ma non potevo fare a meno di essere un po' nervosa non sapendo se Liam sarebbe stato eccitato dal mio corpo una volta che fossi stata effettivamente nuda.

Mi avvolse con le braccia e tirò il mio corpo a contatto con il suo, come se sapesse esattamente quello che volevo.

"Sì" sibilai, mentre la sua pelle calda accarezzava la mia.

"*Dannazione!* Non resisterò» gracchiò.

"Allora, immagino che ci godremo qualunque sia il tempo che abbiamo" replicai.

Mi sollevò il mento. "Non me ne andrò, finché non sarai soddisfatta" giurò.

Chiusi gli occhi, mentre la sua testa si abbassava e mi prendeva la bocca con una ferocia che non avevo mai provato.

Mi lasciai cadere nell'abbraccio, il cuore che batteva all'impazzata, mentre reclamava ogni centimetro della mia bocca. Era esigente e non avevo problemi a dargli tutto ciò che voleva, la mia lingua che si intrecciava con la sua in un duello di bramosia.

La mia figa pulsava per il bisogno di sentirlo dentro di me.

"Liam" mi lamentai, quando finalmente mi lasciò respirare di nuovo.

Misi una mano tra i nostri corpi e palpai il davanti dei suoi jeans.

Era duro come una roccia, ed era tutto per me.

Si allungò per prendere la mia mano, e la tirò via. «No. Non voglio venire come un dannato adolescente con la sua prima donna. Voglio che duri il più possibile."

Lo volevo anch'io, ma il mio corpo era molto più avanti del mio cervello. Volevo correre all'orgasmo, perché soffrivo per lui. "Cosa posso fare?"

"Puoi denudarti" ringhiò. Fece un passo indietro e raggiunse il bottone dei miei jeans.

Li tirai giù, ansiosa di fare quello che voleva.

Capitolo 6

Brooke

Il resto dei nostri vestiti venne tolto freneticamente. Li lasciammo cadere sul pavimento; a nessuno di noi importava niente di dove fossero finiti.

Ogni muro che avevo costruito con cura crollò, quando vidi lo sguardo avido di Liam una volta che eravamo completamente nudi.

Il mio cuore batteva contro la parete toracica così forte che potevo effettivamente sentire i rapidi battiti che pulsavano nel mio corpo.

Lo osservai, realizzando che ero altrettanto affamata nel *vederlo*.

Il mio intimo si strinse dolorosamente, e si inondò di calore umido, mentre notavo ogni glorioso centimetro del suo corpo perfetto. La V ben delineata sotto gli addominali sembrava scolpita nella pietra, e puntava esattamente su quello che volevo. Come un'insegna al neon che indica ad un alcolizzato il bar più vicino.

E Dio... quanto volevo bere.

Feci un passo avanti per toccare il suo enorme fallo, le mie dita che tremavano, mentre lo avvolgevano.

Gemette, quando mi prese il polso. "Non succederà in questo momento, Brooke" disse duramente. "Non adesso."

Il suo braccio avvolse la mia vita, e la sua mano si aggrovigliò tra i miei capelli. Afferrò una manciata di ciocche e mi tirò indietro la testa. "Ho sempre saputo che sarebbe stato così" aggiunse rudemente, i suoi occhi così intensamente verdi da togliermi il fiato.

Ero vulnerabile e nuda. Al momento, tutto quello che volevo era comunicargli il mio bisogno. "Lo sapevo anch'io. Ma forse non così intenso."

Se ci avessi provato, non avrei saputo spiegare cosa mi stava succedendo. Ma avevo sempre saputo che se mi avesse toccata, toccata davvero, allora le mie difese non sarebbero state all'altezza del fuoco che avrebbe consumato il mio corpo in pochi secondi.

Si chinò e mi prese le labbra con una bramosia così potente che non potevo fare altro che sottomettermi.

Non avrei potuto respingerlo in quel momento, anche se avessi voluto, cosa che non pensavo. Dovevo sentirlo, assaggiarlo, provare ogni grammo di piacere che poteva darmi.

"Mia" ringhiò, mentre lasciava le mie labbra. "Sei nata per essere mia."

La sua dichiarazione non fece che peggiorare i miei istinti possessivi. Sapevo esattamente cosa intendeva. Avevo sempre avuto gli stessi sentimenti. Dal momento in cui gli avevo posato gli occhi addosso, l'avevo desiderato ardentemente.

Avrebbe dovuto appartenere a me da quel primo incontro, ma non era andata così.

Adesso ce l'ho.

Forse alla fine l'avrei dovuto lasciare, ma per ora ero tutta sua. *E lui era mio.*

Lasciai ricadere la testa, mentre si faceva strada con un bacio sulla pelle tenera del mio collo e mi mordeva il lobo dell'orecchio. Potevo sentire il suo respiro caldo contro il mio orecchio, e mi faceva impazzire.

I suoi palmi ruvidi mi stavano accarezzando su e giù per la schiena, esplorando la mia pelle, prima che finalmente si abbassasse e mi afferrasse saldamente il sedere.

"Questo bel culetto mi tormenta da sempre" disse rudemente contro la mia pelle.

Misi le mani sul suo didietro, ma non lo afferrai. Accarezzai i muscoli tesi, ricordando ogni volta in cui l'avevo bramato al ristorante.

"Fottimi, Liam" piagnucolai. "Ho bisogno di te."

La sua espressione divenne feroce e cruda, come se fosse completamente sua responsabilità lenire ogni dolore che avevo. "Voglio che duri, Brooke."

Infilai disperatamente le mie mani nei suoi capelli. Avevo sempre voluto sfiorare quelle ciocche per sentire se fossero così sexy come sembravano. Emisi un sospiro tremante, quando le mie dita entrarono in contatto con i folti ciuffi. "Tu vuoi che duri, e io voglio solo che accada prima che impazzisca" replicai tremante.

Mi sollevò e mi mise il sedere sull'isola della cucina. Era l'altezza perfetta per me per avvolgere le gambe intorno alla sua vita, e non esitai a cercare di avvicinarmi.

"Aspetta, Brooke" disse, accarezzandomi le cosce.

Fu accolto da un calore liquido molto allettante.

"Accidenti!" gracchiò, il petto che si sollevava per lo sforzo di trattenersi. "Non posso aspettare questa volta."

"No" supplicai. "Ho bisogno di te adesso."

Le sue dita accarezzarono il mio clitoride, e quasi colpii il soffitto. "Oh, Dio."

Il minuscolo fascio di nervi pulsava ad ogni ruvido passaggio delle sue dita. Aprii le gambe per consentirgli un accesso migliore, il mio corpo che mormorava per l'orgasmo.

"Vieni per me, Brooke. Voglio guardarti. Devo vederlo."

Il pensiero di lui che mi osservava nel mio punto più vulnerabile non era spaventoso. Era erotico da morire.

Mi ero persa irrimediabilmente nelle sensazioni, mentre il suo tocco diventava più esigente. Ero caduta nel calore, e mi consumava.

C'era troppa stimolazione da trattenere. Il solo fatto che stesse guardando con occhi carichi di lussuria che mi sconvolgevano era sufficiente per soddisfarmi.

La sua bocca copriva la mia e io gemevo contro le sue labbra, mentre l'orgasmo mi attraversava con una forza che era quasi terrificante.

Tremavo contro la sua pelle ardente, il mio bisogno di liberazione così disperato che mi sentivo come se non potessi respirare. "Liam" ansimai, mentre mi lasciava andare la bocca.

"Lasciati andare, Brooke. Ti ho presa" disse urgentemente vicino al mio orecchio.

Chiusi gli occhi, mentre il mio orgasmo prendeva il controllo, e mi sentivo come se non avrei mai smesso di tremare per il potente climax.

Qualcosa senza senso uscì dalla mia bocca, perché non riuscivo a formare le parole. Tutto quello che potevo fare era balbettare e gemere per il piacere più soddisfacente che avessi mai conosciuto.

Stavo ansimando, mentre mi riprendevo.

L'intensità degli ultimi minuti mi stava ancora invadendo, quando il ragazzo mi afferrò il sedere con così tanta forza da farmi quasi male. Fu dentro di me, prima che potessi riprendermi del tutto.

"Sì" implorai. "Sì."

Era grosso, ma il mio corpo lo accettò. I muscoli del mio canale si rilassarono per prenderlo tutto, e averlo sepolto fino alle palle dentro di me era così dannatamente incredibile che volevo che durasse, proprio come aveva fatto Liam.

Avevo combattuto una guerra interna tra il volere che la sensazione di essere in contatto con lui andasse avanti a lungo, e l'esigenza che iniziasse a scoparmi per placare i miei istinti carnali.

Le mie gambe si avvolsero intorno a lui e lo tirai forte contro il mio intimo, i miei fianchi che spingevano in avanti senza pensarci.

Grugnì. "Non posso aspettare, Brooke. Ti desidero troppo."

"Fottimi" pretesi, il mio corpo che mi diceva che non si sarebbe accontentato di niente di meno.

Mi spinse il sedere sul bordo del tavolo, portandoci al contatto più stretto che potessimo ottenere.

Liam si tirò fuori, poi spinse di nuovo il suo membro dentro di me. I miei muscoli si stavano sforzando per prendere un ragazzo della sua taglia, ma anche se provavo un minimo dolore, era davvero bello.

"Sì. Più duro" insistetti.

"Piccola, non puoi volerlo così forte come potrei dartelo" disse con voce rassicurante.

Oh sì, lo volevo. La nostra reazione reciproca era cruda e primitiva, e mi sentivo altrettanto bisognosa. "Più forte" lo incoraggiai.

"Fanculo. Non dimenticare che l'hai chiesto tu" rispose con una ferocia della quale la mia figa prese nota.

Adoravo l'intensità di quell'uomo. Era qualcosa che non avevo mai sperimentato, ma era così dannatamente allettante; forse perché mi sentivo pazza quanto lui.

Ero senza fiato, mentre mi mostrava quanto fossimo andati entrambi fuori controllo. Sapevo che avrei avuto dei lividi sul sedere la mattina successiva con quella forte stretta sulle natiche. Ma ogni dolore sarebbe valso la soddisfazione di ricevere da Liam quello che volevo, focoso e duro.

Mi colpì con una ferocia che non sapevo fosse possibile. Tutto quello che potevo fare era aggrapparmi a lui, i nostri corpi bagnati da un sottile strato di sudore che ci faceva scivolare l'uno contro l'altra, mentre entrambi ci sforzavamo per soddisfare i bisogni selvaggi.

Mi persi in lui, ed ero abbastanza sicura che fossi andata al di là del pensiero razionale.

"Liam" gridai, mentre sentivo il mio orgasmo crescere di nuovo.

Questa volta era diverso, e molto più potente del primo.

Quando spinse la sua mano tra di noi e mi accarezzò il clitoride, implosi.

I muscoli dentro di me fremettero violentemente intorno al suo cazzo, e lo sentii gemere. "Brooke. Sei così perfetta, piccola."

Si spinse dentro di me ancora una volta, mentre stringevo il suo pene per soddisfarlo.

Non avevo idea di quanto tempo fossimo rimasti aggrappati l'uno all'altra, i nostri corpi sudati avvolti, fino a quando non sapevo dove finivo io e dove iniziava Liam. Poi, il mio battito cardiaco rallentò, ed entrambi riprendemmo fiato per un periodo di tempo indeterminato.

Ero stata messa a nudo di fronte a lui, e non mi importava. Gli avevo mostrato ogni mia emozione, ma mi sentivo al sicuro nella sua presa possessiva.

"Dobbiamo muoverci prima o poi" dissi senza fiato.

Con riluttanza, iniziò a fare un passo indietro.

Istintivamente strinsi le gambe intorno a lui. "Non andartene" dissi, sentendomi di nuovo vulnerabile.

Gentilmente mi abbassò le gambe, e poi mi sollevò dal tavolo. "Non andrò da nessuna parte, tesoro. Sono qui" replicò con voce roca.

Appoggiai la testa sul suo petto, sollevata dal fatto che non ci stesse separando.

"Bene" risposi in un forte sussurro. Era un tono estraneo, uno che non avevo mai sentito uscire dalle mie labbra.

"Stai bene?" chiese esitante.

Sembrava insicuro, e mi sciolse il cuore che un momento prima potesse essere un maschio alfa conquistatore, e poi in pochi istanti l'amante preoccupato.

Era una specie di combinazione impossibile da non adorare.

Gli sorrisi. "Mai stata meglio."

Un sorriso lento si diffuse sul suo viso, e il mio cuore sussultò, quando vidi la malizia sexy nei suoi occhi. "Doccia?" domandò.

I nostri occhi si incrociarono, ed ero di nuovo senza fiato. Liam era ovviamente insaziabile, ma sapevo che sarei stata in grado di tenere il passo.

Avevamo avuto quasi un anno per arrivare a questo punto, e un suo assaggio non sarebbe mai stato sufficiente. "Sì, grazie" risposi.

Eravamo entrambi maleodoranti, e una doccia sembrava il paradiso.

Mi portò nel bagno, e imparai quanto potesse essere deliziosa un po' d'acqua, prima che mi portasse a letto.

Persi il conto di quante volte c'eravamo svegliati a vicenda, i nostri corpi che bramavano ancora di più l'estasi che avevamo scoperto insieme.

Lo sentii con me tutta la notte.

Sfortunatamente, quando mi svegliai alla luce del mattino, non c'era più.

Liam

"Hai un aspetto di merda. Penso che tu abbia bisogno di dormire di più."

Guardai Xander Sinclair, e gli lanciai un'occhiataccia. Forse *avevo* un pessimo aspetto per aver dormito poco la notte prima, ma di certo non volevo che me lo facesse notare.

Ero già irritabile.

Ignorando la sua osservazione, bevvi un sorso del mio caffè mattutino, sperando che sarebbe stato d'aiuto.

Xander era diventato una persona mattiniera, quindi lo vedevo sempre di più all'ora della colazione. E quel giorno non faceva eccezione. Era entrato, mentre stavo preparando il caffè e, qualche tazza dopo, non se n'era *ancora* andato.

Lasciare Brooke subito prima dell'alba era stata la cosa più difficile che avessi mai fatto. Il mio istinto era di non lasciarla mai andare, ma sapevo che tutto sarebbe stato diverso alla luce del giorno, e dovevo decidere un piano d'azione.

"Torna sulla Terra, Liam. Torna sul pianeta, per favore" disse Xander con un sorrisetto.

Mi piaceva di più quando era triste. Era troppo dannatamente felice da quando aveva conosciuto sua moglie, Samantha.

Alla fine, risposi: "Non ho dormito molto la scorsa notte, ma non è insolito per me."

Scosse la testa. "Cazzate. Hai più o meno lo stesso aspetto da quando una certa cameriera ha iniziato a lavorare per te. Sembri solo peggio del solito oggi."

Aveva ragione. Tutto quello a cui riuscivo a pensare era Brooke, e al fatto che avesse un uomo nella sua vita. Ma non avevo intenzione di dirlo al presuntuoso bastardo dall'altra parte del tavolo. "Sta partendo" lo informai.

Mi diede un'occhiata consapevole. "Quindi, è questo che ti tiene sveglio la notte. Che cos'hai intenzione di fare?"

"Cosa *posso* fare? Il suo ragazzo non è sparito, e lei ha una famiglia numerosa in California."

"Allora, devi farle desiderare di restare, amico" consigliò. "Portala a letto e convincila che starebbe meglio ad Amesport."

"L'ho fatto" replicai irritato. "Non è cambiato nulla."

Fare sesso—un sesso fottutamente fantastico—non aveva fatto altro che incasinarmi la testa. Sì, mi ero masturbato. Parecchie volte. Piuttosto che aiutare, mi aveva solo fatto desiderare di più. Una notte con lei era stata addirittura meglio di quanto avessi fantasticato, ma ora ero ossessionato dal fatto che sarebbe tornata a casa da qualcun altro.

Non sapevo bene cosa fare adesso, e non ero sicuro di come avrebbe reagito Brooke alla luce del giorno. Quella mattina ero sgattaiolato fuori da casa sua come un codardo, temendo di non scorgere lo stesso desiderio nei suoi occhi.

Era destinata a sentirsi in colpa per aver scopato un altro ragazzo. La conoscevo abbastanza bene da sapere che non avrebbe preso quella roba alla leggera. Ne ero certo.

"Cos'è successo?" Xander sembrava confuso.

Non avevo intenzione di discutere della mia vita sessuale con lui. "Niente. Abbiamo fatto sesso. Fine della storia."

Mi guardò sospettoso. "Penso che questo abbia cambiato tutto. Non è più solo una fantasia."

"Fanculo! Come diavolo fai a sapere su cosa fantastico?" Mi stava dando sui nervi.

"Ci sono passato, ricordi? Una volta che hai quel tipo di connessione con la donna giusta, non puoi lasciarla andare. Non che io sia del tutto sicuro che avrei potuto lasciar andare Sam, anche senza quella connessione, ma fare sesso con Brooke ovviamente ha cambiato le cose per te."

Grugnii. "Quindi, ora sei l'esperto dell'amore? Solo perché sei stato abbastanza fortunato da convincere Sam a sposarti?"

"Non è stata fortuna" spiegò. "Lei mi ama."

"Non sono sicuro di aver capito perché" risposi, sentendomi scontroso. "Sei irritante da morire."

Sorrise. "Sai che ti piace ricevere i miei consigli."

Lo guardai di traverso, e poi mi concentrai sul mandare giù il caffè nel mio corpo il prima possibile. Ingoiai il resto della tazza, e poi mi alzai per prenderne un'altra.

"È solo una cosa fisica" gli dissi, desiderando non aver accennato al fatto di essere andato a letto con Brooke. Xander poteva essere implacabile quando voleva.

"Se l'avessi detto un anno fa, ti avrei risposto che non esisteva nient'altro *eccetto* il lato fisico. Ma ora ho Sam, e so tutto sul volere di più. Sfrutta la tua opportunità, Liam, o te ne pentirai. Ti chiederai sempre cosa avrebbe potuto essere."

"Cazzo! Non credi che lo sappia? Voglio pensare che sarebbe più felice se rimanesse qui, ma tutta la sua vita è in California."

Si alzò e si fermò di fronte a me, quando mi voltai con un'altra tazza di caffè. "Ascolta, amico. In tutta serietà, non voglio vederti rovinare la tua vita. Ho visto come sei con Brooke. Posso dire che si sente allo stesso modo. Non so come stiano le cose con il fidanzato, ma a lei importa di te. Devi farle desiderare di restare, perché la tua vita sarebbe uno schifo senza di lei."

"Non voglio che rimanga, perché in qualche modo la sto costringendo a vivere nel Maine." Quello che volevo veramente era che rimanesse perché voleva stare qui... con me.

"*Vuole* restare. Posso dire che lei si sente nello stesso modo. A volte è più facile vedere l'ovvio da estraneo. Se sei coinvolto personalmente, non puoi vedere niente. Hai la testa su per il culo."

Appoggiai il caffè sul tavolo e incrociai le braccia davanti a me. "Allora, che cosa mi suggerisce di fare, Dottore?"

Una storia d'amore andata bene e pensava di essere un esperto? Anche se dovevo ammettere che speravo che la sua visuale dall'esterno fosse accurata.

"Falle sapere cosa provi. Probabilmente sta vivendo le stesse cose che stai vivendo tu in questo momento. La cosa che desidera di più sei tu. Falle sapere che la vuoi."

"Ho già *scopato*" ammisi irritato.

Inarcò le sopracciglia. "Allora, forse dovresti farlo di nuovo. Forse non saresti così dannatamente irritabile."

"Non voglio nessuno tranne lei" confessai con riluttanza. "Non lo faccio da molto tempo, e non mi sono mai sentito allo stesso modo per un'altra donna prima... mai."

Nessun'altra donna poteva catturare il mio interesse. Ero troppo ossessionato dalla mia dipendente, e lo ero dal giorno in cui l'avevo incontrata per la prima volta. Da quando Brooke era arrivata, non avevo nemmeno pensato di uscire con qualcun'altra. Ero troppo preso da lei.

Xander si strinse nelle spalle. "Allora, è meglio che ti assicuri di prenderla. Portala fuori per un vero appuntamento, falle capire che sei serio. *Vuoi* una relazione con lei, giusto?"

Non avevo mai veramente considerato cosa volevo. Brooke era sempre stata irraggiungibile per me, quindi non passavo il mio tempo a pensarci. "Sì, la voglio" dissi infine a bassa voce. "Dal momento che non l'ho mai vista come se non fosse proibita, non credo di averci riflettuto molto."

"Gesù, Liam, sei un bravo ragazzo, ma comincio a mettere in dubbio la tua capacità di ragionamento."

"Non ho molti pensieri razionali, quando lei è nei paraggi."

"L'ho notato" rispose. "E ho capito. Ti incasina la testa. Ci sono passato. Ma non lo sta facendo apposta. Brooke probabilmente non è sicura di cosa diavolo vuoi da lei. Un giorno è proibita, e il giorno dopo fai sesso con lei. Ascolta, penso che sarebbe fortunata ad avere un ragazzo come te. In genere, sei un ragazzo intelligente—a parte in questo momento. So che saresti fedele. Guadagni dannatamente bene, e mia moglie pensa che tu sia di bell'aspetto. Io non saprei, visto che non sono omosessuale, ma hai un ex rock star come migliore amico. Questo deve farti guadagnare dei punti" concluse scherzando.

Gli lanciai un'occhiata impaziente. "Eri incasinato quanto me, e lo sai."

"Probabilmente di più" ammise.

Alzai una mano. Non volevo entrare nella vita personale di Xander ora che aveva messo la testa a posto. "Sono combattuto tra il lasciarla sola in modo che possa tornare a casa e cercare di convincerla che ha bisogno di me nella sua vita."

"Pensa a come ti sentiresti, se non la vedessi mai più. Deciderai abbastanza velocemente. Il tuo tempo è limitato, Liam."

Mi passai una mano tra i capelli con frustrazione. "Hai ragione. Non c'è alcun modo in cui possa lasciarla andare senza combattere."

Si diresse verso la porta. "Ora fissa quel pensiero nella mente, e non pensare a nient'altro. Ho visto quanto puoi essere incredibilmente testardo, quando vuoi esserlo."

C'erano volte in cui avrei voluto prenderlo a pugni, e ora era una di quelle occasioni. Il problema era che sapevo che aveva ragione.

Non avrei dovuto lasciare Brooke quella mattina.

Non avrei dovuto darle il tempo di pensare a quello che era successo, e poi sentirmi in colpa.

Sarei dovuto restare e avrei dovuto convincerla a mollare il fidanzato.

Guardai Xander andarsene senza dire una parola, uscendo dalla porta della cucina che dava fuori.

Ero stato stupido, e forse *era* confusa su quello che volevo. C'erano stati momenti in cui l'avevo tenuta a distanza intenzionalmente, e poi mi ero voltato e le avevo mostrato che la volevo.

Dovevo smettere di combattere me stesso, prima di poter combattere per Brooke.

Chi stavo prendendo in giro con le mie stronzate? Avrei fatto qualsiasi cosa per tenerla ad Amesport e poter stare insieme. Solo che non ero del tutto sicuro di cosa volesse *lei*.

Sapevo che una delle cose che Xander aveva detto era vera: se non avessi provato, me ne sarei pentito.

Mi sarei sempre chiesto cosa sarebbe successo, se fossi stato onesto con lei.

Ma prima doveva accettare di sbarazzarsi del ragazzo.

Eliminare la competizione con me era la priorità.

Presi il caffè dal bancone e mi sedetti al tavolo. Avevo bisogno di svegliarmi abbastanza per arrivare al ristorante più tardi quella mattina.

Brooke aveva il giorno libero, quindi non l'avrei vista, a meno che non avessi fatto uno sforzo per trovarla.

Presi il cellulare dal tavolo, sperando che Tessa fosse disponibile a coprirmi più tardi.

Capitolo 8

Brooke

"Non vedo l'ora che tu sia qui" disse Jade eccitata. "Mi sei mancata così tanto."

"Tornerò a casa la prossima settimana" le ricordai, cercando di mantenere la voce calma al telefono, in modo che non capisse che stavo soffrendo.

Jade percepiva le cose con me, proprio come io potevo dire quando qualcosa non andava bene in lei. Il nostro legame gemello era piuttosto forte, anche se non eravamo identiche.

Mi ero svegliata quella mattina in completa confusione, e non era sparita. Non avevo idea del motivo per cui Liam se n'era andato, o di quando l'aveva fatto, ma era stato una specie di schiaffo in faccia vedere che non aveva nemmeno lasciato un biglietto.

Certo, pensava ancora che avessi un ragazzo.

"Lo so" rispose. "Sono solo contenta che tu possa finalmente tornare."

Volevo disperatamente vederla. "Ti farò sapere quando arrivo. Evan mi ha offerto il suo jet. Non vedo l'ora di rivederti. Sembra un'eternità."

Jade e io non eravamo mai state separate così a lungo, e non avere lei con cui parlare mi stava uccidendo. Avevamo parlato al telefono, ma non era la stessa cosa. Eravamo sorelle, gemelle e facevamo di tutto, dallo shopping alle serate tra ragazze insieme. Era sempre stata la mia migliore amica.

Forse avevo davvero avuto bisogno di tempo da sola. Quando ero arrivata ad Amesport, non ero davvero riuscita a descrivere il dolore e la paura che avevo dovuto superare. E non avevo avuto voglia di parlare.

Ora, avevo un disperato bisogno di vedere la mia famiglia.

"Non vedo l'ora di vedere cosa hai combinato per quasi un anno. Ho sentito così tanto parlare di Amesport che voglio vederla di persona."

"Non ci sono esattamente molte notizie interessanti da qui" la avvertii. "È abbastanza tranquilla fino all'estate."

"Non mi importa. Ho solo bisogno di vederti. Ho bisogno di sapere che stai davvero bene."

"Sto bene. Meglio" la rassicurai.

L'istinto mi urlava che qualcosa non andava bene in lei, ma non riuscivo a capire cosa fosse. "Come sta andando il tuo progetto?"

Prima che me ne andassi, aveva lavorato a un progetto di conservazione della fauna selvatica come parte dei suoi studi universitari.

"La mia tesi è finita" rispose.

"È fantastico" commentai con entusiasmo.

"È un sollievo" confessò.

"Pensavo che ti piacesse farlo" dissi, confusa dal fatto che mia sorella non fosse felice per aver finalmente terminato la scuola e potesse andare a lavorare a tempo pieno come biologa della fauna selvatica.

"Mi piace" replicò vagamente. "Ma sono contenta che sia finita."

"Insegni ancora?" domandai.

Oltre alla sua formazione come scienziata della fauna selvatica, era un'esperta di sopravvivenza nella natura selvaggia primitiva. Era passata da studentessa a insegnante diversi anni addietro.

"Non quanto vorrei, ma in futuro potrei avere un lavoro televisivo. I produttori di quel programma TV sui sopravvissuti mi hanno contattata per vedere se fossi interessata a partecipare allo show."

"Jade" strillai. "Sarebbe fantastico!" Ero così emozionata per lei. Amava essere una scienziata, ma la sua formazione sulla sopravvivenza era altrettanto importante per lei, anche se era ancora un hobby.

Sospirò. "Non sono sicura che sia una buona cosa farlo. Chissà quali stranezze combineranno per la televisione."

"Devi farlo" insistetti. "Se non è quello per cui ti sei iscritta, puoi tirarti indietro."

"Credo."

"Contattali. Per favore. Penso che potresti fare un ottimo lavoro." Non conoscevo nessuno abile come mia sorella.

"Ci penserò. Ma sai com'è quello spettacolo. Se trovo un partner stupido, sarò fregata."

Mia sorella ed io avevamo guardato ogni episodio del programma. Sapevo che trovare il partner giusto era tutto. "Forse troverai qualcuno figo" ribattei scherzando.

"Più che probabilmente, finirò con un sopravvissuto aspirante maschio alfa. Sai quanti di quelli prendono nello show. Ragazzi che vogliono giocare a stare allo stato brado, ma non sanno un bel niente su come sopravvivere."

Ero abbastanza sicura che pochissime persone fossero serie quanto mia sorella riguardo alle loro capacità, ma volevo comunque che ci provasse. "Potresti essere fortunata."

Sbuffò. "Ne dubito. Così tante persone ci si stanno buttando dentro soltanto per lo spettacolo, e non si preoccupano molto del motivo per cui lo stanno facendo. Io lo faccio perché voglio quella connessione con i miei antenati. Voglio sapere com'è stato per loro far fronte a un mondo senza telefoni cellulari, Internet e tutte le altre cose che abbiamo a portata di mano ora."

"Allora, vai e prendili a calci nel culo" consigliai.

"Come ho detto, ci penserò."

"Stai bene?" chiesi. Non era da Jade rifuggire da qualcosa.

"Sto bene" rispose. "Forse mi manchi soltanto."

"Mi manchi anche tu" confessai. "Come stanno tutti a casa? Come sta Owen?"

Mio fratello più piccolo era particolarmente dotato. Aveva appena venticinque anni, e aveva terminato la scuola di medicina. In questo momento, stava facendo la specializzazione.

"Eccelle, come al solito. Era a casa durante le vacanze, ed era troppo tranquillo. Ho provato a convincerlo a parlare con me, ma non mi ha detto cosa lo preoccupasse" spiegò. "L'unica cosa che ha menzionato è che stava avendo difficoltà a gestire la sofferenza umana del suo lavoro. Ma è bravo in questo. Diventerà un ottimo medico."

"Lo immaginavo. Owen è sempre stato il più gentile della famiglia. È incredibilmente intelligente, ma è molto sensibile."

"Lo so" concordò Jade. "Ma spero che non cambi mai."

Onestamente, non volevo vedere il mio fratellino *diversamente* a causa della sua scelta di carriera. Potevo sempre contare su di lui come la voce della ragione.

"Tutti gli altri stanno bene?" sondai.

"Se stai chiedendo se i nostri tre fratelli maggiori stanno bene, posso riferirti che sono ancora tutti dei rompiscatole. Ma per ora sono sani. Fino a quando non li ucciderò per aver cercato di ficcare il naso nei miei affari."

Risi, sapendo che Jade non aveva problemi a farsi rispettare. Non si faceva scrupoli a dire a Noah, Seth e Aiden quanto fossero invadenti.

Sfortunatamente, erano dei ficcanaso quasi sempre.

"Cerca di tenerli in riga" pregai. "Sono sicura che avranno molti consigli fraterni per me, quando tornerò a casa."

Sospirai. Parlavo con tutti i miei fratelli al telefono abbastanza spesso, ed erano sempre pieni di suggerimenti.

"Sono preoccupati per te, Brooke. Lo siamo tutti" disse seriamente.

Sospirai. "Lo so. Ma tornerò a casa, e starò meglio. Spero che le cose tornino alla normalità. È stato un lungo anno."

"Come farai a lasciare il tuo capo sexy?" prese in giro.

Le avevo detto di Liam e di cosa provavo per lui. Era l'unica persona con cui potevo parlare del mio capo incredibilmente attraente.

"Non lo so" risposi onestamente. "Forse è un bene che me ne vada."

"Brooke! Conosco quella voce. Mi stai nascondendo qualcosa. Sei andata a letto con lui, vero?"

Dio, a volte odiavo essere così legata a lei. "L'ho fatto."

"Sputa il rospo, sorella. Dimmi tutto."

Le diedi una breve versione di quello che era successo. Non le avrei detto che Liam aveva completamente sconvolto il mio mondo al punto che non sarei mai più stata lo stessa. Avrebbe cercato di convincermi a sposarlo.

"Quindi, te ne andrai e basta?" chiese. "Come puoi farlo, quando hai trovato l'uomo dei tuoi sogni?"

"Sei così romantica" la accusai.

"Non lo sono. So che non sempre c'è un lieto fine. Ma non ti sei accontentata di qualcosa di meno di quanto meritassi. Hai aspettato di trovarlo."

Alzai gli occhi al cielo. Mia sorella poteva essere un po' drammatica riguardo alle relazioni, il che era strano per me. Jade era così pragmatica nella maggior parte degli altri ambiti della sua vita, ma portava la ricerca dell'uomo giusto all'estremo.

"Non è *quello giusto*" le dissi, sapendo che stavo mentendo. Liam era la persona giusta, ma le circostanze erano impossibili.

"Non ti credo" sfidò. "Cosa c'è che non va?»

"Pensa che io abbia un ragazzo, ricordi?"

"Non gli hai detto che era Noah?"

"No. Mi odierebbe per avergli mentito."

"Brooke, *devi* dirglielo adesso. Sei andata a letto con lui. Vuoi davvero che pensi di aver scopato una donna che era già stata presa?"

Non avevo ancora pensato a come si sarebbe sentito Liam. Ero stata troppo occupata a preoccuparmi di come proteggermi dall'unico uomo che poteva farmi perdere completamente la compostezza. "Probabilmente è meglio che lo pensi. L'alternativa è sapere che gli ho mentito. Odia i bugiardi."

"Non avevi scelta" sostenne. "Non ti biasimerà. Se questo ragazzo è tutto ciò che pensi che sia, è impossibile che non vorrebbe sapere la verità."

Probabilmente aveva ragione, ma non volevo rendere le cose difficili tra me e Liam per le due settimane successive. "Vedremo" dissi vagamente. "Devo capire come stanno le cose, quando lo vedrò. Non gli parlo da quando abbiamo dormito insieme."

"Oh, mio Dio. È appena successo, vero?"

"La scorsa notte" confermai, sapendo che era inutile cercare di nascondersi molto da Jade. Me lo avrebbe tirato fuori.

"Per favore, non lasciare che questo malinteso continui" supplicò. "Dovresti dirgli la verità. Se è un brav'uomo, capirà perché hai mentito. Sa già che sei lì per un motivo. Doveva aver capito che stavi nascondendo chi eri e perché eri lì."

"Non gli ho mai detto il motivo."

"Spiegagli solo tutto quello che è successo. Per l'amor di Dio, hai passato l'inferno. Ora che torni a casa, non hai motivo di nascondere nulla."

Aveva ragione. Potevo dire tutto a Liam. "Ho paura" ammisi.

"Non ne hai motivo. È solo il tuo cervello che ti sta giocando brutti scherzi. Ne hai passate tante" ribatté in tono confortante. "Non pensi che dovresti almeno provare a fargli sapere che ci tieni a lui? Che davvero non volevi mentirgli?"

"E se non capisse, Jade?" domandai.

"Allora, è un coglione" rispose. "Non ti merita."

"E se tutto questo fosse solo per scopare? Una folle cosa fisica?"

"Allora, è ancora più coglione."

Risi. "Non so cosa vuole. Sono confusa."

"E pensi che lui non lo sia? Pensa che tu abbia già un ragazzo, quindi questo ti renderebbe una traditrice. Qualsiasi cosa è meglio di quello. Anche una bugiarda."

La nostra conversazione portò ad altri argomenti, ma quello che mi aveva detto Jade era ancora in agguato nel mio cervello. Liam avrebbe preso meglio il fatto che avessi mentito? La storia del fidanzato lo aveva sempre tenuto a distanza.

Cosa sarebbe successo, se nessuno si fosse messo sulla sua strada? Sarebbe stato diverso?

Dopo aver riattaccato, stavo ancora pensando a cosa avrei dovuto fare.

Avrei dovuto correre il rischio di dirgli la verità o proteggere il mio cuore in modo che non fosse a pezzi, al momento di salutarlo?

Brooke

Più tardi quel giorno, ero raggomitolata con un buon libro sugli investimenti, quando qualcuno bussò alla mia porta. Gettai da parte il tascabile. Non che avessi soldi da investire, ma mi piaceva tenermi aggiornata sulle ultime informazioni dal mondo della finanza.

Mi alzai, chiedendomi chi bussasse alla mia porta alle otto di sera.

Aprii la porta e mi bloccai, quando vidi Liam.

Non avevo sentito una sua parola per tutto il giorno, e le mie insicurezze avevano preso il sopravvento.

Aveva finito con me dopo che avevamo fatto sesso?

Se pensava che fossi una traditrice, forse ero solo l'ennesima avventura di una notte per lui, un modo per alleviare la tensione sessuale che indugiava sempre tra noi.

"Pensavo stessi lavorando" dissi, cercando di non notare che sembrava proprio un bel bocconcino nei suoi jeans blu scuro e un maglione nero.

Non pensavo che fosse un tipo da maglione, ma gli stava bene. Era il genere di ragazzo che poteva far sembrare sexy anche quell'indumento. Davvero, non sapevo molto di lui fuori dal ristorante. L'unica cosa che gli avevo mai visto indossare erano jeans e maglietta.

Varcò la porta ed entrò nel soggiorno, che non era affatto grande. Era un piccolo appartamento.

"Devi mollare il tuo ricco fidanzato" dichiarò bruscamente. "È una linea rossa per me che non supererò."

Deglutii a fatica, mentre chiudevo la porta e lo affrontavo. La sua espressione era così intensa che non potevo rispondere.

Continuò. "Per il resto del tuo tempo qui ad Amesport, usciremo insieme. Ci vedremo in un posto diverso dal Sullivan. Le cose normali. Non siamo mai stati normali, Brooke."

Alzai un sopracciglio, chiedendomi dove volesse arrivare a parare, ma il mio cuore stava martellando, mentre lo guardavo a bocca aperta.

"Posso portarti ovunque tu voglia andare. Diamine, possiamo volare ovunque nel mondo. Sai che non sono esattamente a corto di fondi. Potrei essere solo un milionario, ma ne ho molti di milioni. Potrebbe non sembrare un granché rispetto alla sovrabbondanza di miliardari in questa città, ma potrei non lavorare più un altro giorno nella mia vita, spendere in modo stravagante e avere ancora soldi da bruciare."

Aveva ragione. Liam aveva raggiunto le nove cifre tra liquidità, investimenti e conti bancari. Mi ero occupata io delle sue tasse. Sapevo che era ricco. Ma cosa c'entrava questo con noi?

"Non voglio i soldi" replicai con voce tremante.

Si fece avanti, finché non fu direttamente di fronte a me. "Allora, cosa vuoi, Brooke? Dimmelo, e mi assicurerò che tu lo ottenga. L'unico requisito è che ti sbarazzi dell'altro ragazzo. Non lo ami. Ti conosco abbastanza bene da sapere che non saresti mai andata a letto con me, se fossi stata innamorata di qualcun altro. Dio sa che volevo considerarti infedele, ma c'è dell'altro. So che c'è. Non posso volere bene a una donna che tradisce."

Inspirai profondamente, i miei polmoni affamati di ossigeno. "Mi vuoi bene?" chiesi cautamente.

Si passò una mano frustrata tra i capelli. "Sì. Ho finito con le stronzate."

In quel momento, sembrava così vulnerabile che volevo gettarmi tra le sue braccia e fare qualcosa per sistemare tutto. Ma ero l'oggetto del suo tormento, quindi non mi mossi.

Non mi aveva semplicemente scaricata, dopo aver fatto sesso con me. Conoscevo Liam, e ovviamente aveva rimuginato tutto il giorno su quello che era successo... proprio come me.

"Non sei al ristorante" dissi, senza pensare al fatto che il mio commento non fosse esattamente brillante. Ovviamente *non* era al Sullivan. Era in piedi proprio di fronte a me.

"Tessa è lì" borbottò. "Se accetti le mie condizioni, lei mi sostituirà molto più a lungo, e chiamerò qualcuno per coprirti, così potremo passare un po' di tempo insieme."

Sapevo che dovevo chiudere la bocca e smetterla di guardarlo a bocca aperta, ma non sapevo come farlo.

Voleva... uscire con me? Avevamo già fatto sesso. "Abbiamo dormito insieme" replicai, sentendomi ancora come se tutto quello che stava succedendo fosse surreale.

Non l'avevo mai visto comportarsi in quel modo, ed ero più che un po' sconcertata.

In conclusione... ci teneva a me, ed era difficile da capire. Anche se presumibilmente l'avevo tradito, voleva comunque uscire con me, avere una sorta di relazione normale.

Dannazione! Gli dovevo la verità.

"Non ho un ragazzo" sbottai, incapace di trattenermi. Si era messo in gioco per venire qui. Anch'io dovevo essere sincera.

I suoi occhi si posarono sul mio viso. "Cosa intendi?"

Gli passai accanto e mi sedetti sul divano, in modo da poter avere qualcosa di solido sotto di me. "Il ragazzo con cui mi hai vista era mio fratello maggiore, Noah. È venuto a vedere come stavo. Il jet era di Evan Sinclair."

Fu un sollievo far uscire le parole dalla mia bocca, ma continuavo a sentirmi nervosa.

"Perché mi hai detto che era il tuo ragazzo ricco?" chiese, suonando confuso.

Strinsi le dita sul grembo. "Prima di tutto, la mia famiglia non è ricca. Siamo stati incredibilmente poveri per tutta la vita. Stiamo ancora mettendo insieme i fondi per aiutare mio fratello più piccolo, Owen, a frequentare la scuola di medicina. Adesso è uno specializzando, quindi avrà finito tra un anno o due. Secondo, non ti ho mai detto che Noah era il mio ragazzo ricco. L'hai pensato tu. Semplicemente non ho davvero contraddetto la tua storia. Non potevo. Se lo avessi fatto, penso che ci sarebbero state altre domande a cui non avrei potuto rispondere. Mi stavo nascondendo, Liam. Ed ero spaventata. Inoltre, avevo promesso a Evan e Noah che non avrei rivelato nulla. Non potevo infrangere quella promessa. Entrambi avevano fatto di tutto per aiutarmi e stavano cercando di proteggermi."

La sua faccia era di pietra e difficile da leggere, quando alla fine disse: "Quindi, non c'è mai stato nessun altro?»

Scossi la testa. "No. Hai ragione su di me. Non avrei mai potuto fare sesso con qualcuno, se fossi stata impegnata con un altro ragazzo. Avrei dovuto prima interrompere l'altra relazione."

Ero sia euforica che terrorizzata che Liam fosse stato in grado di vedere così tanto di me senza sapere veramente chi fossi.

"Non posso dire di non essere sollevato, ma avrei preferito che mi avessi detto la verità" borbottò.

"Volevo. Avrei voluto dirtela tante volte. Mi fidavo di te, Liam. Ma ho fatto una promessa che non potevo infrangere." Lo fissai, desiderando che scorgesse la verità nei miei occhi.

Sollevò una mano. "Non farlo, Brooke. Non scusarti. Capisco che hai fatto quello che pensavi di dover fare."

"Ma ciò non significa che mi piaccia" ribattei solennemente. "È stato un anno difficile per me."

"Ma è finita" commentò. "Ora tutto quello che devi fare è uscire con me. Passare un po' di tempo con me, Brooke. Niente pressioni. Sappiamo entrambi che quello che è successo la scorsa notte non accade tutti i giorni. Cavolo, ho trentacinque anni e non mi sono mai sentito così."

"Non è mai successo neanche a me" condivisi.

"Vogliamo davvero allontanarci da questo?" chiese con voce roca.

Il suo sguardo dagli occhi verdi era tumultuoso, e non potei resistere all'entrare nel fuoco per dirgli tutto. "No. Non ho mai voluto ignorarlo e sapevo che l'alchimia era lì dal momento in cui ti ho incontrato. Solo che... non potevo essere me stessa."

Scosse la testa. "Non importa. Ti ho vista."

Il mio cuore sussultò. "Lo so." Mi fermai, prima di chiedere: "Dove possiamo andare, Liam? Non ne ho idea."

"Ci divertiremo insieme. Vuoteremo il sacco su tutto. Non è quello che fanno le persone agli appuntamenti? Spero di convincerti a restare" avvertì. "Voglio che tu lo sappia in anticipo."

Il mio cuore era bloccato in gola, e non potevo parlare. Nessun ragazzo si era mai veramente preoccupato, se fossi rimasta con lui o meno. Avevo avuto esperienze al college. Ma nessuna era mai diventata una vera relazione. "Non ho mai avuto una vera relazione" ammisi.

Mi sorrise. "Non posso dire di averne avuta una nemmeno io. Ma possiamo costruire le cose man mano che procediamo."

Gli sorrisi, ricacciando indietro le lacrime che volevano cadere solo perché gli importava di me. "Affare fatto."

Mi prese in braccio e mi fece roteare sul pavimento del soggiorno. "Mi hai appena reso un uomo felice, Brooke. E non è facile."

Risi, mentre mi rimetteva i piedi per terra. C'era così tanto sotto il suo aspetto rude. Forse era un po' intimidatorio, ma proprio come aveva visto me, anch'io avevo visto lui. Ero attratta da lui sin dal primo giorno in cui mi aveva detto che potevo lavorare al ristorante.

"Penso che mi piaccia renderti felice" dissi, avvolgendogli le braccia intorno al collo.

I suoi occhi diventarono di un verde più intenso. "Gesù! Amo il tuo odore. Sai di vaniglia dolce."

"È solo la mia lozione per il corpo. Ho fatto il bagno prima." Avevo usato la stessa lozione per anni, e nessuno aveva mai commentato il profumo. Onestamente, era piuttosto delicato, quindi ero abbastanza sicura che Liam fosse l'unica persona ad averlo notato.

"È quasi come i biscotti allo zucchero" rifletté.

"Vaniglia e zucchero" confermai.

"Abbastanza buoni da mangiarli. Ti ho mai detto che quelli sono i miei preferiti?"

Provai a liberare il mio cervello a raggi X dall'evocazione di immagini di lui che mi divorava.

Scossi lentamente la testa. "Non lo sapevo."

Si chinò e mi diede un bacio molto appassionato.

Ero senza fiato, quando finalmente alzò la testa.

Mi lasciò andare e attraversò il soggiorno. "Fanculo! Brooke, ho promesso a me stesso che non ti avrei scopata di nuovo, finché non avessimo iniziato a vederci davvero. Abbiamo saltato quel passaggio la scorsa notte. Io ho saltato quel passaggio la scorsa notte. Non che me ne penta. Ma adesso, voglio solo stare con te. Voglio imparare tutto su di te. Non è così facile, quando il mio uccello è duro, il che è quasi ogni volta che ti vedo."

Gli sorrisi. "Anch'io lo voglio."

Non che non volessi fare sesso con lui. L'impulso sarebbe stato sempre lì. Ma sapevo che c'era molto di più in lui che un corpo spettacolare e un bel viso.

"Allora, facciamolo" disse burbero.

"Fare sesso?" lo presi in giro.

Mi guardò di traverso. "Dovrai aiutarmi."

"Non sono sicura di essere molto d'aiuto" scherzai. "Voglio quasi che mi inchiodi tutto il tempo."

La sua bocca si trasformò in un sorriso felice. "Per fortuna devo tornare al ristorante. Ho promesso a Tessa che avrei chiuso io. Ma lei mi coprirà per un po', e tu avrai delle notti libere non programmate."

"Lavorerò ancora domani?"

Tornò da me e mi sollevò il mento. "Sì, intelligentona. Certo. Ma nessuna promessa per dopo. Sto rifacendo il programma."

Incontrare i suoi occhi direttamente quando eravamo così vicini era intenso. Il mio corpo lo desiderava ora, ma cercai di scrollarmelo di dosso. Volevo conoscerlo. E se il mio corpo avesse fatto a modo suo, non sarei mai uscita dalla camera da letto.

"Mi dispiace" mormorai, il cuore che mi si stringeva nel petto per avergli mentito.

Mi mise le sue dita sulle labbra. "No. Non è stata tutta colpa tua. Non so esattamente cosa sia successo, ma aspetterò finché non vorrai parlarne. Nel frattempo, sono contento di sapere che non sei coinvolta con un altro uomo."

Lasciai andare un sospiro, mentre muoveva le dita e mi baciava. Fu breve, ma così dannatamente dolce.

"Ci vediamo domani" disse rudemente, lasciandomi andare.

Lo lasciai uscire, sapendo che probabilmente avrei dormito molto poco per un'altra notte.

Capitolo 10

Brooke

Durante la settimana successiva, Liam e io eravamo riusciti a trascorrere molto tempo insieme. Avevamo fatto alcuni turni al lavoro, ma la maggior parte del tempo uscivamo insieme dal ristorante.

In quei giorni, avevo scoperto che amava il cibo tanto quanto me. Era venuto con me a cena con Evan e Miranda.

E io l'avevo accompagnato a cena a casa di Xander e Samantha.

Avevamo mangiato benissimo a Boston, perché Liam aveva giurato che lì tutti i ristoranti erano migliori. Non ero sicura che lo *fossero*. Il Sullivan serviva del cibo davvero incredibile. Ma i ristoranti erano decisamente più *sofisticati*.

Essendo cresciuti poveri, mangiavamo tutto ciò che potevamo permetterci, che di solito consisteva in una casseruola che potevamo mettere insieme con gli avanzi e molti panini economici. Non era l'ideale per una bambina ossessionata dal cibo, ma non ci avevo pensato molto, fino a quando Liam non aveva iniziato a portarmi da un orgasmo gastronomico all'altro. Ero abbastanza sicura di aver messo su diversi chili negli ultimi sette giorni, ma ero certa che non mi sarei lamentata.

In un brevissimo periodo di tempo, stare con lui era diventato naturale come respirare. Finora avevamo mantenuto il nostro accordo di conoscerci senza sesso, ma andavo a letto ogni notte pensando a lui, bramandolo con un dolore lancinante che peggiorava sempre di più ogni giorno che passava.

"Sto diventando molto viziata" mormorai tra me e me, mentre entravo nel vialetto della casa di Liam, situata fuori Amesport.

Sebbene non fosse il tipo di persona che ostentava la sua ricchezza, aveva i suoi *giocattoli*. Quando aveva ristrutturato la sua residenza d'infanzia, i nuovi piani avevano incluso sei garage per i veicoli, e ognuno di essi era pieno. Mi ero rifiutata di guidare le costose auto sportive, ma avevo accettato la sua offerta di guidare uno dei due SUV che aveva nei garage.

La vita era semplicemente più facile con una macchina.

"Non abituartici" mi ricordai ad alta voce, mentre parcheggiavo sull'asfalto accanto a casa sua.

Non avevo idea di come sarebbe finita quella fiaba. Mi fidavo di lui, ma non avevamo discusso della mia partenza, che diventava sempre più imminente ogni giorno.

Non voglio essere distrutta, quando dovrò partire.

Mentre spegnevo il motore del SUV, sapevo che probabilmente non sarebbe finita bene. Ero già abituata a vederlo ogni giorno, e anche se il mio corpo lo desiderava, il mio cuore lo voleva ancora di più.

Non mi ero pentita del tempo che avevo trascorso con lui. Che ci fossimo visti o meno dopo la settimana successiva, quei giorni sarebbero sempre stati i più felici di tutta la mia vita. Sapevo che stavo correndo un rischio, ma dovevo farlo.

Se devo affrontare le conseguenze dell'avvicinamento a Liam, me ne preoccuperò più tardi.

L'ultima cosa che volevo fare era passare la settimana successiva ad aspettare che sganciasse una bomba.

Afferrai la busta di cibo cinese che avevo preso, mentre andavo da lui, sorridendo, mentre scendevo dall'auto.

Si era vantato delle sue capacità di pesca, quindi avremmo dovuto mangiare pesce appena pescato per cena. Xander e Liam erano usciti con la barca di Liam per pescare quella mattina.

Erano tornati a mani vuote.

Mi chiedevo se fosse ancora arrabbiato, perché avevo riso e mi ero offerta di prendere il cinese.

Era perlopiù di buon carattere, ma avrei potuto ferire leggermente il suo ego maschile.

"Liam" chiamai, entrando dalla porta. "Ho portato del cibo."

"Intelligentona" borbottò, mentre usciva dalla cucina per salutarmi.

Cosa si aspettava? Avevo quattro fratelli. Dovevo avere una sorta di meccanismo di protezione da quel trauma infantile. La mia arma migliore era sempre stata il sarcasmo.

Gli passai accanto per prendere dei piatti, ma mi afferrò la vita, prima che potessi superarlo. "Ma ti perdono" disse con voce roca, ricevendo un bacio, prima di lasciarmi andare.

Rabbrividii, quando mi lasciò. Amavo il modo in cui non mi lasciava mai oltrepassarlo senza toccarmi.

"Non volevo ferire il tuo ego virile" dissi con una risata.

"Non l'hai fatto" replicò burbero. "Sono abbastanza sicuro della mia mascolinità."

"Lo so" borbottai, mentre andavo in cucina. La sua mascolinità non era mai stata messa in discussione. Produceva molto più testosterone di quanto avrebbe dovuto.

Mi schiaffeggiò scherzosamente il sedere, mentre posavo le buste sul tavolo della cucina.

Strillai. "Per cos'era quello? Ho portato il cibo" dissi con finto oltraggio.

Incrociò le braccia davanti a sé e sorrise. "Il tuo culetto è troppo bello per poter resistere."

Mi strofinai la natica, sorridendogli. "Ricordami che diventi scontroso, quando non riesci a prendere un pesce."

Fece spallucce. "Succede, ma è stata una mattinata sprecata. Avrei preferito passare il tempo con te."

Dato che Xander e Liam avevano programmato di andare a pescare quella settimana, lo avevo incoraggiato ad andare. Avrei trascorso una piacevole mattinata in giro con Samantha. "Mi piace il cinese" dissi. "E io sono qui ora."

Era patetico, ma mi era mancato tanto quanto a lui ero mancata io.

"Grazie a Dio" borbottò. "Se avessi dovuto ascoltare Xander piagnucolare ancora una volta sul fatto di non aver preso alcun pesce, lo avrei gettato in mare. La prossima volta verrai con me. Ti insegnerò a pescare."

Lo guardai a bocca aperta. "Mi *insegnerai* a pescare?" Pensava che l'avessi incoraggiato ad andare con Xander perché non volevo andare? O perché ero inutile su una barca? "Pesco da quando ero abbastanza grande per camminare" ribattei con tono brusco.

"Sai pescare?"

"Certo. Mio fratello, Aiden, mi ha insegnato quando ero piccola, e ci vado ogni volta che posso. È un pescatore professionista, e a volte è un po' competitivo, ma ignoro la sua arroganza per avere la possibilità di uscire in acqua."

"Allora, immagino che non dovrei raccontarti le mie storie sui pesci."

Sorrisi. "No. I miei fratelli ci hanno provato tutto il tempo. Smettiamo di ascoltare, quando arrivano alla parte in cui il pesce è scappato."

Quando una donna ha quattro fratelli come me, impara ad essere tollerante. Ma Jade e io dovevamo tracciare la linea da qualche parte.

Presi alcuni piatti dalla credenza e iniziai a riempirli. Liam afferrò l'argenteria e le bevande, in modo che potessimo sederci al tavolo.

Dopo esserci seduti con un piatto di cibo cinese, chiese: "Quindi, siete tutti molto legati?"

"Quanto possa essere legata una femmina a dei fratelli che sanno tutto. Onestamente, non è stato facile crescere con tutto quel testosterone, ma io e Jade siamo riuscite a sopravvivere" scherzai.

"Com'è?» domandò. "Crescere con così tanti fratelli?"

"Per noi a volte è stato spaventoso, e posso solo immaginare come sia stato per Noah. Quando mia madre è morta, lui era tutto ciò che avevamo. E non era davvero abbastanza grande per prendersi cura di quattro ragazzini di età inferiore ai diciotto anni. È cresciuto troppo presto. Ma eravamo abituati a collaborare per aiutare. Mia madre lavorava molto. Vivevamo con un reddito piuttosto limitato, quindi cercavamo tutti di raccogliere dei soldi per aiutarla. È stato lo stesso una volta che è morta."

Aggrottò la fronte. "Non avevate una famiglia che potesse aiutarvi?"

"Nessuno di noi conosceva veramente nostro padre. È morto quando eravamo tutti abbastanza piccoli. Mia madre era figlia unica. I suoi genitori sono morti quando lei aveva diciannove anni. Parlava di alcune persone, ma non sono mai venute a trovarci in California."

"È dura" osservò Liam con voce roca.

"Non è stato così male" spiegai. "Tutti noi abbiamo imparato ad essere indipendenti, e ci siamo presi cura l'uno dell'altro."

Stava inalando il suo cibo. Immaginavo che non avesse mangiato molto quel giorno.

Quando si fermò per prendere l'acqua, chiese: "Mi racconterai mai della tua vita lì e del perché te ne sei andata?"

Quasi mi strozzai sul mio lo mein. Non era che non mi aspettassi quella domanda, ma non nel bel mezzo del riso e del kung pao. Bevvi un sorso d'acqua, prima di rispondere. "Sono davvero sorpresa che tu non l'abbia sollevato prima."

"Non è che non voglio saperlo, Brooke. Immagino volessi solo darti il tempo di fidarti di me."

Esaminai il suo splendido viso e l'espressione seria nei suoi occhi. Il mio cuore si sciolse. "Oh, Liam. Non è che non mi fido di te. Solo che non so da dove cominciare."

Alzò le spalle. "Dovunque tu voglia. Ma prima finisci di mangiare."

Ricominciai a mangiare, fermandomi, quando ebbi lo stomaco pieno.

Guardando il suo piatto, notai che aveva completamente demolito il suo cibo.

"Ce n'è altro" offrii.

Sollevò una mano. "Basta così."

Ci mettemmo subito a pulire, e poi andammo a sederci nel soggiorno. Mi ero versata un bicchiere di Merlot, e lui si era procurato una soda.

C'eravamo messi a nostro agio sul divano, prima che parlassi. "Non sono una cameriera. Almeno, non lo sono sempre stata in California."

Immaginavo che la mia carriera fosse un buon punto di partenza per la mia spiegazione.

"Non l'avrei mai immaginato" rispose. "Sei dannatamente brava."

"Le mie referenze erano reali. Sono una cameriera da quando ho potuto lavorare legalmente, fino a quando ho completato la laurea. Sono un'analista finanziaria. Prima di venire qui, lavoravo in una piccola filiale di una banca nazionale a Citrus Beach."

"Avrei dovuto sapere che avevi un lavoro finanziario, visto che stranamente ami i numeri." Si fermò, prima di chiedere: "Si tratta di un ragazzo? Uno stalker?"

Potevo vedere che Liam era pronto a uccidere lo strambo ragazzo immaginario della mia vita, mentre gli sorridevo. "No. Non è quello."

Sembrava sollevato. "Grazie al cielo."

Non ero sicura che la verità fosse migliore. "Ho lavorato in banca per un anno. Amavo il mio lavoro. Poi, una mattina, la banca è stata rapinata."

Diventò visibilmente teso, ma continuai a parlare. "Ero in un ufficio sul retro, ma ho sentito gli spari. Quando sono andata a vedere cos'era successo, tutti i miei amici e colleghi erano morti. Il bastardo aveva sparato ai due cassieri e al vicedirettore." Il mio cuore batteva all'impazzata per aver rivissuto quel giorno orribile, ma non riuscivo a calmarmi. "Sarei dovuta morire anch'io. Ma la polizia è entrata nel parcheggio, mentre lui stava riempiendo un sacchetto di carta con i soldi dei cassetti. È dovuto scappare dal retro."

Liam mi prese la mano e mi tirò contro il suo petto, le sue braccia avvolte intorno alla mia vita per tenermi.

"Non devi parlarne per forza, Brooke. Non devi" disse con voce roca.

Scossi la testa. "Voglio farlo."

"Stai piangendo" sostenne.

"Va tutto bene. A volte fa bene piangere." L'avevo capito subito dopo essermi trasferita ad Amesport. Avevo bisogno di piangere in privato, e la piccola città costiera mi aveva dato questa opportunità. Stavo vedendo uno psicologo locale che aveva tenuto al sicuro i miei segreti, e lentamente avevo superato la paura, la rabbia, il senso di colpa e la disperazione.

"Allora, finisci" concordò.

"Mi ha vista, Liam. Ma ha visto anche la polizia. Quindi, immagino che abbia deciso di lasciare una testimone per evitare di essere arrestato." Mi fermai per prendere un respiro tremante. "Tutti i miei colleghi sono morti per un totale di milleduecento dollari."

Una volta aver tirato fuori l'intera storia, lo abbracciai e singhiozzai.

Capitolo 11

Brooke

Non ero sicura di quanto tempo avessi passato a scaricare il mio dolore sulla spalla di Liam, ma mi sentivo bene a piangere. Non piangevo così tanto per i miei amici da mesi. Anche se avevo superato le loro morti senza senso, non ero del tutto guarita dal trauma di quello che era successo in banca quel giorno.

"Gesù, piccola! Mi dispiace così tanto" disse Liam con la bocca sui miei capelli.

Annuii e mi ritrassi, in modo da poter vedere la sua faccia. "Erano miei amici."

Mi baciò la fronte. "Lo so." Si fermò, prima di chiedere: "L'hanno catturato?"

"Sì. Era già noto alle forze dell'ordine, quindi non è stato poi così difficile per loro trovarlo. Ho deposto come unica testimone, ed è stato mostrato il video. Era facilmente riconoscibile sui nastri, e la polizia aveva tutti i tipi di prove a sostegno. Non uscirà mai di prigione."

"Dev'essere stato un periodo difficile per te" osservò, mentre scuoteva dolcemente il mio corpo. "Non riuscivi a superarlo, perché dovevi testimoniare."

"Dopo il processo, è stato un circo mediatico" spiegai. "I giornalisti volevano la mia storia come unica sopravvissuta. E non ero pronta a parlare. Non avevo pianto i miei amici. Non avevo capito tutto. Mi sentivo come se stessi camminando in trance, Liam, e avevo i giornalisti di tutte le principali reti fuori dalla porta. Inseguivano persino la mia famiglia. Sono dovuta scappare."

"Immagino che abbiano smesso" suppose con calma.

"Alla fine, si sono arresi e sono passati alla storia successiva, più attuale. Abbiamo pensato che prima o poi l'avrebbero fatto. Ma Noah ed Evan erano preoccupati, quindi mi hanno fatto giurare di tacere su chi fossi e su cosa fosse successo. Entrambi volevano solo darmi un po' di tempo."

Mi accarezzò i capelli. "Sono contento che l'abbiano fatto."

"Anche se ho dovuto mentire?"

"Non me ne frega niente, se hai dovuto mentire a tutte le persone di Amesport. Riguardava la tua sicurezza e la tua sanità mentale, Brooke. Niente è più importante di questo."

Il mio cuore si scaldò alle sue parole, e poi mi si strinse forte il petto. Liam era così forte, ma stava ancora male per me. Lo potevo sentire.

"Amesport mi ha dato una via di fuga" condivisi. "Anche tu. Te ne sarò sempre grata. Sono guarita qui. Forse non mi sono completamente ripresa, ma ho superato la parte difficile, credo. E i giornalisti non se ne sono interessati negli ultimi due mesi. Ho il via libera a casa."

Il suo volto era cupo. "Sei sicura di averla superata?"

"Di tanto in tanto ho gli incubi, ma mi rifiuto di lasciare che un criminale cambi il modo in cui conduco la mia vita. Non posso vedere mostri dove non ce ne sono. I miei amici non lo avrebbero voluto. Non vivranno le loro vite, quindi mi sento come se, in qualche modo, dovessi farlo per loro."

"Vuoi tornare al tuo lavoro?" chiese con voce triste.

Scossi la testa. "Non alla banca. Non posso tornare lì. Ma mi piacerebbe tornare alla mia professione."

Avevo sempre saputo che non sarei mai potuta tornare nella stessa banca. La vista dei miei amici, il sangue e il terrore che avevo provato quel giorno mi avrebbero perseguitata. Ma mi mancava lavorare come analista finanziaria.

"Avrei dovuto capire che eri un mago della finanza" borbottò. "Dio sa che l'hai dimostrato lavorando sui miei conti incasinati e sulle tasse."

"Non è esattamente la mia specialità" replicai, asciugandomi le lacrime sul viso. "Solo che mi piacciono la matematica e i numeri."

"Sì. C'è qualcosa di completamente sbagliato in questo" rispose.

Gli rivolsi un debole sorriso. Liam era un uomo d'affari straordinario, ma non era portato per i dettagli. "Adoro i numeri. La matematica è così concreta. O si somma... o no. Non sono brava con l'incertezza" spiegai.

"So perché non me l'hai detto. Ma non posso fare a meno di desiderare di averlo saputo. Avrei potuto aiutarti. Avrei potuto essere qualcuno con cui parlare" disse con voce scontenta.

"Amici?" lo presi in giro.

"Se era quello che volevi. Sarei stato quello che diavolo avessi voluto, se ciò ti avesse aiutata a superare i momenti difficili."

I miei occhi si riempirono di nuovo, ma ricacciai indietro le lacrime. Il ragazzo mi scioglieva il cuore con la sua volontà di essere di supporto. "Non ci conoscevamo davvero" gli ricordai. "E non sono sicura che sarei stata pronta a parlarne."

"Non so come migliorare le cose" confessò, e poi si passò una mano frustrata tra i capelli.

"Non devi" sostenni. Anche i miei fratelli avevano cercato di migliorare le cose, scoraggiandosi, quando non ci riuscivano. Immaginavo fosse una cosa da ragazzi. "Non è possibile. Ma apprezzo che tu sia qui per me adesso."

"Non andrò da nessuna parte, Brooke. Sarò qui per te ogni volta che avrai bisogno di me."

Sospirai, mentre mi sdraiavo accanto a lui. Mi prese la mano, e io gliela diedi, appoggiando la mia nella sua. "La vita non è sempre come vorremmo che fosse" commentai, emotivamente esausta per avergli raccontato cos'era successo. Non era ancora facile parlarne senza avere dei flashback.

"Lo so" concordò. "Ma è quello che facciamo della merda che ci viene lanciata che conta."

Mi alzai e presi il bicchiere di vino che avevo lasciato sul tavolino. Bevvi qualche sorso e poi mi appoggiai di nuovo a lui.

Conosceva bene le sfide della vita. Ne aveva avute in abbondanza. Ma adoravo il suo atteggiamento.

Bevvi un altro sorso del mio Merlot.

"È meglio che ci vada piano" avvertì. "Di solito ti fa perdere le mutandine."

Risi e poggiai di nuovo il bicchiere sul tavolo. "Solo una volta" ribattei. "E volevo perdere tutti i miei vestiti *e* i tuoi. Ma quella notte non ero ubriaca. Sapevo quello che volevo."

"Davvero?" chiese con voce roca.

"Liam, ti desideravo da quasi un anno. Ovviamente lo sapevo."

Forse il vino mi aveva rilassata un po', ma non mi ero ubriacata dai tempi del college.

"Cosa volevi?"

"Volevo *te*."

"Mi hai preso" dichiarò seccamente. "Ma sicuramente non ero nella mia forma migliore."

"Mi vedi lamentarmi?" scherzai. "Mi sei sembrato piuttosto straordinario."

"Buongustaia" disse in tono divertito.

"È stata una notte incredibile per me, Liam" replicai in tono più serio. Forse pensava di essere andato troppo in fretta, ma non avevo mai voluto che si pentisse di quello che era successo. Io di sicuro non l'avevo fatto.

"Anche per me" confessò. "Avrei solo preferito che il mio uccello non avesse preso il sopravvento sul cervello. Non volevo solo scopare."

"Cosa volevi?"

"Volevo questo." Mi strinse la mano. "Volevo noi."

Capivo. Il mio bisogno di lui andava molto più in profondità del solo lato fisico, anche se il mio corpo soffriva per lui.

"Quindi, non ci sono problemi, se non facciamo sesso?" chiesi con curiosità.

"Dannazione, no" si lamentò. "Ci sono problemi, e ho avuto le palle blu nell'ultima settimana. Ma dovrei esserci abituato. Ti desidero dal giorno in cui sei entrata nel ristorante. Ed è solo peggiorato nel tempo."

Sentii una vampata di calore tra le cosce, mentre si sistemava sul divano.

Sapevo che stava provando lo stesso desiderio tagliente che stavo provando io.

Ero pronta a farmi scopare.

"Sopravvivrò» mormorò.

Mi alzai e mi voltai a guardarlo. "E se dicessi che sono pronta?" chiesi senza fiato.

Scosse lentamente la testa con un'espressione di rammarico. "Direi che è stata una notte difficile per te. Quando sarai davvero pronta, sarò qui."

Sono pronta! Sono così dannatamente pronta!

Il mio corpo gli stava urlando di scoparmi, ma il mio cuore tremò notando lo sguardo pensieroso sul suo viso. "Allora, immagino che sopravvivrò anch'io."

Mi mise una mano dietro il collo e mi strinse a sé. "Baciami" pretese.

Non dovette chiedermelo due volte. Gli avvolsi le braccia intorno al collo e incontrai le sue labbra con audacia, baciandolo con tutte le emozioni represse che si nascondevano dentro di me.

Mi sollevò il maglione e mi accarezzò la pelle nuda della schiena, mentre mi divorava la bocca.

Potrei averlo iniziato io, ma lui terminò in modo spettacolare. Quando mi lasciò andare, stavo ansimando.

"Non puoi baciarmi così e aspettarti che non risponda." *Gesù!* Quale donna poteva frenarsi dal desiderare un ragazzo che baciava come se volesse assorbire la sua dannata anima?

Era come una droga a cui non potevo rinunciare.

"Voglio che tu risponda" gracchiò. «Ma è un inferno, quando lo fai."

Mi tirò sopra di lui e avvolse le sue braccia attorno al mio corpo.

"Grazie" sussurrai vicino al suo orecchio.

L'unica cosa di cui avevo bisogno dopo aver condiviso così tanto con lui era sentirmi al sicuro. Mi aveva dato questo e molto altro ancora.

"Per cosa?" chiese.

"Per essere te" risposi. Non c'era altro modo per dirgli quanto significava per me che potessi fidarmi abbastanza da condividere il mio dolore.

"Prego. Ma faccio schifo la maggior parte del tempo" replicò.

Ridacchiai alla sua risposta. Minimizzava ogni cosa dolce che dicevo di lui, quindi non rimasi esattamente sorpresa.

Si prendeva in giro, ma sapeva esattamente chi era, un tratto che trovavo affascinante.

Oltre ad essere il maschio più sexy che conoscessi, era anche uno dei più premurosi, anche se gli piaceva fingere di non esserlo.

"Sono sorpresa che nessuna donna abbia mai visto attraverso le tue stronzate" dissi, chiedendomi ancora una volta come potesse essere ancora single.

Era tutto ciò che una donna avrebbe mai potuto desiderare in un uomo.

"Ti stavo aspettando" ribatté quasi immediatamente.

Non avevo commenti arguti da fare. Liam Sullivan mi aveva completamente rubato il cuore.

Capitolo 12

Liam

"**C**ome sarebbe a dire... *se n'è andata?*"

Sapevo che probabilmente stavo urlando alla mia unica sorella, ma non avrebbe mai dovuto darmi la notizia che Brooke era partita per la California nella sala da pranzo del Sullivan.

Per fortuna, Tessa aveva appena chiuso, quindi eravamo soli.

Ero tornato dalla mia riunione a Boston appena in tempo per fare le pulizie, in modo che lei potesse rientrare a casa.

Era stato un lungo viaggio in auto. Forse avrei dovuto passare la notte in città. Ma non vedevo l'ora di tornare a casa da Brooke. Erano passati alcuni giorni dall'ultima volta in cui aveva parlato di quello che le era successo, e sembrava stare bene, ma non mi sentivo così a mio agio nel lasciarla sola per tutto il giorno. Sfortunatamente, avevo dovuto partecipare ad un incontro con i miei fornitori che non ero riuscito ad annullare, e avevo un altro motivo personale per voler essere in città.

Tessa smise di caricare i piatti e si voltò a guardarmi. "Ha detto che sarebbe tornata. Aveva solo bisogno di un paio di giorni per sistemare

alcune cose sulla Costa Occidentale. Onestamente, sembrava un po'
scossa."

"Quali cose?" chiesi sospettoso. Brooke non aveva nemmeno fatto
le valigie il giorno prima, e avevo programmato di elaborare i dettagli
del suo soggiorno con lei quella notte o l'indomani.

Accidenti, avevo pianificato tutto, certo che sarebbe stata disposta
a restare.

E ora se n'era andata.

"Non lo so" spiegò Tessa. "Non mi ha dato molte informazioni
tranne che sarebbe tornata. Non è andata via per sempre, Liam."

"Non ha detto nient'altro?" *Dannazione!* Volevo che Tessa mi
dicesse qualcosa di più. Non aveva senso che Brooke se ne fosse
andata.

Mia sorella scosse la testa con rammarico. "Il suo turno era finito
ed Evan era qui per accompagnarla. Ha lasciato le chiavi del SUV nel
tuo ufficio. Non ha detto molto. Sembrava un po'... agitata."

Evan? "Ucciderò il bastardo" ringhiai. "Perché diavolo era qui?
Che cosa ha a che fare con la partenza di Brooke?"

"Avrei dovuto fare più domande" replicò Tessa. "Ma avevo dei
clienti. Mi ha solo chiesto di dirti che sarebbe tornata."

"Non è poi così confortante in questo momento" risposi
bruscamente. "Ma non è colpa tua, Tessa."

Mia sorella era solo la messaggera. Se Brooke se n'era andata, non
avevo dubbi che Evan Sinclair avesse qualcosa a che fare con la sua
assenza. Ma perché diavolo aveva *voluto* che partisse? Perché avrebbe
dovuto spingerla? Quando avevamo cenato con lui e Miranda, erano
sembrati entrambi desiderosi di convincerla a restare e ad accettare
un lavoro a livello locale.

Tessa si fece avanti e mi mise una mano confortante sul braccio.
"Forse non è colpa mia, ma mi dispiace comunque. Non sapevo che
avrebbe creato un grosso problema andando via per qualche giorno."

Mi passai una mano tra i capelli e cercai di fare un respiro
profondo. "Non è davvero un grosso problema, ma sento che c'è
qualcos'altro qua sotto."

"Perché pensi questo?"

Spiegai rapidamente cos'era successo a Brooke, e perché era qui. Dissi a mia sorella del nostro accordo per frequentarci e conoscerci. Non che Tessa non sapesse già cosa provavo per la ragazza. Negli ultimi nove o dieci giorni eravamo stati insieme in tutta la città.

Annuì, mentre finivo. "Sei pazzo di lei" affermò. "Ma la cosa è reciproca. Anche lei ti vuole."

"Ma non ha mai pianificato di andarsene, Tessa. Lo so. Avevamo programmi per i prossimi giorni."

"Forse è successo qualcosa in California. Ha molti parenti lì, Liam."

Uno dei membri della sua famiglia era malato? Era una possibilità. "Sembrava turbata?" chiesi.

Aggrottò la fronte, sollevando le sopracciglia, mentre considerava la domanda. "Non esattamente turbata" rifletté. "Sembrava più sciccata che turbata. Come se si stesse muovendo come uno zombi. Non credo che fosse del tutto lucida. Era piuttosto vaga, come se non capisse bene perché se ne stesse andando."

"Scommetto che Evan sappia perché" dissi con rabbia. "Senza dubbio lui l'ha convinta ad andare. A che ora è partita?"

"Ha fatto il turno di giorno, e poi è tornata a casa. Sembrava felice, finché non è tornata con Evan per lasciarti il messaggio che sarebbe tornata. È via da ore."

Lo sapevo. Si era scambiata con uno dei miei dipendenti part-time per fare il turno mattutino, in modo che potesse finire prima del mio ritorno a casa.

Tirai fuori il cellulare e composi il suo numero. Rispose la segreteria telefonica.

"Fanculo!" imprecai. "Perché diavolo non mi ha chiamato?"

"Ha detto che non riusciva a contattarti."

Rimisi il telefono in tasca e cercai di riprendere il controllo per il bene di mia sorella. "Torna a casa" dissi con voce più calma. "Me ne occuperò io più tardi."

"Pensi che stia bene?" chiese.

L'espressione di mia sorella era carica di preoccupazione.

Cavolo, dovevo essere furente dalla rabbia. Tessa non sapeva cosa avesse passato Brooke, né si era resa conto che stavo per rendere permanente la mia relazione con lei, se mi avesse voluto. "Sono sicuro che stia bene" la rassicurai, sapendo che probabilmente Brooke non stava affatto bene. "Vai a casa. Grazie per aver coperto il posto per me."

Qualcosa era successo. Brooke non era una donna volubile. Non c'era modo che avesse preso una decisione impulsiva di andare. *Qualcosa* l'aveva spinta a prendere quella decisione.

"Sei sicuro?" chiese esitante.

"Vai" ripetei con la voce più calma che potessi raccogliere.

Mia sorella si gettò tra le mie braccia e mi abbracciò, dicendo: "Chiamami. Voglio sapere cosa le è successo."

L'abbracciai di nuovo. "Ti chiamo più tardi."

Non appena se ne fu andata, programmai di affrontare Evan per vedere cosa diavolo aveva detto a Brooke per farla tornare in California.

Osservai Tessa arrivare sana e salva alla sua auto, prima che io saltassi sulla mia.

* * *

Mezz'ora dopo, mi ritrovai a non ottenere alcuna soddisfazione da Evan per la seconda volta negli ultimi mesi. La volta precedente ero rimasto senza risposte. Non sarebbe andata di nuovo così.

"Non capisco" gracchiai. "Quali cose doveva sistemare con la sua famiglia?"

Era seduto sul divano del suo soggiorno, troppo lontano perché potessi tirargli un pugno dalla mia sedia di fronte a lui. Ma potevo saltare sul tavolinetto tra noi abbastanza facilmente, e calcolavo quanto tempo avrei impiegato per arrivarci.

Aveva tenuto la bocca fastidiosamente chiusa sul fatto che Brooke se ne fosse andata.

"Non so se posso dirtelo. È la *sua* vita privata."

"Non mi ha nemmeno chiamato" urlai. "Non ho avuto una sola fottuta parola da lei. Stamattina avevamo programmi per i prossimi giorni, e stasera se n'è andata? Che diavolo è successo, Evan? Eri lì con lei. Devi sapere qualcosa."

In precedenza, avevo apprezzato e rispettato Evan Sinclair. In quel momento, non così tanto. Si rifiutava ostinatamente di darmi informazioni sulla ragazza o su ciò che le aveva detto per farla andare via.

"In realtà, so molte cose" spiegò con calma. "Ma non sono autorizzato a dirtele, a meno che non sia certo che questo la aiuterà. Ha bisogno di tempo, Liam. Ha intenzione di tornare ad Amesport. Ha lasciato qui la maggior parte delle sue cose."

"Non posso darle del tempo, perché sono preoccupato da morire" risposi conciso.

"Ah, sai la sua storia" suppose.

"La so" confermai irritato. "E sono mezzo fuori di testa dal giorno in cui mi ha detto che era quasi morta per mano di uno stronzo che non aveva rispetto per la vita umana."

Mi ero trattenuto per lei, ma avrei voluto vomitare le budella dopo che mi aveva detto la verità, e mi sentivo ancora protettivo per la sua sicurezza. Non avevo dubbi che non sarebbe mai passato.

Se la polizia non fosse intervenuta esattamente nello stesso momento in cui lo aveva fatto, se fossero arrivati anche solo pochi secondi dopo, Brooke sarebbe morta.

"Sai che le possibilità che qualcosa del genere accada di nuovo sono ridottissime" disse Evan con calma. "Le probabilità che potesse accadere la prima volta erano piuttosto scarse."

"Non importa" replicai. "Tutto quello che so è come mi sento. Ha passato l'inferno, e mi assicurerò che non accada mai più."

Si strinse nelle spalle. "A volte non abbiamo alcun controllo sugli eventi che accadono nelle nostre vite."

Razionalmente, lo sapevo. I miei genitori erano morti in un tragico incidente, e mia sorella era diventata sorda per una malattia. Non c'era modo di sapere che quelle cose sarebbero accadute. Il problema era che non stavo pensando come un uomo ragionevole.

"Ho bisogno di sapere che è al sicuro" dissi, sentendomi così nervoso che ero pronto a saltare oltre il tavolo e strangolarlo, finché non mi avesse dato ulteriori informazioni.

"È al sicuro" rispose amabilmente. "Sta volando sul jet di Jared. Verrà accompagnata a casa. Non è sola."

"Perché il jet di Jared?" Di solito Evan non aveva problemi a prestare il suo. Di questi tempi viaggiava raramente.

Mi fissò, esaminandomi come un campione da laboratorio. "Perché avevo la sensazione che avresti avuto bisogno del mio" rispose seccamente.

La mia rabbia divampò. "Sei un bastardo manipolatore" ringhiai. "Sapevi che sarei andato a cercarla."

Annuì. "Lo immaginavo, sì."

Mi alzai in piedi, incazzato che stesse manipolando Brooke e me. "Cosa ti dà il diritto di interferire in tutto questo?" gridai. "Non sei nessuno per lei. Almeno, io ci tengo a lei. Per te è solo un'altra pedina."

Si alzò piedi, il suo viso che passò da impassibile a furioso. "Non è un'altra *pedina*" mi corresse. "E ho sempre le mie ragioni per interferire" spiegò. "In questo caso, ho *tutte* le ragioni. Il vero cognome di Brooke è Sinclair. Lei è mia *sorella*."

Capitolo 13

Liam

Il mio culo atterrò di nuovo sulla sedia, mentre mi sedevo per assorbire l'ammissione di Evan. I pensieri mi attraversavano la mente, e cercai disperatamente di comprendere la bomba che aveva appena sganciato.

"Lei lo sa?" chiesi con un tono distante e sconcertato.

Assunse la sua precedente posizione sul divano. "Adesso sì. Ho dovuto dirglielo. I suoi fratelli e le sue sorelle lo sanno da quasi un anno. Non potevo più nasconderle quella verità."

Quindi, per tutto quel tempo, i mesi in cui Brooke era stata qui, non si era resa conto che Evan era imparentato con lei? Scossi la testa, non ancora pronto a credere che la mia Brooke fosse effettivamente una Sinclair. "Come?" Quella parola era tutto ciò che potevo far uscire dalla mia bocca.

"Lo avrebbe già saputo, se la sparatoria in banca non fosse avvenuta prima che Noah e io potessimo dirlo a tutti i miei fratelli. Ma avevamo a malapena scoperto la verità, quando è avvenuto l'incidente. Brooke era già afflitta da un enorme e comprensibile dolore, e non volevamo che avesse a che fare con dell'altro."

"Non sapevo che il suo cognome fosse Sinclair." Era sempre stata chiamata con il cognome Langley.

"Il suo cognome fittizio" disse con un cenno del capo. "È sempre stata una Sinclair. Pensava che il nostro cognome condiviso fosse una coincidenza. Non è raro."

Non le avevo mai chiesto se il suo cognome fosse vero. Non era mai stata una priorità. "Come ha fatto tua sorella a finire sulla Costa Occidentale? Non capisco."

"La maggior parte delle persone non lo capisce" affermò in modo uniforme. "È una lunga storia" avvertì.

"Ho tempo" borbottai. "Ho bisogno di sapere. Se vado in California, voglio sapere esattamente cosa aspettarmi."

Evan si appoggiò allo schienale del divano. "Ti ho detto la verità, perché so che ci tieni a lei. Se non fosse così, non avremmo questa conversazione."

Aspettai con impazienza che continuasse. Avrei saputo tutto quello che c'era da sapere da lui, prima di cercare di capire cosa stava succedendo con Brooke. Traevo un po' di conforto dal fatto che fosse al sicuro, ma non abbastanza per i miei gusti. E ora ero preoccupato per il suo stato d'animo.

"Anche se non è mai stato di dominio pubblico, mio padre era un bastardo violento" condivise. "Quando ero piccolo, si è preso la responsabilità di *addestrarmi* a diventare il suo erede. Erano lezioni dolorose, ma non erano *sempre* fisiche, anche se il più delle volte quelle sessioni *erano* abusi fisici. Una cosa che cercava sempre di usare mentre cercava di spezzarmi era l'esistenza di un'altra famiglia, la sua, e come sarebbe stato molto meglio se quei bambini fossero stati i suoi veri eredi. Recentemente, ho scoperto da Noah che loro non conoscevano molto bene nostro padre. Ogni tanto andava per qualche giorno. Lo vedevano per pochi minuti e poi li lasciava per stare con la loro madre per un giorno o due. Sembra che abbia usato le informazioni per provocarmi. Non ha mai veramente conosciuto gli altri suoi figli."

Ero incredulo. "Anche tutti i fratelli e le sorelle di Brooke sono tuoi fratelli?"

Annuì, prima di continuare. "Fratellastri e sorellastre" corresse. "Condividiamo tutti lo stesso padre. Quando è morto, ho esaminato tutti i suoi averi per cercare di scoprire la loro identità. Tutto quello che ho trovato erano un paio di foto, qualcosa che presumo la madre di Brooke abbia dato a mio padre. Non avevo nessun posto dove cercare. Non ero nemmeno sicuro che fossero cittadini statunitensi. Mio padre viaggiava molto all'estero."

"Allora, cos'hai fatto?"

"Al momento della morte di mio padre, ho messo via una parte dei suoi soldi, sperando che alla fine avrei scoperto chi fossero. Speravo che venissero da me."

Lo guardai acutamente. "E l'hanno fatto?"

Scosse la testa. "Non intenzionalmente. Ma quando si sono sviluppati i siti di DNA e di discendenza, ho messo un campione del mio DNA su ogni sito web che ho trovato. C'è voluto molto tempo, ma finalmente ho trovato una corrispondenza."

"Noah?" tirai a indovinare.

"Jade" corresse. "La sorella di Brooke ha alcune abilità di sopravvivenza primitive impressionanti, ed era curiosa di sapere se avesse sangue nativo americano, poiché sapeva molto poco di suo padre. Non ha trovato antenati nativi americani, ma ha trovato me. L'ho abbinata come sorellastra. Ci siamo scoperti a vicenda subito prima della rapina in banca. Non ho avuto la possibilità di parlare con nessuno tranne Noah e Jade, prima che accadesse."

"Quindi, Brooke è stata tenuta all'oscuro e spedita sulla Costa Orientale?" ringhiai, odiando il fatto che la sua famiglia avesse nascosto tutto per quasi un anno.

"Pensi che sia quello che volevo fare?" scattò Evan. "Brooke aveva passato l'inferno. Non potevo rivelarle una cosa simile."

"Quindi, presumo che abbia un'eredità significativa." Dovevo ammettere che era stato dannatamente carino da parte di Evan riconoscerli come possibili eredi, anche se non doveva. Ma ero ancora incazzato con lui.

"Ti importa?" chiese, fissandomi intensamente.

"No. Ho più soldi di quanti ce ne potranno mai servire."

Si alzò. "Penso di aver bisogno di un drink. Posso portarti qualcosa?"

"Birra, se ne hai una" risposi distrattamente. Non me la concedevo molto spesso, ma quella sera mi sembrava perfetta per spezzare la mia solita astinenza.

Mi appoggiai allo schienale della sedia, tutto il mio corpo teso per aver assorbito quelle informazioni.

Tornò velocemente, porgendomi una bottiglia di birra, mentre beveva qualcosa che sembrava leggermente più forte. Iniziò a parlare di nuovo, sedendosi. "Come ho detto, ero in una brutta situazione" disse con voce roca. "Volevo dirlo a Brooke, ma non volevo ostacolare la sua guarigione da qualcosa che la maggior parte delle persone non dovrà mai vedere."

"Lo capisco" ammisi a malincuore. "Immagino che ciò che non ha senso sia il fatto che non abbiano mai saputo chi fosse loro padre."

Si strinse nelle spalle. "Forse la loro madre aveva intenzione di dirlo un giorno, ma si ammalò. D'altra parte, non la biasimerei, per non aver mai parlato. I suoi figli erano convinti che fosse morto, il che era vero, ma non ha mai detto loro che il matrimonio che pensava fosse legale non era valido. Mio padre ha sposato la madre di Brooke a Las Vegas. Probabilmente era ubriaco, e doveva sapere che il matrimonio era illegale, ma era un forte bevitore. Presumo che pensasse che non sarebbe mai stato scoperto, e non gliene importava."

"La madre di Brooke l'ha mai saputo?"

Evan annuì. "Per quanto ne so da Noah, l'ha scoperto quando è morto mio padre. Ha detto che lei piangeva molto, ma era anche arrabbiata. Suppongo che abbia scoperto che mio padre era già sposato e aveva una famiglia. Se non l'avesse fatto, non avrebbe mai rinunciato a trovare il suo presunto marito. La mia ipotesi è che lo abbia trovato dopo la sua morte, e poi abbia scoperto che aveva una moglie legale e altri figli."

Feci un respiro profondo, e poi rilasciai l'aria, chiedendomi quale diavolo di situazione dovesse essere. Scoprire che avevi dato a tuo marito così tanti figli, e lui non era davvero tuo marito. "Dev'essere stato difficile per lei" dissi comprensivo.

"Sono sicuro che lo fosse" concordò. "Vorrei solo che fosse venuta da me."

Sembrava davvero dispiaciuto, e dovetti dargli credito per il suo senso di responsabilità. "La maggior parte delle famiglie miliardarie non le avrebbe parlato" sottolineai.

"I Sinclair non sono la *maggior parte delle famiglie*" replicò. "Mio padre non era l'espressione di questa famiglia. I suoi figli lo sono. Tutti loro."

Il mio rispetto per lui crebbe, quando mi resi conto che si sentiva responsabile dei suoi fratellastri e sorellastre quanto dei suoi fratelli e sorelle di sangue al cento per cento. "Brooke ha detto che è cresciuta povera."

"È vero. Penso che mio padre probabilmente desse a sua madre abbastanza soldi in contanti quando la vedeva per tenere a galla la famiglia. Ma una volta morto, non arrivarono più soldi."

"Quindi, ha vissuto come un miliardario, mentre metà dei suoi figli viveva appena al di sopra della soglia di povertà?"

Evan annuì bruscamente. "Dopo la sua morte, non avevano niente. La mamma di Brooke non aveva davvero esperienza lavorativa. Era giovane, quando lui l'ha sposata, ed è morta prematuramente di cancro al seno. Tutto quello che faceva era lavorare secondo Noah. Fino a quando... è morta."

"Che fottuta vita miserabile" imprecai. "Per tutti loro."

"Stranamente, si sono rivelati tutti delle persone rispettabili" mi informò. "Hanno lavorato duramente per avere una vita migliore. Deve averglielo insegnato la madre. Di certo non mio padre. Infatti, vedo pochissime somiglianze tra loro e mio padre."

"Sono legati, perché si sono aiutati a vicenda" aggiunsi.

Aveva l'accenno di un sorriso sul viso, mentre diceva: "In realtà, sono piuttosto straordinari."

Notai che sembrava orgoglioso dei bastardi Sinclair, ma ero più interessato a quello che era successo a Brooke. "Allora, perché è dovuta partire?"

"Temo che sia un po' sospettosa delle mie motivazioni. Non so se sia perché non si fida di me, o temesse che tutta la sua famiglia fosse cambiata, mentre era qui ad Amesport."

"È così?" domandai.

"Non per la maggior parte. Ammetto che ho dovuto dar loro un po' di tempo per digerire le informazioni, ma alla fine ci siamo visti di persona. Non era colpa nostra, ma sicuramente non era nemmeno loro. I responsabili sono morti, e siamo stati tutti vittime delle circostanze. I miei fratelli e io avevamo i soldi, ma tutti noi abbiamo sopportato gli abusi di nostro padre. La famiglia di Brooke aveva un vero legame che i soldi non avrebbero mai potuto togliere, ma hanno lottato perché erano poveri. Non sono sicuro di quale situazione fosse peggiore o migliore. Ci sono voluti anni perché mia sorella e i miei fratelli si legassero. I fratelli di Brooke non hanno mai saputo cosa significhi non proteggersi a vicenda."

"Quindi, sono tutti improvvisamente ricchi?" Quello doveva essere uno shock per i Sinclair californiani.

"Miliardari" precisò. "Ho lavorato sulla loro parte dell'eredità tanto duramente quanto sulla mia. Hanno ricevuto tutti oltre un miliardo di dollari, una volta che ho separato i fondi."

Ero cresciuto in una famiglia della classe media, e non ero ancora abituato ad essere un milionario. Potevo solo immaginare come si dovessero sentire Brooke e i suoi fratelli.

"Hanno accettato tutti?" chiesi con curiosità.

"Non subito. Hanno impiegato un po' per rendersi conto di averne diritto. Erano eredi, anche se il matrimonio della loro madre con mio padre non era legale. Era già sposato e aveva figli, quando ha deciso di diventare bigamo, ma sono tutti figli di sangue."

"Sei sicuro che non ci siano altre famiglie?"

Bevve un sorso dal suo bicchiere e deglutì, prima di rispondere: "Sicurissimo. Penso che ormai probabilmente lo saprei. Le foto che ho visto erano sicuramente di Noah, Seth e Aiden. L'hanno verificato."

"Che razza di persona fa qualcosa del genere?" mi chiesi ad alta voce.

"Non hai mai conosciuto mio padre" rispose seccamente. "Sii felice di non averlo fatto. Non avrebbe mai dovuto essere un padre. Non solo era psicotico, ma anche sadico. La vita non era facile nella nostra famiglia, e ognuno di noi viveva nella paura di una delle sue invettive. Era un sollievo per noi, quando era fuori città."

"Hope e i tuoi fratelli lo sanno?" domandai, chiedendomi se qualcun altro a parte Evan fosse informato.

"Non ancora. Non potevo rischiare che qualcuno di loro lo dicesse a Brooke, ma ci vedremo nel fine settimana. Lo dirò, quando saranno tutti qui. Posso affermare con gioia che dubito che uno solo di loro avrà altro che amore da dare ai nostri fratellastri."

Sembrava orgoglioso di questo, e non potevo biasimarlo. Sapevo che aveva ragione. A Xander sarebbe piaciuto avere più famiglia, ed ero pronto a scommettere che Hope avrebbe voluto incontrare le sue nuove sorelle e la sua famiglia. L'unica sorella Sinclair era in inferiorità numerica da anni. "Hope adorerà Brooke" dissi senza riflettere.

"So che lo farà" confermò Evan. "Finalmente avrà le femmine dalla sua parte."

"Penso che Brooke sarà distrutta dal fatto che tutta la sua famiglia glielo abbia tenuto nascosto" avvertii.

"Alla fine capirà che eravamo in una brutta situazione. O dirle una bugia o scaricarle tutto addosso, quando non poteva sopportare altro emotivamente. A nessuno di noi piace mentirle o tenerle le cose nascoste."

"Quindi, è tornata in California per vedere la sua famiglia?"

"Più per affrontarla" spiegò. "Ha avuto un sacco di brutte parole per me, e sono sicuro che ne avesse molte altre per la sua famiglia. È arrabbiata. E ovviamente ferita. Tutto è cambiato a Citrus Beach. Penso che avesse bisogno di vedere se tutti erano ancora gli stessi."

"Cambiato... come?"

Evan trangugiò il resto del suo drink, prima di rispondere: "I suoi fratelli hanno iniziato a sfruttare i loro soldi mesi fa. Noah ha lasciato il suo lavoro di programmatore per dedicarsi alla propria attività. Aveva sviluppato un'app di appuntamenti che in realtà è abbastanza intelligente. Ora ha finalmente le risorse per lanciare le proprie idee. Anche Seth e Aiden hanno lasciato il loro lavoro regolare. Seth lavorava nelle costruzioni, e Aiden pescava a fini commerciali. Ora stanno facendo start-up nei loro campi di interesse. Jade può fare molto di più che lavorare per altre persone ora che ha conseguito il dottorato. Owen sta ancora facendo la specializzazione, ma non deve più preoccuparsi di come pagare i suoi prestiti studenteschi."

Quante persone avrebbero voluto avere lo stesso cambiamento di vita? Non che non pensassi che tutti i fratelli di Brooke lo meritassero, ma dovevano essere rimasti completamente sbalorditi. "Perché ho la sensazione che tu abbia le mani in tutte le loro attività?" dissi sospettosamente.

"Non è così" affermò. "Li aiuto, quando hanno bisogno di me, e sono felice di farlo. Ma non ho alcun interesse finanziario con nessuno di loro. Sono abbastanza sicuro che anche i miei fratelli e Hope interverranno per offrire la loro esperienza."

Non avevo mai dubitato che Evan non stesse cercando di trarre profitto da ciò che stavano facendo i suoi nuovi fratelli. Ero solo certo che non lo avrebbero fatto senza alcuni dei migliori consigli di affari. "Sapevo che li avresti aiutati" chiarii.

Avere l'assistenza di Evan Sinclair era probabilmente il sogno di ogni imprenditore.

Era solenne, mentre rispondeva: "Tutto quello che voglio per loro è poter avere la vita che avrebbero dovuto avere."

Mi alzai, non potendo più restate seduto senza cercare di raggiungere Brooke. "Devo mettere insieme alcune cose, così potrò partire per la California. Devo vedere Brooke."

"Volevo proteggerla da qualsiasi cosa potesse ferirla dopo tutto quello che aveva passato, ma non ci siamo lasciati in modo positivo" disse Evan con un rimorso insolito.

"Dovresti metterti in fila per proteggerla" borbottai. I miei istinti possessivi erano alle stelle, e non volevo altro che essere lì per cercare di proteggere Brooke da tutto questo. Forse alla fine avrebbe visto l'intera faccenda come una cosa positiva—il che lo era— ma considerando quello che le era successo, aveva davvero bisogno della normalità in quel momento. E diventare un'erede della famiglia Sinclair era quanto di più lontano dal normale potessi immaginare.

Annuì. "Immagino che accetterai la mia offerta di trasporto?"

"Sì." Non mi importava davvero come fossi arrivato in California, ma l'aereo di Evan era il più veloce.

"Prenditi cura di lei" chiese.

"Contaci" concordai, tendendogli la mano.

"Verremo tutti al matrimonio" avvertì.

Potevo dire che era preoccupato, anche se esternamente non lo mostrava molto. "Alla fine apprezzerà quello che hai fatto" gli dissi burbero, mentre mi avviavo verso la porta d'ingresso. "In questo momento Brooke sarà immersa nelle sue emozioni."

Ovviamente non si era fermata a riflettere prima di andarsene. Se l'avesse fatto, sarebbe arrivata alla stessa conclusione che avevo appena tratto io: Evan aveva fatto tutto il possibile per lei e i suoi fratelli, anche prima di avere la conferma di chi fossero.

Avevo ancora delle domande, ma nessuna era vitale quanto il mio bisogno di trovarla. *Dovevo* sapere che stava bene.

La sua casa non sarebbe più stata la *stessa*, poiché tutto era cambiato. Se avesse avuto bisogno di una cosa stabile nella sua vita in quel momento, sarei stato io.

Senza un'altra parola, uscii a grandi passi dalla porta principale, non volendo fermarmi, finché non avessi saputo con certezza che stava bene.

Capitolo 14

Brooke

"Mi dispiace tanto, Brooke. Nessuno di noi ha mai avuto intenzione di ferirti."

Mia sorella, Jade, piangeva, mentre si sedeva sul divano del mio appartamento a Citrus Beach.

Grazie a Dio, una di noi viveva ancora nello stesso posto.

Pensavo di essere stata l'unica nella mia famiglia ad aver avuto una vita che si era fermata, mentre ero via.

Ogni membro della mia famiglia, tranne me, ora possedeva una residenza sull'acqua nella zona più prestigiosa della città di Citrus Beach. Non avevo ancora visto nessuna delle case dei miei fratelli, ma ero confortata dal fatto che l'appartamento in cui avevo vissuto per diversi anni fosse rimasto *uguale*.

"Lo so" risposi a malincuore.

Volevo rimanere arrabbiata per il fatto che ogni membro della mia famiglia mi avesse tradita, incluso Evan, ma la realtà stava lentamente venendo a galla. Tutti loro avevano agito per amore e preoccupazione.

"Mi ha quasi ucciso ogni volta che ti parlavo. Sei la mia miglior amica. Volevo poter condividere tutto con te" disse in lacrime.

Mi si strinse il cuore, sapendo che mantenere la verità era stato difficile per tutti loro.

Avevo avuto con me una scorta delle forze di sicurezza di Evan, finché finalmente non ero entrata nel mio appartamento. Li avevo congedati, ma in realtà non avevano smesso di vegliare su di me, finché Jade non era arrivata a casa mia. Dovevano aver ricevuto istruzioni da lui di non andarsene, finché la mia famiglia non fosse stata con me.

Avevo lasciato Amesport con la mente completamente sovraccarica, e non mi ero fidata di Evan. Ma quando l'intera immagine era stata messa a fuoco, e Jade mi aveva detto di più su tutto ciò che Evan aveva fatto per la mia famiglia, non avevo potuto fare a meno di essere pentita per le cose sconsiderate che gli avevo detto.

"Evan non meritava le cose che gli ho detto" confessai a Jade.

Si asciugò le lacrime, mentre rispondeva: "Non ha fatto altro che cose carine per aiutare da quando ci ha trovati. Ha scherzato sul fatto che non gli sarebbero mai mancati i soldi, e forse a loro non sarebbe mancato lui. Ma la mia mente è ancora sbalordita dal fatto che abbia risparmiato e investito per noi tutti quegli anni. Immagino che ora ci fidiamo tutti del suo giudizio. È una delle menti imprenditoriali più intelligenti del mondo."

"Ero arrabbiata" spiegai. "Gli ho detto alcune cose cattive che non meritava. Onestamente, penso di aver avuto paura."

"Perché le cose erano cambiate?" chiese pensierosa.

Annuii. "Sembra irragionevole ora, ma immagino che stessi cercando di far tornare le cose alla normalità, e sono tutte così diverse. Tutto è cambiato."

"Noi non siamo cambiati, Brooke" replicò Jade dolcemente. "I nostri fratelli sono ancora tutti degli stupidi, proprio come quando eravamo poveri. Non credo che i soldi abbiano cambiato nessuno di noi. Ci permettono solo di fare le cose che avevamo sempre desiderato fare prima. E abbiamo più famiglia. Sfortunatamente, include altri fratelli ficcanaso, ma vivono su un'altra costa, il che è un vantaggio secondo me."

"Abbiamo una sorella" dissi, ancora sbalordita da tutto quello che era successo, mentre ero via.

La mia rabbia si stava dissolvendo. Ora che avevo sentito l'intera storia da lei, potevo mettermi nei panni della mia famiglia. Per loro era stata una situazione impossibile. Non potevo dire che non avrei fatto lo stesso, se i ruoli fossero stati invertiti e fosse stata Jade ad aver bisogno di tempo per guarire.

Certo, pensavo che avrebbero potuto dirmelo un po' prima, ma l'intera situazione era incerta. I giornalisti non avevano smesso di setacciare Citrus Beach fino a un mese o due addietro, e nessuno sapeva se si sarebbero presentati di nuovo.

Sorrise malinconicamente: "Com'è? L'hai incontrata, vero?"

"L'ho fatto. Ma non sapevo che fosse mia sorella" risposi, pentita di non aver conosciuto meglio Hope Sutherland, quando ero ad Amesport. La bella rossa aveva incrociato il mio cammino diverse volte, ma non le avevo parlato molto.

Ero la sua cameriera; lei era una cliente.

Quello era più o meno il grado di conoscenza della mia nuova sorella.

"È simpatica" le dissi. "È bellissima. E posso dire che ama suo marito. Sono una coppia piuttosto potente, ma non diresti che sono mega-ricchi."

Jade mi lanciò un'occhiata dubbiosa. "Erano entrambi miliardari prima di sposarsi" mi ricordò.

"Non sono così, Jade. Hope è una fotografa naturalistica, ed è brava in quello che fa." Avevo visto la mia nuova sorella da lontano scattare foto molte volte nell'ultimo anno. "Nessuno dei Sinclair di Amesport se la tira. Hanno donato milioni per aiutare la città, e la maggior parte di loro mette meno in soggezione di Evan. Hope sembra solo... felice."

Le poche volte in cui avevo visto lei e suo marito, Jason Sutherland, nel ristorante di Liam, erano stati proprio come qualsiasi altra coppia che si adorava.

Annuì. "Bene. Speravo che nessuno di loro avesse la puzza sotto al naso. Evan cerca di comportarsi come se non gli importasse di niente e di nessuno, ma so che non è così."

"Adora sua moglie" riflettei pensierosa. "In realtà, ogni singolo matrimonio Sinclair mi sembrava felice."

"Che tipo è Xander Sinclair?" chiese con curiosità. "La sua carriera è stata così tragica. Adoravo la sua musica."

Anch'io ero una fan della musica di Xander, quindi vederlo come una persona reale era stato un po' scoraggiante. "È divertente, ma non lo era in passato. Da quello che ho capito, era praticamente un recluso in convalescenza, quando ha incontrato sua moglie, Samantha."

"Ma ora sta bene?" domandò con ansia.

Avrei impiegato un po' per riconoscere Xander come mio fratello, ma potevo vedere che Jade aveva già superato quel punto. Era preoccupata per qualcuno che non conosceva, perché era di famiglia.

"Sì. È uno dei migliori amici di Liam. Si sfidano a vicenda costantemente, un po' come fanno i nostri fratelli, ma si può dire che c'è un legame tra loro due.»

"Mi piacerebbe incontrarli tutti" disse con voce malinconica.

Mi spostai nella mia poltrona, cercando di mettermi a mio agio. Avevo appena avuto il tempo di abituarmi a tornare nel mio appartamento, prima che Jade volasse attraverso la porta in lacrime, sconvolta, perché aveva dovuto nascondermi la verità per mesi.

"Sono sicura che li *incontrerai*" risposi. "Evan ha detto che avrebbe dato loro la notizia subito dopo avermelo detto. Probabilmente ormai lo sanno."

Mi guardò attentamente. "Guarda, so come ti senti. Abbiamo affrontato tutto questo insieme, mentre eri via. È piuttosto surreale. Non sentirti sola. Non lo sei. Nessuno di noi si è abituato a tutto."

L'avevano attraversato, e ora avevano almeno superato lo shock iniziale. Io stavo ancora arrancando, incredula. "Non riesco ancora a credere che mamma non l'abbia detto a nessuno."

"Eravamo bambini" sottolineò Jade. "I suoi figli. Penso che stesse cercando di proteggerci."

"Non ha nemmeno avuto la possibilità di confrontarsi con lui sul fatto di essere un bigamo" considerai. "Evan ha detto che suo padre probabilmente è morto prima che mamma conoscesse la verità."

"Era davvero sola" mormorò Jade.

"Mi piace pensare che alla fine ce l'avrebbe detto, ma Noah aveva già finito il liceo, quando è morta, e non gliel'ha rivelato" dissi.

"Non credo che nessuno di noi possa sapere se alla fine ci avrebbe detto o meno la verità" rispose.

"È difficile credere che non l'abbia riconosciuto. È sempre stato uno degli uomini più ricchi del mondo" replicai, chiedendomi come fosse potuto sfuggire a mia madre vederlo sui media.

"Non operava esattamente in quei circoli, e quando aveva il tempo di leggere le notizie sui ricchi? Lavorava sempre" osservò ironicamente. "Ho pensato la stessa cosa, fino a quando Noah ha sottolineato che non guardava mai la TV, e il padre di Evan non mostrava spesso la sua faccia al di fuori del mondo della finanza. Non era esattamente un tipo di uomo generoso o filantropico."

"Lo chiami ancora il padre di *Evan*" dissi, leggermente divertita. "È anche *nostro* padre."

Jade arricciò il naso. "Forse non voglio davvero rivendicarlo" ammise. "Era squallido."

Incrociai le braccia. "Allora, non avresti alcun collegamento con Evan."

"Va bene... visto che la metti in questo modo, rivendicherò il bastardo, se posso ancora avere tutti quei nuovi fratelli" scherzò.

Risi. "Cavolo, mi sei mancata."

Ero tornata a casa con un sacco di rabbia, ma non così tanta come quando avevo lasciato Amesport. Avevo avuto molto tempo per ragionare, tornando a casa, e non potevo restare arrabbiata con Jade o con i miei fratelli. Non era davvero colpa loro. Ero stata solo confusa e spaventata per la mia famiglia. A metà del volo, mi ero pentita di aver lasciato Liam senza parlargli. Sì, stavo progettando di tornare, ma si meritava molto di più delle informazioni maldestre che avevo dato a Tessa.

Mi avvolsi le braccia intorno al corpo, sentendomi vulnerabile e desiderando avere la forte presenza di Liam lì a Citrus Beach. Forse non parlava molto, ma potevo sempre *sentirlo* lì per me. Era così solido e reale che sarei arrivata a contare sul fatto che fosse con me.

"Mi sei mancata anche tu, Brooke" rispose enfaticamente.

C'eravamo già abbracciate, fino quasi a strangolarci a vicenda, e avevamo frignato come bambine subito dopo che lei era entrata nel mio appartamento.

"Non vedo l'ora di vedere i miei fratelli domani, ma devo tornare ad Amesport. Non ho mai veramente detto addio a Liam" le dissi con rammarico nella voce.

"Hai *intenzione* di dirgli addio?" insistette.

Alzai le spalle. "Non lo so. Non siamo mai arrivati così lontano."

Liam ed io eravamo solo stati felici nel momento. Forse entrambi c'eravamo resi conto che il domani non era mai scontato, e ci stava bene solo goderci il nostro tempo insieme. Sfortunatamente, pensavo che mi fosse piaciuto troppo stare con lui. Ero completamente dipendente da lui e sentivo già i dolori dell'astinenza. "Spero di no" condivisi finalmente.

"Sei innamorata di lui" concluse Jade, sforzandosi di ottenere maggiori informazioni da me.

Sospirai. "Sono abbastanza sicura di esserlo sempre stata." Ero in un posto sicuro con la sorella di cui mi fidavo. Se non avessi potuto ammettere con lei come mi sentivo, non lo avrei detto a nessuno. "Non so se all'inizio fosse solo lussuria, ma è diventato qualcosa che non avrei mai potuto immaginare. Mi conosci. Non sono mai stata una grande sostenitrice del lieto fine. Siamo sopravvissuti."

"Le persone cambiano" disse dolcemente. "So che abbiamo sempre dovuto lavorare sodo per sopravvivere, ma questo non significa che non possiamo tutti avere il nostro lieto fine."

"E il tuo?" azzardai.

Sbuffò. "Mi sembra di essere tormentata dagli uomini ricchi all'improvviso. Beh, forse non *molti* ricchi visto che li evito, se posso. Non sono tutti gentili come i Sinclair. Ma solo uno è più che sufficiente."

Sollevai un sopracciglio. "Hai conosciuto qualcuno?"

Si fermò un momento, prima di rispondere con riluttanza: "Eli Stone. È uno stronzo completo."

Conoscevo il nome. Non aveva bisogno di dire un'altra parola. "*Quell'*Eli Stone? Il sexy e schifosamente ricco *Eli Stone*?"

La maggior parte delle persone conosceva il miliardario per nome, soprattutto le donne. Rendeva i tatuaggi sexy, e io non ci andavo pazza, tranne per quelli di Liam, perché avevano uno scopo ed erano ben fatti. Dato che Eli Stone aveva così tanti hobby fisici, era abbastanza facile vedere una sua foto senza maglietta.

"È un coglione viziato e snob" disse velenosamente.

Raramente avevo visto Jade reagire negativamente a qualcuno, quindi ero più che un po' sorpresa. "Così pessimo?"

"Ci siamo... scontrati un paio di volte."

"Hai una testa piuttosto dura" risposi in tono divertito.

"Volevo prenderlo a pugni in faccia, ma ho dovuto ricordare a me stessa che è ricco, e probabilmente sarei stata arrestata per aggressione, quindi ho dovuto trattenermi" spiegò con disappunto.

Essendo state cresciute da tre fratelli maggiori, Jade e io eravamo perfettamente in grado di combattere sporco, quando dovevamo.

"Mi è sempre sembrato un tipo rilassato" riflettei, pensando alle cose che avevo letto e visto sul giovane miliardario.

"Credimi sulla parola, non lo è" replicò con una risposta secca.

"Potresti sempre lasciarlo ai nostri fratelli maggiori" dissi con una risata.

"Non lo farei. Il bastardo si vendicherebbe. Non è un tipo piacevole." Esitò, prima di cambiare argomento. "Dimentica Eli Stone. Allora, cos'hai intenzione di fare con Liam? Non vedo l'ora di conoscerlo."

Sapevo che stava deliberatamente cambiando argomento, e glielo permisi. La sua antipatia per il ragazzo sembrava metterla di cattivo umore, qualcosa che non ero abituato a vedere da mia sorella. A Jade piacevano praticamente tutti, e non aveva mai serbato rancore.

A quanto pareva, Eli Stone non era un tipo che chiedeva scusa.

"Tornerò ad Amesport con un jet privato di proprietà di nostro fratello e chiederò scusa a Liam per essere partita così bruscamente. Immagino che vedrò dove andremo a finire, dopo che avremo parlato."

"Forse dovresti solo sedurlo" rifletté.

Non avevo dubbi che se avessi insistito, Liam avrebbe infranto la sua promessa di non fare sesso con me in un minuto appassionato, ma avevamo sviluppato una fiducia tra di noi, una che non volevo davvero rovinare. "Penso che sarebbe meglio parlare prima" replicai.

Annuì. "Allora, non potete fare sesso."

Alzai gli occhi al cielo. Ovviamente aveva il sesso nel cervello, e dovetti chiedermi se il suo odio per Eli Stone fosse così profondo. Non l'avevo mai vista reagire con così tanta rabbia verso un ragazzo.

Mi alzai. "È meglio che dorma un po'. Penso che ne abbiamo bisogno entrambe e, ovviamente, domattina avrò a che fare con i nostri fratelli. È tardi."

Al mattino avrei visto i miei tre fratelli maggiori. Apparentemente, avevano lasciato che fosse Jade a spiegare. In quel momento, ero esausta. Non ero sicura se fosse stanchezza emotiva o fisica, ma mi sentivo come se avessi raggiunto il limite di ciò che avrei potuto assorbire in un giorno.

Jade saltò in piedi e mi abbracciò, e io la strinsi un po' più a lungo del solito. Dopo la rapina, tenevo tutto ciò che avevo a cuore ancora più stretto di prima, forse perché avevo imparato quanto velocemente sarebbe potuto sparire tutto.

Una volta chiusa la porta dopo che mia sorella era andata via, vagai per il mio piccolo monolocale, sentendomi disconnessa.

Non appartenevo più a quel posto. Essere a casa non aveva la stessa piacevole sensazione che aveva sempre avuto prima della sparatoria in banca.

Ma non appartenevo nemmeno ad Amesport. Sì, sapevo di avere una famiglia lì adesso, ma non conoscevo nessuno di loro.

Avevo imparato che il posto in cui vivevo era solo un luogo. Il mio unico posto sicuro era con Liam, e lui non era qui.

Le lacrime mi uscivano dagli occhi, mentre vagavo per la camera da letto singola del mio appartamento, non sentendomi più a *casa*.

Disgustata da me stessa per aver permesso così tanta autocommiserazione, cercai nei miei cassetti un vecchio pigiama e biancheria intima. Avevo portato molto poco qui in California, ma avevo ancora alcune cose che mi ero lasciata alle spalle.

Mi spogliai, sentendo la stanchezza in ogni parte del corpo, i miei movimenti lenti e pesanti, mentre entravo nella mia piccola doccia.

Per un momento, mi sentii leggermente ravvivata dai getti d'acqua che si riversavano sul mio corpo stanco, ma il mio momento edificante terminò bruscamente. Il mio sollievo si trasformò in terrore, quando un grosso corpo sbatté contro di me, entrando nella mia doccia.

Capitolo 15

Brooke

"Liam?" Rimasi senza fiato, mentre mi voltavo, pietrificata. Era meravigliosamente nudo, ma impiegai un momento per riconoscere esattamente chi fosse con me, anche se conoscevo e fantasticavo spesso su quel corpo maschile particolarmente splendido.

"Ti ho spaventata?" chiese con una voce roca che mi fece arricciare le dita dei piedi. "Non hai risposto alla porta, ma era aperta, un fatto di cui dovremo parlare più tardi."

Anche se Citrus Beach era una piccola città, mi ero sempre sentita relativamente al sicuro nel mio appartamento qui. Di solito chiudevo a chiave, ma dovevo essere stata così distratta che me ne ero dimenticata.

Feci un paio di respiri profondi, desiderando che il mio cuore rallentasse. Eravamo vicini, perché il box era piccolo, ma non mi toccò. Sapevo che stava aspettando che registrassi la sua presenza senza aver paura.

Alla fine, lo guardai, il mio cuore che batteva all'impazzata per qualcosa di *diverso* dalla paura. Il suo bel viso era la cosa più accogliente che avessi mai visto. "Liam" dissi con più sicurezza, e poi mi gettai tra le sue braccia.

Mi prese saldamente, tirandomi contro il suo corpo potente e bagnato.

"Mi sei mancato così tanto" gli dissi in fretta, il mio cuore che batteva perché era qui con me.

Tutto quello che avevo scoperto sui miei genitori in così poco tempo mi aveva oppressa, ma avevo tenuto tutto dentro, non volendo parlarne davanti a Jade. Era già stata nella situazione in cui mi trovavo adesso. Non volevo farcela tornare di nuovo. I miei fratelli avevano già avuto il tempo di parlare ed elaborare la verità. Io no.

Accolsi con favore le sue braccia forti intorno a me. La sua forte presenza mi fece crollare, e singhiozzai tutta la mia confusione, paura e rabbia sulla sua spalla solida.

Le sue braccia si strinsero intorno a me, e mi abbracciò, mentre piangevo, accarezzandomi i capelli bagnati e sussurrandomi con voce rauca nell'orecchio: "Andrà tutto bene, tesoro. Lo prometto."

Gli credevo. Finché era qui con me, sentivo che *sarei* stata bene.

Mi teneva con i piedi per terra, permettendomi finalmente di esprimere il dolore che provavo da quando avevo saputo di come mia madre era stata tradita.

"Non meritava quello che le ha fatto, Liam" balbettai, mentre piangevo. "Tutto quello che ha sempre voluto era proteggerci. Ma era così sola."

"Era uno stronzo, piccola" cantilenò. "C'è un posto speciale all'inferno per uomini come lui" ringhiò.

Ci vollero alcuni minuti perché le mie lacrime si placassero e la mia testa si schiarisse. "Cosa ci fai qui?" domandai con voce tremante, dopo aver versato amare lacrime.

"Secondo te?" chiese in un pigro baritono. "Sono venuto per te."

"Grazie" risposi tremante, mentre facevo scorrere le dita lungo la sua mascella. "Avevo davvero bisogno di te. Domani sarei tornata ad Amesport dopo aver visto i miei fratelli, ma sono contenta che tu sia qui. Ovviamente sai tutto. Come l'hai scoperto?"

Era abbastanza chiaro che Liam sapesse di mio padre.

"Ero pronto a pestare Evan, ma ha spifferato le informazioni prima che dovessimo arrivare a quel punto. Ero fottutamente preoccupato, Brooke. Ho perso il conto di quante volte ho provato a chiamarti."

Sembrava preoccupato. Lo vedevo nei suoi occhi. "Mi dispiace. Avrei dovuto aspettare per venire qui, ma ero... sopraffatta. Non sapevo più di chi fidarmi."

Dato che eravamo stati entrambi in volo, ovviamente non eravamo riusciti a sentirci. Avevo provato a chiamarlo anch'io.

Mi spinse contro la parete della doccia, inchiodandomi contro le piastrelle fredde. "Puoi fidarti di me" ringhiò. "Non ti ho mai mentito. Forse mi sono trattenuto a causa del tuo ragazzo, ma non sono un bugiardo."

Annuii. "Lo so."

"Non farlo mai più" chiese.

"Non lo farò" accettai prontamente. Sapevo che non mi sarebbe piaciuto, se lui avesse fatto la stessa cosa con me.

"Non posso credere che tu sia qui" dissi, facendo scorrere le mani sul suo corpo scolpito per dimostrare a me stessa che fosse vero e non un'illusione.

"Ci sarò sempre, quando avrai bisogno di me" giurò solennemente.

"Avrò sempre bisogno di te" replicai, ipnotizzata dal suo sguardo irresistibile. Mi persi nel verde intenso dei suoi occhi, non sicura se avrei mai voluto essere ritrovata.

"Ho finito con la mia promessa" borbottò. "Ho smesso di fingere di non aver bisogno di scoparti, finché non riesci a pensare lucidamente. Ti conosco, Brooke. E tu conosci me. Ci siamo conosciuti molto tempo fa. Forse non sappiamo tutto quello che c'è da sapere l'uno dell'altra, ma so quello che voglio. I dettagli possono essere aggiunti in seguito."

Il mio cuore sussultò, quando vidi la determinazione nei suoi occhi. Ogni giorno imparavo qualcosa di nuovo che avrei potuto amare di Liam.

Avevo la sensazione che sarebbe stato sempre così.

Sospirai. "Grazie a Dio" dissi sbuffando. "Non avrei resistito a lungo."

Il modo in cui lo volevo era inesorabile, e il mio corpo mi chiedeva l'orgasmo da diversi giorni.

"In questo momento, voglio solo sapere che stai bene" disse con tono rauco.

Capivo che era determinato a prendersi cura di me, ma avevo bisogno di qualcosa di più di una semplice spalla su cui piangere.

Avevo bisogno di *lui*.

"Non respingermi stasera, Liam" ribattei con tono fermo.

I nostri occhi si incrociarono e si fissarono, e il mio sguardo non nascondeva più nulla.

"Dannazione!!" Sbatté la mano sulla piastrella accanto alla mia testa. "Voglio essere di supporto, Brooke. Voglio aiutarti a gestire tutte le stronzate che devi assorbire—"

Gli misi le dita sulla bocca. "Non adesso. Dovrò affrontare tutto ciò che è cambiato, ma in questo momento, voglio che tu mi fotta più di quanto io voglia qualsiasi altra cosa."

Lo desideravo. Era qui. Era reale. E amavo quell'uomo più di quanto potessi esprimere veramente.

La sua faccia era feroce, mentre rispondeva: "Il tuo desiderio sarà esaudito."

Catturò la mia bocca, e la mia risposta fu istantanea. Ci baciammo come due persone che avevano un disperato bisogno di toccarsi, di stare insieme nel modo più elementare possibile. Lo bramavo, ed ero avida di toccare qualsiasi parte della sua pelle potessi raggiungere.

Quando mi lasciò andare le labbra, ansimai: "Liam. Oh, Dio, ti voglio così tanto."

La sua espressione era tesa, quando si voltò per chiudere l'acqua, poi mi sollevò fuori dal box.

Ero ancora bagnata, quando mi sistemò sul ripiano del bagno. "Mia" ringhiò. "Sei sempre stata destinata ad essere mia."

Non riuscivo a parlare, mentre lo guardavo leccare singole gocce d'acqua dai miei seni, la sua lingua che sferzava i miei capezzoli per catturare le goccioline che minacciavano di cadere sulle cosce.

Gemetti, afferrandogli la testa, ma allontanò le mie mani, mentre si inginocchiava sul pavimento per divaricarmi le gambe.

Una vampata di calore saettò tra le mie cosce, la vista della sua testa in una posizione così intima e così erotica che dovetti chiudere gli occhi.

Rabbrividii, quando sentii il suo respiro caldo contro la mia figa, il mio corpo teso perché sapevo cosa stava per accadere.

Avevo fatto sesso, ma non avevo mai avuto un uomo—nessun uomo—affamato di assaggiarmi. Non mi ero mai sentita così a mio agio nell'essere così vulnerabile.

Ma con Liam, accoglievo con favore qualunque cosa mi desse. Mi fidavo di lui.

Ma non ero preparata per il momento in cui passò la lingua dal basso verso l'alto della mia pelle rosa e sensibile, spostandosi lentamente sul clitoride.

Gridai, un verso insensato che liberò un po' della tensione che stava rapidamente crescendo dentro di me.

Non mi diede pietà, la sua bocca e la sua lingua che divoravano ogni goccia di umidità che si era riversata nella mia figa nel momento in cui mi ero resa conto che mi aveva *seguita* nella doccia.

Cercò, esplorò e consumò, facendolo più e più volte, finché il mio corpo si sentì più come se non mi appartenesse.

Come aveva appena dichiarato, ero *sua*, anche se sperimentavo ogni suo tocco.

Conficcai le mie dita nei suoi capelli e rimasi così, avendo bisogno di qualcosa che mi tenesse a terra, mentre mi sentivo come se fossi pronta a volare via.

Mi appoggiai allo specchio, sentendomi impotente a fare qualsiasi cosa tranne provare sensazioni.

"Liam" piagnucolai, e poi gli strinsi a pugno i capelli. "Per favore."

Avevo bisogno di più. Avevo bisogno di *qualcosa*, ma non sapevo come dirgli quello che volevo così disperatamente.

Ma non aveva bisogno di istruzioni. Mentre le sue mani mi passavano sotto il sedere per tirarmi contro la sua bocca vorace, si concentrò sul minuscolo fascio di nervi che pulsava per la sua attenzione.

"Sì" gemetti. "Sì."

Ansimava sulla mia carne tremante, come se fosse intossicato dal sapore della mia figa, e ne avesse bisogno per il sostentamento.

Il mio corpo rispose rilasciando un potente climax che mi lasciò tremante, ogni emozione esposta.

Non avevo il tempo per considerare la mia debolezza, e Liam non aveva approfittato della mia vulnerabilità.

Mi avvolse le gambe intorno alla vita, aspettando che gli mettessi le braccia intorno al collo, poi mi portò in camera da letto.

"Anche tu sei mio" gli dissi con voce seducente che quasi non riconoscevo come mia, quando mi lasciò cadere sul letto. Non ero mai stata un tipo possessivo, ma volevo reclamarlo con un dolore tale che faceva male fisicamente.

Mi lanciò un'occhiata possessiva. "Forse volevo negarlo, quando pensavo che appartenessi a qualcun altro, ma non ho alcun desiderio di credere a nient'altro ora" replicò burbero, i suoi occhi verdi pieni di lussuria e splendenti di calore. "Cazzo, mi hai avuto dalla prima volta in cui ti ho vista sorridermi."

Sì, le sue parole mi facevano sentire una sorta di seduttrice, cosa che sapevo benissimo di non essere. Ma venendo da lui, l'ammissione era stata sexy come l'inferno.

Mi aveva resa nervosa dal primo momento in cui l'avevo guardato.

"Bene" dissi, avvolgendo le braccia e le gambe intorno a lui, mentre si accasciava sopra di me. "Prenderò ciò che mi appartiene" scherzai.

Aspettai un momento mozzafiato, il suo uccello che non mi penetrava ancora, mentre guardava il mio viso.

Sollevò un sopracciglio. "Chi sta prendendo chi?"

Sollevai i fianchi, sforzandomi di prenderlo dentro di me. "Non mi importa" risposi in tono disperato. "Fallo c basta."

"Di' che sei mia" insistette con voce bassa e gutturale. "Di' che starai con me, così non perderò la testa."

Comprendevo la sua urgenza. Non sapevo come avrei fatto a sopravvivere, se non fossimo stati insieme. Non ora che avevamo avuto un assaggio di come sarebbe stato avere una vita insieme. "Tua" balbettai. "Sarò sempre con te."

"Bene" replicò, imitando il mio tono soddisfatto, quando avevo pronunciato la stessa parola.

Entrò dentro di me con una potente spinta, scacciando ogni pensiero dal mio cervello.

"Liam" gracchiai, la voce che mi sfuggiva, mentre lo sentivo seppellirsi fino alle palle, riempiendomi, finché non riuscivo a respirare del tutto.

"Stai bene?" chiese.

"Sì."

Sollevai i fianchi, assaporando la sensazione dei nostri corpi uniti così strettamente. Era grosso, ma il mio corpo lo accettava come se il suo posto fosse tra le mie cosce tremanti.

"Voglio restare così" borbottò. "Perché quando non sono dentro di te, ho una grande voglia di esserci, cazzo."

Rilasciai un respiro affannoso e strinsi le gambe attorno ai suoi fianchi. "Anch'io" confessai.

La potente chimica tra di noi non aveva mai voluto essere negata.

"Purtroppo, io lo voglio di più" aggiunse con voce frustrata, mentre si tirava indietro e si tuffava di nuovo dentro di me.

Volevo la stessa cosa. Volevo che mi fottesse, finché non fossimo entrambi esausti e sazi.

"Allora, fallo" incoraggiai con urgenza. "Scopami, Liam."

Lo avrei voluto per sempre, come non avevo mai voluto un altro ragazzo.

Abbassò la testa per baciarmi, mentre iniziava a scoparmi come voleva, la sua lingua che entrava e si ritirava con le stesse spinte audaci che stava iniziando a fare con il suo uccello.

Le mie unghie gli graffiarono la schiena, ed ero disperata di prenderlo il più possibile, quel desiderio sempre presente di arrampicarmi nel suo corpo che mi spingeva a muovermi con lui.

I nostri corpi erano ancora leggermente umidi, e il calore della sua pelle mi marcava ovunque ci toccassimo.

Ti amo, Liam. Ti amo così tanto che non riesco a respirare.

Volevo urlare le parole ad alta voce, ma non ero del tutto sicura di essere pronta per essere così figurativamente nuda, quindi cercai di mostrargli quanto avessi bisogno di lui con il mio corpo. Sollevai i fianchi, cercando di unirci.

"Vieni per me, Brooke" disse, mentre la sua bocca si staccava dalla mia, la sua voce insistente, mentre il corpo potente continuava a sbattere contro di me con forza.

Il tormento dentro di me cominciò a sciogliersi.

Il mio corpo era fisicamente esausto per la lunga giornata e il mio precedente orgasmo, ma potevo ancora sentire il climax iniziare ad attraversarmi, una sensazione dominante che non riuscivo a controllare.

"Sei così fottutamente bella" lodò, guardandomi con un'espressione feroce che avrebbe dovuto farmi un po' paura, ma non lo faceva.

Fu un momento crudo e intimo, entrambi che ci fissavamo senza speranza.

Quando finalmente chiusi gli occhi, fu perché stavo raggiungendo l'orgasmo così fortemente che ero schiava di ogni sensazione, e non potevo più sopportare la stimolazione.

Gemette, quando la mia figa tremante gli strinse il membro come se volesse impedirgli di andarsene.

Le sue spinte divennero più dure e più urgenti, più veloci di quanto potessi eguagliare, quindi mi aggrappai a lui, mentre il mio orgasmo raggiungeva il picco. "Liam" urlai. "Fottimi più forte."

Si sollevò dentro di me con un'ultima enorme spinta, mentre gemeva il mio nome più e più volte trovando il suo orgasmo.

Mi abbracciò e rotolò, lasciandomi distesa su di lui.

Nessuno di noi due parlò, mentre riprendevamo lentamente il respiro.

Alla fine, ruppe il silenzio. "Un giorno mi ucciderai."

Gli sorrisi. "Ti stai lamentando?"

Scosse lentamente la testa, un sorriso che si diffuse sul suo bel viso. "Mai."

Sbadigliai, mentre scivolavo per riposarmi accanto a lui, e poi mi sistemai lungo il suo fianco.

"Sei stanca" disse scontento.

Appoggiai la testa sulla sua spalla. "Colpa tua" mormorai, chiudendo gli occhi.

"Colpa mia" concordò, accarezzandomi i capelli delicatamente. "Dormi. È stata una giornata difficile."

"Non più" ribattei in disaccordo, mentre i miei occhi si chiudevano. "Adesso sei qui."

"Ci sarò sempre" rispose in un rilassante baritono.

Volevo assaporare il momento. Godermi la sensazione di beatitudine che mi attraversava.

Invece, sospirai e mi addormentai.

Capitolo 16

Liam

"Se fai del male a mia sorella, ti ammazzerò."

Girai la testa per guardare la persona che aveva parlato avvicinarsi, mentre prendevo una bevanda proteica dal frigorifero di Brooke. Dopo la notte precedente con lei, avevo bisogno di tutta l'energia possibile.

Supponevo che quando uno aveva una casa piena di Sinclair, uno di loro dovesse trovarmi da solo e minacciare la mia vita, ma le parole di Noah mi colsero comunque di sorpresa, mentre si avvicinava.

Tutti i fratelli di Brooke si erano fatti vivi al mattino presto nel suo appartamento. Adesso che era pomeriggio, stavo affrontando la realtà di non essere in grado di farli andare via.

Aprii il coperchio della lattina, grato che, perlomeno, fossero arrivati con drink e viveri.

Chiusi il frigo e mi appoggiai al tavolo. "Cosa ti fa pensare che la ferirò?"

Mi passò accanto per tirare fuori una birra. "Non ho detto che lo farai" precisò con voce scontenta. "È solo un avvertimento."

Avevo scoperto che Noah non aveva mai molto da dire, ma quando lo faceva, era minaccioso o di supporto. Ovviamente aveva tenuto a freno i suoi fratelli, ma almeno lo aveva fatto in modo incoraggiante.

Rovesciai la parte superiore della bevanda energetica e trangugiai metà della lattina, prima di rispondere. "Lo capisco. Ho una sorella minore."

Mi lanciò un'occhiata che sembrava voler dire che non sapevo nulla di quello che aveva passato.

E forse era vero.

Onestamente, ammiravo il ragazzo, anche se era uno stronzo. Non riuscivo a immaginare come fosse stato prendersi cura di tutti e cinque i suoi fratelli e sorelle dopo la morte di sua madre.

Stappò la sua birra e bevve diversi sorsi, prima di rispondere: "Brooke ne ha passate tante, e ora deve affrontare tutte queste stronzate. Voglio che *questa* sia l'ultima volta che la vedo sconvolta per almeno un decennio."

"Non voglio più vederla piangere" confessai, ricordando vividamente come il mio cuore fosse stato tagliato in un milione di minuscoli pezzi la scorsa notte, quando aveva lasciato andare il suo dolore e la sua confusione. "Ma non credo che lascerò più che qualcuno la controlli. Non era turbata per colpa mia."

"Non la *controllo*" gracchiò, gli occhi lampeggianti di rabbia e indignazione.

"Cazzate. Avresti potuto dirglielo prima di quanto hai fatto."

Avevo la mia parte di rabbia nei confronti di Noah Sinclair, ma ero disposto a lasciarla andare per Brooke.

Aveva dovuto ricoprire molti ruoli nella vita dei suoi fratelli, quando erano più piccoli. Non potevo dire di essere mai stato nei suoi panni.

Onestamente, l'intero clan Sinclair aveva fatto quello che riteneva fosse meglio per Brooke, ma sapevo che era risentita per non essere stata informata prima.

"Non potevo" ribatté Noah con calore. "Pensi che non mi sia agitato per ogni singola decisione che abbiamo preso per lei? Non era pronta ad affrontare nient'altro."

"Questo è quello che hai pensato tu" sfidai. "Stavi prendendo decisioni per una donna adulta. Brooke è molto più forte di quanto pensi che sia."

"Penso ancora a lei come a una ragazzina" ammise.

"Non lo è" lo informai senza esitazione.

"Non ho mai voluto essere suo *padre*. L'ultima cosa che volevo fare era trattenere i miei fratelli" disse con rimorso. "Volevo solo che tutta la mia famiglia stesse fottutamente bene."

Potevo vedere la preoccupazione sul suo viso, e la pesante coltre di responsabilità che sembrava ancora pesare sulle sue spalle. "Non posso dire di sapere completamente come ti senti" replicai. "Ma so che dev'essere stata dura per tutti voi. Concediti una pausa. Hai avuto un sacco di cose da gestire. Ma i tuoi fratelli e le tue sorelle sono tutti cresciuti adesso." Avevo la sensazione che Noah avesse bisogno di iniziare a vivere la propria vita, qualcosa che aveva dovuto mettere da parte per la sua famiglia all'inizio della loro vita.

Brooke mi aveva raccontato abbastanza su com'era stata cresciuta da farmi capire l'inferno che doveva aver passato Noah, quando aveva dovuto assumersi la responsabilità di una famiglia cresciuta per metà, quando era appena abbastanza grande per poter votare. L'avevano visto tutti e, in cambio del suo sacrificio, avevano cercato di aiutare il più possibile.

Non molte persone avrebbero potuto farlo e far crescere una famiglia così brava come quella di Noah.

Il suo volto era cupo, mentre rispondeva: "Non ne hai idea. Sapevo che se non avessi potuto sostenerli, li avrei persi. Ho avuto momenti in cui ho pensato che sarebbe stato meglio con una famiglia affidataria o adottiva. Ma non potevo vederlo accadere."

Capivo. I bambini affidatari o adottati non avevano sempre un lieto fine, e non finivano sempre con una buona famiglia. Sarebbe stata una questione di fortuna e, come lui, dubitavo che avrei potuto correre il rischio con Tessa, se mi fossi trovato in quella situazione. "Ora sono tutti cresciuti, amico" dissi in tono più calmo. "Ce l'hai fatta, anche senza l'aiuto del nome Sinclair o dei soldi. Devi esserne orgoglioso."

Avevo incontrato tutti quella mattina tranne Owen. Il fratello più piccolo di Brooke era fuori dallo Stato per la specializzazione.

Jade le somigliava tanto, ma non erano identiche. Ed entrambe avevano personalità diverse. Ma potevo percepire la stessa gentilezza intrinseca in Jade che percepivo in Brooke.

Okay, Seth e Aiden erano entrambi degli stronzi, ma sapevo che stavano cercando di proteggere i fratelli nei loro modi odiosi.

Contro ogni previsione, tutti i Sinclair della California si erano rivelati in qualche modo normali, anche se erano un po' rudi.

Noah si passò una mano tra i capelli scuri, mentre mi guardava accigliato. "Penso di avere uno stress post-traumatico per averli cresciuti tutti. È difficile lasciarsi andare."

Immaginavo che concedere a tutti loro un po' di spazio adesso per fare i propri errori fosse difficile. Noah era stato un fratello maggiore e un padre sostituto per molti anni. Avevo visto il modo in cui ascoltava tutto ciò che i suoi fratelli e sorelle dicevano e facevano, e poi interveniva con un consiglio. Mi ricordava me stesso con Tessa. "A volte devono capire le cose da soli. Ho una sorella che è diventata sorda in tenera età. I nostri genitori sono morti in un incidente, quindi ero tutto quello che aveva."

Inghiottì un po' della sua birra. Impiegò un minuto di riflessione per rispondere: "Se fosse successo a una delle mie sorelle, non so come avrei reagito."

"Ha recuperato l'udito con un impianto cocleare e ha sposato uno dei tuoi cugini, Micah. È felice, ma gli istinti protettivi rimangono con una persona anche dopo che non sono più necessari."

"Penso che Seth, Aiden e io ci sentiremo sempre come se dovessimo stare attenti a Brooke, Jade e Owen" ammise scontento.

Alzai le spalle. "Non andrà mai via. Ma migliora con il tempo. Alla fine ti rendi conto che sono tutti cresciuti e in grado di prendersi cura di se stessi."

"Ne dubito" rispose.

Avevo i miei dubbi sul fatto che i fratelli di Brooke l'avrebbero mai vista come un'adulta, ma ero sicurissimo che non ne avrei parlato con Noah. "Mi prenderò cura io di lei" dissi.

"Sarà meglio per te" borbottò. "Vedo il modo in cui ti guarda. Potresti ferirla peggio di qualsiasi altro ragazzo sul pianeta."

"Ha lo stesso potere di ferirmi" risposi. "Lo so da quando è arrivata ad Amesport."

"Non voglio che si trasferisca sulla Costa Orientale" borbottò.

"Questa decisione spetta a lei" replicai, non volendo lasciare che la sua famiglia cercasse di influenzarla. "Sono disposto a restare qui."

"E il tuo ristorante? Evan ha detto che appartiene alla tua famiglia da generazioni."

Feci spallucce. "Le priorità cambiano."

Se Brooke voleva vivere sulla Costa Occidentale, ero più che disposto a trasferirmi. Lei era la mia priorità. Mi sarebbe mancato dirigere il Sullivan, ma avevo i soldi per iniziare in un altro posto. In diversi posti se volevo. E c'era solo una Brooke.

"Lasceresti casa tua e tua sorella per lei?" chiese con attenzione.

Annuii bruscamente. Avevo impiegato un po' per giungere alla conclusione che non importava dove vivessimo. Volevo solo assicurarmi che saremmo stati sempre *insieme*. "Tessa ha Micah, ed è indipendente, anche se ho cercato di non notarlo. Mia sorella ha un sacco di amici e la famiglia Sinclair che ama ad Amesport. E non è che non potrei raggiungerla, se avesse bisogno di me."

"E il ristorante?" chiese.

"Assumerò un manager. Mi piace gestirlo da solo, ma nel quadro generale, non ha molta importanza. Brooke è molto più importante per me."

"Evan ha detto che sei ricco" disse, studiandomi come se fossi un esemplare al microscopio.

"Non così ricco quanto Brooke con la sua eredità, ma non credo che i soldi avranno molta importanza. Non hanno mai significato molto per me. Ma se domani perdesse tutto, potrei prendermi cura di lei per il resto della sua vita."

Grugnì. "Credo di sì. Un tempo, sarei stato elettrizzato, se avesse trovato un ragazzo con una buona professione. Ora stiamo spaccando il capello in quattro sui milionari o miliardari. Sembra fottutamente ridicolo."

Il fratello di Brooke sembrava fare ancora fatica ad accettare così tanti soldi. "Ti ci abituerai" assicurai. "Il denaro non cambia chi sei."

Mi lanciò un'occhiata cupa. "Ma a volte cambia le persone intorno a te."

Scossi la testa. "Non se frequenti le persone giuste."

"I miei fratellastri e mia sorella ad Amesport sono le persone giuste?"

Sapevo che Noah stava cercando di chiedermi come fossero. Era ovviamente curioso sulla sua seconda famiglia. "Sono tutte brave persone. Conosci già Evan, e anche se è uno stronzo, ha a cuore le persone che ama."

Forse i fratelli e la sorella di Brooke erano un po' rudi. Forse erano cresciuti senza l'influenza del denaro, ma probabilmente avrebbero apprezzato molto di più essere ricchi, perché avevano vissuto poveri.

"Evan può essere un idiota" confermò. "Ma non è così difficile vedere attraverso di lui. Non doveva includerci, quando ha sistemato la proprietà di nostro padre. Non doveva spaccarsi il culo per far crescere ancora di più quella fortuna. Ma lo ha fatto."

"Avrebbe dovuto dirlo al resto della sua famiglia" gli dissi. "Non riesco a immaginare che tutti saranno felici, quando scopriranno che voi ragazzi esistete e non lo sapevano."

Si strinse nelle spalle. "Io avrei fatto la stessa cosa. Non ha senso turbarli, se i fratellastri non si trovano."

Sorrisi. Noah era un maniaco del controllo, anche se non voleva ammetterlo. Mi ricordava molto Evan, quindi non era una sorpresa che si sarebbero capiti.

Cambiai argomento, tornando alla sua minaccia originale di uccidermi. "Brooke sarà felice ovunque andremo a finire. Puoi contarci."

"Sei sicuro che rimarrà con te?" chiese subito dopo aver scolato la sua lattina di birra.

No, non ero affatto certo che si sarebbe impegnata per tutta la vita con me, ma dovevo credere che l'avrebbe fatto. Non sarei valso nulla in caso contrario. "Lo spero."

Finii il mio drink e gettai la lattina nella spazzatura. Noah lanciò la sua da un po' più lontano e centrò perfettamente il bersaglio. "Faresti meglio a riportarla spesso a farci visita" borbottò.

"Come fai a sapere che tornerà nel Maine con me?" chiesi.

Mi lanciò un'occhiata consapevole. "La conosco da molti più anni di te" spiegò. "Brooke è sempre stata la gemella più sensata. Ma Jade poteva facilmente metterla nei guai, quando erano più piccole. Quando sono cresciute, erano... diverse."

"Come?"

"Brooke non aveva molto interesse per gli uomini. Se le piaceva un ragazzo, la relazione non sarebbe durata a lungo. Sembrava sempre che aspettasse con calma qualcosa di straordinario."

"Come me?" scherzai.

"Forse quello giusto" concordò, facendosi sfuggire completamente la mia battuta.

"E Jade?" chiesi con curiosità.

"È completamente disillusa" rispose triste. "È rimasta scottata, quindi non si fida facilmente. È ancora romantica con altre persone, ma non tanto per se stessa."

"Alla fine, troverà qualcuno di cui fidarsi" lo consolai. "Tessa era allo stesso modo."

Mia sorella era stata gravemente scottata, ma era guarita dopo aver trovato Micah.

"Voglio che tutti i miei fratelli siano felici" disse con voce tesa.

"E tu?" Mi resi conto che Noah era così preoccupato per la sua famiglia che probabilmente non si era mai preso il tempo per considerare la propria felicità.

"Non importa" borbottò. "Avevo troppe responsabilità per preoccuparmi di me stesso."

"Importa" ribattei.

"Non a me" disse solennemente.

Guardai la sua espressione seria, mentre iniziavo a tornare nel piccolo soggiorno pieno di più Sinclair di quanti volessi veramente affrontare in quel momento. "È importante per la tua famiglia" replicai a bassa voce.

"L'ho notato" rispose con voce grave. "Jade sta cercando di mettermi in contatto con ogni donna che pensa mi renderebbe felice.

Non capisce che in questo momento sono sposato con la mia attività. Voglio essere degno dei soldi che ho ereditato."

Sbuffai. "Sei nato degno."

"Evan e la sua famiglia hanno successo" sostenne.

"Forse le cose sarebbero andate diversamente, se non fossero nati nel denaro. Non puoi confrontare le vostre situazioni."

"Forse no" concordò. "Ma ho sempre desiderato avere successo nella mia attività. Ho questa opportunità adesso."

Il mondo era spalancato a Noah adesso come non lo era mai stato prima. Poteva essere quello che voleva. Anche se non erano cresciuti allo stesso modo, potevo vedere così tanto di Evan in lui. Il fratellastro di Evan aveva la sua stessa ambizione e la sua stessa determinazione.

Mentre tornavamo nel soggiorno affollato, speravo solo che non diventasse un grosso coglione come il suo fratellastro.

Brooke

"So che è stata una giornata pesante oggi" dissi esitante, mentre camminavo mano nella mano lungo Citrus Beach con Liam.

La mia famiglia era *sempre* un po' eccessiva, quando eravamo tutti insieme nello stesso posto, ma vedere e parlare con tutti loro era stato un sollievo per me. Avrei voluto che Owen potesse essere qui, ma sapevo che non era possibile.

Sospirai guardando le onde che si infrangevano sulla riva. Non c'erano molte persone sul bellissimo tratto di spiaggia che avevo attraversato quando ero più giovane. Faceva troppo freddo per nuotare, ed era nuvoloso, ma era bello essere in un luogo così familiare.

Le cose erano cambiate per tutta la mia famiglia, e niente era più come quando me ne ero andata, ma erano cambiamenti positivi.

Noah stava costruendo lentamente il suo impero.

Seth e Aiden sembravano un po' amareggiati per quello che nostro padre aveva fatto a nostra madre, ma non potevo biasimarli per questo. Pensavo che ognuno di noi odiasse nostro padre e le stronzate che aveva fatto subire a nostra madre essendo un bigamo.

Alla fine, forse avremmo visto tutto in modo diverso, ma ne dubitavo. Un giorno, speravo che Seth e Aiden potessero almeno essere meno arrabbiati per quello che era successo. Adesso erano in affari insieme, e sembravano felici del loro destino.

Jade era l'unica che sembrasse turbata, ma si rifiutava di condividere ciò che la preoccupava.

Liam mi strinse la mano, mentre rispondeva: "Sono la tua famiglia. Non devo amarli tutti."

"Ti piaceranno col tempo" lo avvertii con un sorriso.

Stava vedendo il peggior lato dei miei fratelli in quel momento. Erano iperprotettivi. Ma quando univano le forze per una causa comune, erano decisamente pericolosi.

Si fermò e si voltò per guardarmi. Il mio respiro si bloccò, mentre lo guardavo, i suoi capelli leggermente agitati per la brezza e la sua espressione cupa.

"Non li conosco davvero" spiegò. "Ma voglio farlo."

Cercai il suo viso. Sapevo che stava cercando di dirmi qualcosa. "Cosa intendi?" sondai, il mio cuore che batteva all'impazzata.

"Voglio restare qui con te, Brooke. Voglio costruire una bella casa e crescere i nostri figli qui, se vuoi averli."

Il petto mi faceva male, mentre guardavo la sua espressione sincera. Volevo avere dei figli, semplicemente non avevo trovato la persona giusta, quindi non ci avevo pensato molto.

Lo vidi rovistare nella tasca dei suoi jeans, e poi finalmente tirò fuori quello che stava cercando.

Aprì la piccola scatola e il respiro che stavo trattenendo uscì dal mio corpo, quando vidi il bellissimo diamante all'interno.

Guardai dalla sua faccia al diamante, il mio cuore che rimbombava nelle orecchie.

"Ti amo, Brooke" borbottò. "Probabilmente dalla prima volta in cui ti ho vista, ma allora non volevo pensarci. Detesto quello che hai passato, ma voglio la possibilità di mostrarti com'è la vera felicità." Fece una pausa, prima di aggiungere: "Sposami."

Il tempo si fermò per un momento, mentre cercavo di capire cosa mi stava chiedendo.

Era disposto a restare qui per me?

Voleva che fossi sua moglie?

"Ti amo anch'io" dissi velocemente, sentendomi sollevata di poter finalmente esprimere come mi sentivo.

All'improvviso, sorrise maliziosamente. "Sai da quanto tempo volevo sentirlo?"

"N-no" balbettai, ancora troppo sbalordita per capire cosa stesse succedendo.

Sapevo che mi voleva bene, ma non mi aspettavo che si offrisse di lasciare Amesport per vivere con me in California.

"L'ho comprato a Boston" spiegò. "Ecco perché non mi dava fastidio andarci."

Sollevò il bellissimo anello dal suo letto di velluto e si ficcò di nuovo la scatola in tasca.

"È stupendo" riuscii a dire.

"Sposami" ripeté, il suo tono esigente.

"Non sembra che tu me lo stia chiedendo" scherzai, ma mi tremavano le mani e il mio cuore sembrava pronto a volarmi fuori dal petto.

Liam sarebbe sempre stato esigente, ma non mi dava fastidio. Sapevo cosa c'era sotto tutta quella spacconaggine: *l'uomo che avrebbe dovuto essere sempre mio.*

"Immagino di non volere che tu abbia la possibilità di dire di no" replicò con voce cruda e gutturale.

"Non ho intenzione di dire di no" lo informai, la mia voce tremante, mentre rispondevo. "È decisamente un *sì*."

Mi gettai tra le sue braccia, assaporando la sensazione della sua stretta avvolgente.

Come avrebbe dovuto reagire una donna, quando aveva appena ottenuto ogni singola cosa che il suo cuore desiderava?

Mi sentivo libera, ma protetta.

Proprio come lui, avevo sempre sentito il modo in cui eravamo connessi.

Era il ragazzo che stavo aspettando, ma all'inizio le circostanze non erano state favorevoli.

"Penso di averti sempre aspettato" dissi con un singhiozzo felice.

Mi tirò a sé e mi baciò, le nostre bocche che si incontrarono e si mescolarono con la fame surreale che mi aveva sempre consumata ogni volta in cui eravamo insieme.

Il mio corpo fu immediatamente pronto affinché lui scuotesse il mio mondo, proprio come faceva ogni volta che mi toccava.

Lasciando andare le mie labbra, mi prese per le spalle e mi spinse indietro. "Voglio questo anello al tuo dito."

Acconsentii tendendo la mia mano tremante, e trattenni di nuovo il respiro, mentre armeggiava per infilare l'anello nel mio dito.

"Mi va bene" osservai, mentre rilasciavo un respiro represso.

"Certo che ti va bene" replicò. "Pensavi che te lo avrei lasciato togliere? Ma misurare il dito con una cordicella mentre dormivi non è stato esattamente facile."

Risi, in grado di immaginare quanto fosse frustrato nel provare a maneggiare una piccola corda con le sue grandi mani. Era tanto accattivante quanto divertente.

"Possiamo cambiarlo se non ti piace" disse, la sua voce che rivelava un po' di insolito nervosismo.

Mi portai la mano al petto. "Lo adoro" risposi categoricamente, sapendo che non l'avrei mai cambiato con qualcosa di diverso, anche se non l'avessi apprezzato così tanto. Potevo dire che aveva pensato molto alla scelta, e mi aveva fatto venire le lacrime agli occhi.

"Ti amo" disse sinceramente, mentre mi prendeva la mano sinistra dal petto e se la portava alle labbra.

Le lacrime mi rigarono le guance, quando risposi immediatamente: "Ti amo anch'io."

L'uomo alto e bello davanti a me era diventato il mio tutto. Probabilmente sapevo che era possibile fin dall'inizio, ma entrambi c'eravamo allontanati.

In un certo senso, l'enormità di come amavo Liam era spaventosa, ma ero disposta a correre il rischio.

Mi prese tra le sue braccia e mi tenne come se fossi la cosa più preziosa del mondo per lui. "Gesù, Brooke! Non ho mai pensato potessi essere tuo."

"Forse è per questo che è così speciale" ribattei con una voce piena di lacrime vicino al suo orecchio.

Restammo in silenzio per alcuni istanti, assorbendo entrambi il fatto che non avremmo mai dovuto essere separati di nuovo.

Non lo lasciai andare, mentre mormoravo: "Voglio trasferirmi ad Amesport."

Si tirò indietro quel tanto che bastava per vedere la mia faccia. "Che cosa?"

"Voglio tornare sulla Costa Orientale." Avevo imparato ad amare la piccola città costiera, e non sarebbe stato difficile trovare un lavoro lì.

Cavolo, avrei potuto avere i miei affari lì, se avessi voluto. La mia eredità mi apriva delle porte dentro cui non era mai stato possibile guardare, prima di diventare schifosamente ricca.

"Perché vuoi tornare con me?" chiese con un'espressione incredula.

"Mi piace avere i migliori involtini di aragosta del Paese" scherzai. "E mi mancherebbero il caffè e la cioccolata."

"Ma la tua famiglia—"

"Saranno qui ogni volta che torno a casa per vederli, e possono venire a trovarci ad Amesport. Tutti i miei fratelli vorranno incontrare e conoscere i Sinclair del Maine."

"Brooke, dobbiamo parlare di questo—"

"Non dobbiamo" gli assicurai. "Amo la mia famiglia, ma è tempo per me di fare ciò che mi rende felice. Non c'è alcuna garanzia che rimarremo tutti qui in modo permanente. Abbiamo tutti bisogno di vivere le nostre vite. Non che non possiamo salire su un aereo ogni volta che vogliamo fare una visita."

"Sei sicura?"

Annuii. "Quando siamo passati accanto alla banca prima, ho capito che era il momento di ricominciare."

Quella sarà stata pure la mia città natale, ma ero pronta a spiegare le ali e volare. Ero rabbrividita, quando eravamo finiti di fronte al luogo della sparatoria, sapendo che sarebbe stato per sempre un luogo di dolore per me. Per tutti gli altri, la città era tornata alla normalità dopo l'incidente, ma per me non sarebbe mai più stata la stessa cosa.

"Brutti ricordi" disse dolcemente, mentre mi toglieva una ciocca di capelli dal viso.

"Sì. Penso che essere qui mi ricorderà sempre quello che è successo."

"Allora, vivremo ad Amesport" concordò prontamente.

"Non è solo la sparatoria" lo rassicurai. "Voglio stare lì con te.»

Ormai adoravo il Sullivan's Restaurant e tutte le persone che vedevo lì regolarmente. Volevo conoscere i miei fratellastri e la mia sorellastra senza la necessità di nascondere la mia identità.

Condivisi tutte le ragioni per cui volevo tornare a vivere ad Amesport con Liam, mentre ascoltava.

Quando ebbi finito, sembrava sollevato, mentre diceva: "Evita di conoscere Xander" consigliò. "È un coglione."

Gli diedi un pugno sulla spalla scherzosamente. "Non dici sul serio" lo accusai. "Non passeresti tanto tempo con lui, se non ti piacesse."

"È un idiota."

Ridacchiai, sapendo che lui e Xander adoravano inimicarsi a vicenda. "Ho l'altra famiglia lì" gli ricordai.

"Sì" disse infelice. "So che dovrò abituarmi alla presenza di tutti loro. Non mi dispiace così tanto Micah, ma potrei fare a meno di Evan."

Gli sorrisi ampiamente. Sapevo che per quanto protestasse, avrebbe dato il benvenuto a tutti loro per me. "Ti amo, Liam."

Il mio cuore sembrava pronto a esplodere di felicità, una sensazione che sicuramente non ero abituata a provare.

Mi baciò la fronte con riverenza. "Ti amo anch'io, piccola. Non pensare che non sappia quanto sia dannatamente fortunato."

Anch'io ero stata fortunata, e avrei passato il resto della mia vita grata per un uomo che era disposto a fare un così grande sacrificio per me, anche se non avevo accettato.

Gli accarezzai la guancia barbuta, mentre gli suggerivo: "Andiamo a casa."

"Ad Amesport?" chiese con voce roca.

"Per ora, possiamo usare il mio appartamento" risposi, il corpo che mi chiedeva a gran voce di spogliare l'uomo che amavo. "Possiamo andare ad Amesport domani."

"Possiamo andare ad est quando vuoi. Non sono contrario all'idea di darti tutto il tempo che vuoi" rispose con voce roca. "In questo momento, non sono sicuro che ti lascerò alzare dal letto domattina."

"Non sono sicura di volerlo" replicai.

Mi prese in braccio e mi fece girare, prima di rimettermi in piedi. "Lo scopriremo" disse, i suoi occhi ardenti, mentre mi trafiggeva con uno sguardo avido. "In questo momento, ti voglio solo nuda."

Mi prese la mano e iniziammo a tornare alla macchina.

Fortunatamente, volevo esattamente la stessa cosa che voleva lui.

Capitolo 18

Jade

Sapevo che era lì dal momento in cui era entrato nel ristorante. Non che l'avessi visto. Non ne avevo bisogno. La sua presenza provocò un *brivido* di consapevolezza lungo la mia spina dorsale, una sensazione così scomoda che dovetti sforzarmi per non dimenarmi sulla sedia.

Rivolsi di nuovo la mia attenzione al grande tavolo di persone, tutte di famiglia. Brooke aveva rimandato la sua partenza di un altro giorno, in modo che potessimo cenare tutti insieme prima della sua partenza.

Avevamo scelto un bel ristorante a San Diego, un posto di proprietà di Eli Stone. Avevo pensato che le possibilità che si presentasse di persona fossero quasi nulle.

Ma mi sbagliavo.

Dannazione! Cosa ci fa qui?

Certo, era il proprietario del posto, ma possedeva molti ristoranti di prima classe.

Girai la testa e lo guardai. Non impiegai molto per vederlo seduto in un séparé privato con un altro uomo vestito su misura. Non riconobbi il suo amico, ma in base a tutte le indicazioni sembrava ricco quanto lui.

"Jade? Stai bene?"

Non sapevo da quanto tempo la mia gemella stesse parlando con me, ma fui riportata alla realtà dal suono della sua voce preoccupata.

"Sto bene" risposi subito.

"Non sembri stare *bene*" osservò. "Sembra che tu abbia appena visto un fantasma."

"Pensavo di aver visto qualcuno che conoscevo" spiegai. "Ma mi sbagliavo."

Brooke era seduta proprio accanto a me, il suo nuovo fidanzato sul lato opposto. Mi lanciò un'occhiata curiosa, ma le sorrisi.

Questa era la notte di mia sorella. Eravamo qui per celebrare il suo fidanzamento. Mi rifiutavo di lasciare che uno stronzo con un completo perfetto mi rovinasse la serata.

Detestavo il fatto che avrebbe vissuto dall'altra parte del Paese, ma ero disposta a soffrire. La mia unica sorella era felice, e se avessi dovuto portare il mio culo su un aereo per andare a trovarla, non avrei avuto problemi. Ne sarebbe valsa la pena, se fosse rimasta contenta e allegra come adesso.

"Sono preoccupata per te" disse, sembrando a disagio.

"No" insistetti. "Sto bene."

Accidenti, chi non si sarebbe considerato assolutamente benedetto, se avesse ereditato una fortuna? Eli Stone non era altro che un parassita che volevo sterminare. Non valeva la pena pensarci.

"Non ti credo. C'è qualcosa che non va."

Brooke e io avevamo sempre avuto un legame gemello. Proprio come io potevo dire che era davvero euforica per aver trovato l'uomo dei suoi sogni, lei poteva percepire che ero nervosa.

Odiavo quella connessione in questo momento.

"È solo roba di lavoro" risposi. "Niente di importante."

Mi piaceva considerare Eli Stone come non importante. Forse perché *era* insignificante per me.

Brooke mi mise una mano sul braccio. "Potrei vivere lontano, ma sarò sempre nei paraggi, se avrai bisogno di me. Il viaggio non è più un vero problema."

Risi. "Non lo è, se hai i soldi per viaggiare."

Non ero ancora abituata ad essere una miliardaria. A volte mi sentivo come se stessi cercando di interpretare un ruolo che non era così adatto a me. Ma mi piaceva prendere le mie decisioni, e non avrei lasciato che un coglione come Eli Stone mi ostacolasse il cammino.

"Si tratta dei soldi?" chiese.

Annuii. "È strano, vero? Un giorno stiamo lottando per sopravvivere, e il giorno dopo stiamo tutti vivendo il sogno."

"È strano in senso buono" concordò.

Mia sorella rivolse la sua attenzione a Liam, e il mio sguardo si spostò sul séparé dove era seduto Eli.

Mi detestavo per averlo guardato, ma Eli Stone era come un brutto disastro ferroviario. Non sarei dovuta restare a bocca aperta, ma non riuscivo a distogliere lo sguardo.

Sussultai, quando notai che la sua attenzione era rivolta verso di me. I nostri occhi si incontrarono e lui alzò il bicchiere—che immaginavo fosse pieno di superalcolico—in un calmo saluto.

La mia testa tornò di scatto alla mia famiglia, mentre bruciavo per l'irritazione.

Avrei dovuto tenere gli occhi lontano da lui. Il sorrisetto sul suo viso era stato più fastidioso che accogliente, come se sapesse qualcosa che io non sapevo.

Non che Eli avesse alcun desiderio di essere amichevole. Non lo era mai stato.

Eravamo nemici. Non c'era spazio nel mio mondo per vederlo come qualcosa di diverso da una minaccia.

"Scusami un momento" borbottai educatamente, alzandomi dalla sedia.

"Qualcosa non va?" chiese Brooke guardandomi.

Le sorrisi. "Bagno" spiegai, mentre lasciavo cadere il tovagliolo sul tavolo. "Torno subito."

Avevo bisogno di un minuto per ricompormi, così scappai dall'altra parte della sala e corsi nell'elegante toilette.

Una volta entrata nel lussuoso bagno, mi fermai davanti allo specchio, fissandomi.

L'abito che indossavo era costato più di quanto la maggior parte delle persone avrebbe speso per i vestiti in un decennio. L'avevo adorato, quando l'avevo provato. Ora, avevo cambiato idea sull'abito da cocktail nero che mi faceva sentire seminuda.

Misi un po' più di rossetto e mi lavai le mani solo per avere qualcosa da fare.

Non avevo bisogno di fare pipì. Era stata solo una scusa per allontanarmi dallo sguardo penetrante di Eli.

Quando ebbi finito, gettai il tovagliolo di carta nella spazzatura e feci un respiro profondo.

Non posso lasciarmi influenzare da lui.

Non avrebbe voluto altro che farmi innervosire. Il suo obiettivo era vedermi piegare, e non avevo intenzione di dargli quella soddisfazione.

Non sarebbe successo.

Dovevo ignorare persone come Eli Stone, ricchi bastardi che pensavano di possedere il mondo solo perché avevano i soldi.

Purtroppo, mi rendeva davvero difficile ignorarlo.

Feci ancora qualche respiro rilassante, poi uscii dal bagno, determinata a godermi la mia ultima serata insieme a tutta la mia famiglia.

Eli era un idiota, e non potevo cambiare il suo modo di fare maturato in anni di incoscienza ed eccessiva indulgenza. Non volevo nemmeno provarci.

Scivolai di nuovo sulla sedia al nostro tavolo, cercando di non attirare l'attenzione su di me.

Ci volle uno sforzo quasi sovrumano per non guardare di nuovo dalla sua parte, ma ci riuscii.

Quando ci alzammo per andarcene, lui non c'era più.

Epilogo

Brooke

Due Mesi Dopo...

Avevo ricevuto tutto l'aiuto per pianificare il mio matrimonio. Parlavo con Jade ogni giorno in videoconferenza, mostrandole esempi di ciò che volevo come abiti, torte, catering, fiori e tutti gli altri dettagli che non sapevo esistessero per una sposa.

Inoltre, ogni moglie Sinclair mi aveva aiutata. Almeno una delle mogli dei miei fratellastri era stata in giro quasi ogni giorno, e il più delle volte erano *tutte* con me a casa di Liam per aiutare con la pianificazione.

Avevo rinunciato al mio appartamento e mi ero trasferita da lui. Avevamo rinunciato a mantenere residenze separate, poiché eravamo quasi sempre insieme la sera e ogni singola notte.

Ero diventata amica di tutte le mogli dei miei fratellastri, ma il rapporto che amavo di più era quello con la mia sorellastra, Hope.

Era stata lei ad aiutarmi a superare le brutte cose che mi erano successe. Dopo averla sentita parlare della sua vita come cacciatrice di tempeste prima che sposasse Jason, e dell'orrore che aveva sopportato mentre era in un altro Paese durante un tifone, le mie esperienze erano quasi apparse banali. Non che Hope le avesse mai fatte sembrare altro che un incubo per me. Era stata paziente e gentile, empatica, visto che aveva attraversato lo stesso trauma.

Ma la mia sorellastra era la prova vivente che da una tragedia potevano nascere buone cose.

Onestamente, quasi tutte le mogli Sinclair avevano subito il loro inferno privato un tempo, quindi legare con loro era stato facile. Erano così vere, così aperte che mi sembrava di conoscerle tutte da sempre.

Sì, c'erano delle volte in cui mi mancava la mia famiglia in California, ma avere un'altra famiglia qui ad Amesport mi alleviava il dolore dalla mancanza di mia sorella e dei miei fratelli.

Ma ora sono tutti qui.

Sospirai, mentre mi guardavo intorno al Centro Giovanile Amesport, stupita che il grande luogo di ritrovo potesse servire a così tanti scopi. Il mio ricevimento era in pieno svolgimento, e la sala da ballo sembrava incredibile. Avevo dovuto ringraziare gli uomini Sinclair della città per questo. Tutti loro avevano investito un sacco di soldi nel centro fatiscente, assicurandosi che potesse ospitare una pletora di eventi, dalle partite di basket giovanile alle feste in città.

Era stato il posto migliore per il mio ricevimento di matrimonio, poiché c'erano tantissimi ospiti che volevano partecipare. Solo la famiglia Sinclair da sola occupava molto spazio, ed ero abbastanza sicura che almeno metà della città fosse lì. Liam e Tessa erano cresciuti qui e avevano molti amici.

I miei fratelli, Liam e Hope erano tutti riuniti a un grande tavolo nell'angolo più lontano, e sembrava che stessero tutti bene insieme. Quando li guardai raggruppati, la somiglianza tra loro era perfettamente evidente.

Mi chiesi perché non avessi mai sospettato di Evan. Ma avevo stabilito che era difficile vedere qualcosa che non era nemmeno possibile pensare. O almeno, non mi *sarebbe* stato neanche lontanamente possibile immaginare, prima di scoprire la verità.

Quando le cose non si cercavano, rimanevano nascoste. Il cervello era davvero buffo.

Mi feci strada nel caos, tornando nella sala da ballo, dopo aver passato molto tempo a cercare di capire come fare la pipì con l'abito da sposa. Non era stato facile, ma finalmente c'ero riuscita.

Lo sguardo di Liam fu il primo a trovarmi in mezzo alla folla, mentre tornavo verso il tavolo. La sua testa si alzò di scatto e si voltò guardandomi con l'espressione calda e possessiva che avevo imparato ad amare così tanto.

Era come se percepisse la mia presenza, proprio come io potevo sentirlo quando entrava in una stanza. Ci perdemmo di vista, mentre mi facevo strada tra la folla, ma la sensazione di consapevolezza non se ne andò mai.

Negli ultimi mesi, ero riuscita lentamente a sentirmi più a mio agio nella mia pelle, e stavo imparando ad accettare di essere incredibilmente ricca. Evan, dopo aver ricucito la nostra discussione, era stato per me un mentore straordinario, quando avevo iniziato a costruire la mia ricchezza personale. Era stato lì per calmarmi, quando avevo dubitato di me stessa e del mio senso di investimento. Accidenti, quando una persona investiva a sette o otto cifre in varie opportunità, anche se aveva ricercato e scoperto che erano un buon rischio che avrebbe dato un buon guadagno, era piuttosto spaventoso.

Avevo deciso di non accettare un lavoro retribuito. Il solo fatto di gestire la mia ricchezza era più che sufficiente per tenermi occupata. Quando ero andata al college per la mia laurea in finanza, non avrei mai immaginato che sarei finita per essere un'investitrice di me stessa. Era allo stesso tempo liberatorio e scoraggiante.

Evan aiutava. Avere il suo consiglio era inestimabile. Averlo come fratello era ancora meglio.

Ricevetti un mare di suggerimenti da tutti i miei fratellastri. Ognuno di loro aveva una mente per gli affari straordinaria, e lo stesso valeva per il marito di Hope, Jason. Ero come una spugna, mentre assorbivo tutto ciò che condividevano con me. Un giorno, speravo di poter entrare a far parte dei ranghi dei maghi degli affari Sinclair. Ma per ora, ero felice di essere un'apprendista.

Sorprendentemente, avevo scoperto quanto fossero incredibilmente generosi i miei fratellastri con la loro fortuna, e quanto fosse dannatamente bello donare a cause meritevoli per aiutare a cambiare il mondo. Probabilmente quella era una delle parti più appaganti del trovarmi improvvisamente ad essere una miliardaria.

Liam mi sorrise, quando finalmente raggiunsi il tavolo, alzandosi in modo da poter tirare fuori la sedia accanto a lui.

Era da mozzare il fiato in smoking, e mi lasciai sopraffare dall'orgoglio che sentivo ora legalmente mio, prima di prendere posto.

Avevo appena sposato un uomo incredibile, e probabilmente mi sarei pizzicata ancora per settimane, prima di abituarmi ad essere sua moglie.

Aveva deciso di assumere un manager per il Sullivan. Era quasi la stagione intensa, e aveva assunto anche altro personale. Non che avesse intenzione di essere meno coinvolto, ma voleva concentrarsi di più sulla crescita del business che sulle attività quotidiane.

Mi sedetti con attenzione, e lui si sistemò accanto a me.

"Non so te, ma io sono pronto per la luna di miele" borbottò vicino al mio orecchio con una voce destinata solo a me.

Mi morsi il labbro per non ridere, mentre mi voltavo a guardarlo. "Il ricevimento è appena iniziato" gli ricordai. "E non partiremo fino a domani."

Saremmo stati via per un mese. C'erano stati così tanti posti in cui sarei voluta andare in luna di miele che Liam li aveva inclusi tutti. Avremmo fatto un folle viaggio intorno al mondo per visitarli tutti, ma sapevo che sarebbe stato perfettamente comodo, dato che avremmo usato il jet privato di Evan.

"Sì, quindi dobbiamo andare a letto presto per essere riposati" replicò burbero.

Questa volta risi. Non potei trattenermi. "Liam, sono appena le cinque, e sto morendo di fame. Possiamo almeno aspettare che arrivi la cena e la torta?"

"Posso aspettare, allora" ribatté immediatamente, i suoi occhi che vagavano amorevolmente sul mio viso.

Lo baciai, un bacio lento e dolce che mi fece desiderare di avere quell'uomo gloriosamente nudo, in modo da poterlo abbracciare come volevo adesso. Se volevo qualcosa, era sempre paziente. Mi faceva male il cuore sapere che era così dannatamente disposto a mettere i miei desideri e bisogni prima dei suoi. Non ne approfittavo, perché ero disposta a fare la stessa cosa per lui. Ma c'era qualcosa di così dolce in un ragazzo che avrebbe dato così tanto solo per rendermi felice.

"Grazie per aver aspettato" dissi senza fiato, la mia voce toccata dall'umorismo.

"Ti aspetterò sempre, Brooke. Mi sento come se l'avessi già fatto" replicò con voce tranquilla, mentre mi cingeva con un braccio.

Sospirai, sentendo il calore del suo corpo massiccio accanto al mio. "Anch'io" mormorai.

Mia sorella, Jade, si stava facendo strada tra la folla, e sembrava agitata, mentre si sedeva sulla sedia davanti a me.

Le sue guance erano rosse come un pomodoro maturo, mentre beveva un grande sorso del suo drink.

Mi chinai sul tavolo, quando chiesi: "Stai bene? La tua faccia è arrossata."

Si portò una mano alla guancia, come se stesse cercando di spazzare via il calore della sua pelle. "Sto bene" scattò. "Non sapevo che Eli Stone sarebbe venuto."

Avevo incontrato l'eccentrico miliardario subito dopo il matrimonio. "È amico della maggior parte dei Sinclair qui ad Amesport. Neanche io sapevo che sarebbe venuto. Ma sembra abbastanza simpatico."

Una cosa che avevo scoperto sui ricchi era che la maggior parte di loro si conosceva, e molto spesso erano amici. Oppure si odiavano a vicenda. Ero abbastanza sicura che i miei fratellastri conoscessero così tante persone ricche, perché era così che erano cresciuti. Forse altre persone con soldi erano le uniche di cui potersi fidare.

"Lo odio" replicò lei con veemenza. "Non possiamo nemmeno essere civili l'uno con l'altra."

"Perché?" domandai.

Scosse la testa, sembrando pentita del suo sfogo. "Non è niente. Non devo parlargli di nuovo" disse con tono più calmo.

"Ha fatto qualcosa per offenderti?" chiese Liam, sembrando infastidito dal fatto che un ospite al suo matrimonio potesse aver turbato mia sorella.

Jade e Liam si erano conosciuti negli ultimi due mesi, e provavano reciproco rispetto e affetto l'uno per l'altra. Se qualcuno avesse ferito la mia gemella, sarebbe stato determinato a rimediare.

"No. Davvero. Sto bene" rispose Jade. "Mi dà solo fastidio. Non lascerò che un tipo ricco e arrogante mi faccia incazzare." Sorrise un po' troppo ampiamente. "È un giorno speciale."

Le sue labbra sorridevano, ma i suoi occhi sembravano turbati. Ero preoccupata per lei, ma finché non fosse stata pronta a parlare di qualunque cosa la stesse infastidendo, non c'era molto che potessi fare.

"Voi due piccioncini dovete dire al ristoratore di portare il cibo. Sto morendo di fame" suggerì Aiden a voce alta e tonante giù dal tavolo a me e Liam.

"Quando non muori di fame tu?" replicò seccamente Liam, ma fece cenno ai camerieri di iniziare il servizio di ristorazione. "Smette mai di mangiare?" chiese in tono più tranquillo.

Sorrisi. Tutti i miei fratelli potevano mangiare come maiali. "No. Sono così dacché ricordi."

Non dissi che c'erano state così tante volte in cui i miei fratelli maggiori avevano sacrificato il loro cibo per me, Jade e Owen. Stavano recuperando il tempo perso ora che non avrebbero mai più dovuto preoccuparsi di avere cibo a sufficienza per tutta la famiglia.

"Sono contento di aver ordinato del cibo extra" disse Liam bonariamente.

Aveva ordinato un sacco di cibo; più di quanto i miei fratelli avrebbero potuto mangiare. E sapevo che l'aveva fatto perché sapeva quanto amassero mangiare.

"Ti amo" sbottai, voltandomi a guardarlo, il cuore in gola, mentre pensavo a quanto fossi fortunata ad avere un uomo che si prendeva cura della mia famiglia.

"Ehi, cosa c'è che non va?» chiese, quando vide una lacrima scorrere lungo la mia guancia.

Scossi la testa e asciugai la lacrima vagante. "Niente. Mi stavo solo chiedendo cosa abbia mai fatto in vita mia per meritare un uomo come te."

Sorrise, mentre mi sollevava il mento per costringermi a guardarlo in faccia. "Niente. Non dovevi fare nulla. Dovevi solo essere te stessa. E per la cronaca, ti amo anch'io."

Sapevo che mi amava. Lo dimostrava con le azioni oltre che con le parole. Guardai il suo bel viso, pensando ancora una volta a quanto fosse dannatamente attraente in abbigliamento formale. "Forse possiamo saltare la torta" dissi, con una voce abbastanza alta da farglielo sentire.

All'improvviso, non mi importava davvero se mangiassi o meno. Volevo portarlo a casa e togliergli ogni capo di abbigliamento, finché non avessi potuto toccare la sua pelle calda. Le parole non sembravano abbastanza adesso. Volevo... lui. Avevo bisogno di dimostrargli che lo amavo oltre a dirlo ad alta voce.

Rise. Un suono forte, profondo e completamente divertito che mi sciolse il cuore. "Tesoro, prima possiamo mangiare."

Gli avvolsi le braccia intorno al collo. "Non credo di poter aspettare" gli sussurrai all'orecchio.

"Sei affamata—"

"Voglio di più te" ribattei, la mia bocca vicino al suo orecchio.

"Fanculo!" replicò in un tono frustrato. "Ho visto alcune stanze vuote, mentre camminavamo verso la sala da ballo, ma non è esattamente quello che avevo programmato per la nostra prima volta insieme come marito e moglie."

"Potremmo tornare, prima che il nostro cibo sia freddo" proposi in tono suggestivo. Non avevo bisogno di una luna di miele perfetta. Tutto ciò di cui avevo bisogno era Liam.

Sentii le sue spalle irrigidirsi sotto le mie braccia. "Ti senti avventurosa?" chiese con voce roca.

"Molto."

Si alzò senza aggiungere altro. Potevo vedere la giocosità nei suoi occhi, mentre mi tirava in piedi.

"Torneremo, così potrò nutrirti" disse con insistenza. "Non possiamo restare via a lungo."

"Immagino di poter aspettare" replicai, anche se volevo ancora urgentemente stare da sola con lui.

"Sì, beh, posso aspettare" rispose burbero, tirandomi dolcemente verso l'uscita. "Considera questa un'anteprima di ciò che accadrà in seguito."

Risi, mentre osservavo gli sguardi spalancati che la mia famiglia ci stava rivolgendo, mentre Liam mi trascinava risolutamente lontano dal nostro ricevimento di matrimonio.

"Torneremo" gridai allegramente alle mie spalle al tavolo pieno di fratelli che avevamo appena lasciato.

Più tardi, l'avrei ricordato come il ricevimento più felice e più bello che avrei potuto desiderare, anche se Liam e io avevamo avuto bisogno di riscaldare la nostra cena.

Ma non avevo intenzione di lamentarmi.

Mio marito aveva reso più che degno il sacrificio.

~ *Fine* ~

Ringraziamenti dell'Autrice

Come sempre, i miei ringraziamenti vanno alla mia nuova editor, Maria Gomez, e a tutto il team di Montlake Romance per il loro continuo supporto ai Sinclair. Ho amato scrivere questa serie, e sono davvero grata di avere così tante persone a Montlake che adorano i libri quanto me.

Alla mia squadra personale di KA... siete i migliori. Grazie per tutto quello che fate per me ogni singolo giorno, in modo che io possa concentrarmi sulla scrittura.

Alle mie Gems e a tutte le blogger che organizzano la promozione per le mie nuove pubblicazioni e le vendite... ragazze, mi stupite ad ogni singola uscita. Grazie per essere individui così straordinari.

Enormi abbracci ai miei lettori che mi permettono di continuare a fare ciò che amo!

Xxx Jan

Libri di F. S. Scott

disponibili in italiano

Serie L'Ossessione del Miliardario

L'Ossessione del Miliardario – Simon
Il Cuore del Miliardario – Sam
La Salvezza del Miliardario – Max
Il Gioco del Miliardario – Kade
Il Miliardario Fuori Controllo – Travis
Il Miliardario Smascherato – Jason
Il Miliardario Indomito – Tate
La Miliardaria Libera – Chloe
Il Miliardario Impavido – Zane
Il Miliardario Sconosciuto – Blake
Il Miliardario Svelato – Marcus
Il Miliardario Non Amato – Jett
Il Miliardario Indiscusso – Carter
Il Miliardario Inarrivabile – Mason
Il Miliardario Sotto Copertura – Hudson
Il Miliardario Inaspettato – Jax
Il Miliardario Inosservato ~ Cooper

I Sinclair

Un Miliardario Fuori dal Comune (I Sinclair Vol. 1)
Un Miliardario Inavvicinabile (I Sinclair Vol. 2)
Il Tocco del Miliardario (I Sinclair Vol. 3)
La Voce del Miliardario (I Sinclair Vol. 4)